The State of Race

Edited by

Nisha Kapoor
Duke University, US and University of York, UK

Virinder S. Kalra
University of Manchester, UK

and

James Rhodes
University of Manchester, UK

First published 2013 by
PALGRAVE MACMILLAN

Palgrave Macmillan in the UK is an imprint of Macmillan Publishers Limited,
registered in England, company number 785998, of Houndmills, Basingstoke,
Hampshire RG21 6XS.

Palgrave Macmillan in the US is a division of St Martin's Press LLC,
175 Fifth Avenue, New York, NY 10010.

Palgrave Macmillan is the global academic imprint of the above companies
and has companies and representatives throughout the world.

Palgrave® and Macmillan® are registered trademarks in the United States,
the United Kingdom, Europe and other countries.

ISBN 978-1-349-34967-8   ISBN 978-1-137-31308-9 (eBook)

DOI 10.1057/9781137313089

This book is printed on paper suitable for recycling and made from fully
managed and sustained forest sources. Logging, pulping and manufacturing
processes are expected to conform to the environmental regulations of the
country of origin.

A catalogue record for this book is available from the British Library.

A catalog record for this book is available from the Library of Congress.

Contents

List of Contributors

Gargi Bhattacharyya is Professor of Sociology and Public Policy, Aston University.

David Theo Goldberg is Professor of Comparative Literature and Criminology, Law and Society at the University of California, Irvine, and is a Fellow of the UCI Critical Theory Institute. He is Director of the University of California Humanities Research Institute.

Virinder S. Kalra is Senior Lecturer in the Department of Sociology, University of Manchester.

Nisha Kapoor is Samuel DuBois Cook Postdoctoral Fellow in the Centre for Race, Ethnicity and Gender in the Social Sciences (REGSS), Duke University, and Lecturer in the Department of Sociology, University of York.

Shamim Miah is Senior Lecturer in the School of Education and Professional Development, University of Huddersfield.

Heidi Safia Mirza is Professor of Equality Studies in Education at the Institute of Education, University of London.

James Rhodes is Lecturer in the Department of Sociology, University of Manchester.

Ala Sirriyeh is Lecturer in Sociology, School of Social and International Studies, University of Bradford.

Sivamohan Valluvan is ESRC Doctoral Student in the Department of Sociology, University of Manchester.

Vron Ware is Research Fellow based at the Centre for Socio-Cultural Change (CRESC), and the Centre for Citizenship, Identities and Governance (CCIG), Open University.

Introduction: The State of Race

Nisha Kapoor and Virinder S. Kalra

The context

As the turn of the twenty-first century marked a significant shift in geopolitical frameworks, namely from communism to Islamism as the targeted enemy of the West, together with the advancement of neoliberalism on a global level, so the politics of racisms in Britain entered a new moment. Shortly following the 2001 riots in the northern towns of Bradford, Burnley and Oldham, the 9/11 attacks on the US came to denote a defining moment for the re-framing of race-relations policy in Britain. Just as the label 'mugging' came to symbolise, represent and thus mobilise a whole referential context of black ghettos, urban crime, drug addiction and related criminalisation, and a decline in 'law and order' in the 1960s and 1970s (Hall et al. 1978), so in 2001 the terms 'terrorist' and 'terrorism' came into play on new levels to mobilise the cultural context of panic and fear of the suicide bomber, of endless war on our doorstop anytime, anyplace, and of a barbarian, backward, premodern, uncivilised culture threatening 'our' way of life. This phantasm, a threat imagined, has justified an associated escalation of state militarisation and securitisation for the purposes of retaining 'law and order'. The shift from mugger to terrorist equated to a shift from the 'criminal' to the 'unlawful enemy combatant', a shift from an object whose crime could be dealt with within the law to an object that ultimately required suspension of the law (or its extension) in order to curtail legal rights and freedoms. The mobilisation and manipulation of the law to protect the sovereign and target the enemy, in essence the blurring boundaries of legality and illegality, has created an unprecedented institutionalisation of the state of exception – the normalisation of the state of exception, if you will. The heightened level of panic created by the boundless,

1

amorphous, global War on Terror has been tapped into regionally and globally to legitimate and justify the implementation of a permanent police state. This managed state response is of course complicated by the specifics of the political economy of our times. The rapid advancement in biotechnologies now available to govern, monitor and control enable the practice of much more sophisticated biopolitics, increasingly covert in their implementation even as they are ever more intrusive.

So the War on Terror in the colony saw to the creation of a label, then 'ready-made' for its mobilisation to govern 'the terrorist' at home. The technologies used to discipline and control and the ideologies which inform strategies for war have been transferred to the home front. Post 9/11, we witnessed a rethinking of the way in which (British)Muslims would be besieged and disciplined in Britain, as they became the targeted enemy within. Much work was done to construct the figure of the 'terrorist threat' which encompassed drawing on age-old notions of the oriental Muslim; the male simultaneously barbaric, pre-modern, hyper-aggressive and hyper-sexualised, whilst also displaying homophobic and patriarchal tendencies denying the Muslim woman – veiled, submissive and without her own agency –the rights and freedoms deemed the foundations of liberal, democratic civilisations. The potential violence of 'the terrorist' became the cash cow for Western allies, particularly the US and Britain, which mobilised such a threat to step up their programmes of militarisation and the securitisation of everyday life. The response of the state and key political commentators was to argue the failure of, and consequently to call for an end to, multiculturalism as a state response to governing racialised minorities. The new approach was a politics of integrationism (Kundnani 2007) which in essence brought to the forefront, yet again, the problem of 'cultural difference', artificially posing a clash of Islamic and Western belief systems as reasons for social tensions and unrest, prompting instead a series of measures designed to promote the Britishness of Britain's Muslim citizens. As the politics of integrationism set to pummel out any allegiance British Muslims might have to diasporic links abroad, or indeed to mute them from speaking out against Britain's attacks on fellow Muslims in Iraq, Afghanistan, Pakistan and elsewhere, this reinvigoration of (racist) British nationalism went hand in hand with a strategy of heightened discipline and control.

Framed through the state's revised Counter-terrorism Strategy, (CONTEST), which encompasses the four central themes of Prevent, Pursue, Protect and Prepare, the War on Terror in Britain is fought as much within the state's welfare functions as within its policing arms. The strategy of pre-emptive action, from which 'Prevent' takes its cue, has been rolled out through schools and youth clubs as well as higher education, just as we have witnessed a glut of terrorism legislation and escalation of police powers. We find ourselves in a moment where our children are actively taught to be aware of potential 'terrorist threats' just as they are taught to be aware of the dangers of crossing the road; where Muslim girls in particular are taught to play their role in the prevention of terrorism; and where teachers, many of whom have never been in contact with Muslim communities in their personal everyday lives, are trained in how to identify indications of 'extremism and radicalisation' amongst their students, while anti-racist education and training receives scant mention or attention. It is a situation where youth workers are expected to exploit the trust they have developed with young people, as youth-services provision is eroded to a bare minimum, to spy and report on any suspect behaviour. It is a state where protocols are sent out to universities setting out guidelines and recommendations for monitoring Muslim students and societies, encouraging campus police patrolling for this very purpose. And it is a state which actively encourages community self-policing, whether it be for users of public transport to be extra vigilant and report anyone or anything which embodies 'suspicion' or the Muslim communities themselves to scrutinise each other using spy boxes placed in mosques. This indoctrination of threat and suspicion is then backed up by the conflation of 'hard' and 'soft' policing which sees to the increasing use of closed-circuit television (CCTV) cameras, the proliferating use of stop and search, control orders, detention without trial and a drastic removal of legal (and human) rights. Thus, there can be no doubt that the most pervasive form of racism in the current political moment is that conducted through the War on Terror which centres the Muslim as the ultimate folk devil. Yet this focus, which dominates the narratives in this book, sits alongside continuities of racist institutional practices and responses that are all too familiar. As racism extends to the new, it of course builds on the old, so that its articulations and representations overlap as they also reform, becoming ever more complex. The cause and response to the urban disturbances of 2011 and the media hysteria around sexual exploitation are cases in point.

On 4 August 2011, Mark Duggan, a young black man from Tottenham, was shot dead by the police. The operation, involving officers from the specialist firearms team CO19 and from Operation Trident, a police initiative which specifically targets black communities for gun crime, sparked uproar in the local black community as they confronted yet another incident of police brutality. It seemed that despite key historical moments which have unveiled entrenched institutional racism within the police and wider state structures, the most infamous example in recent history being the 1999 Stephen Lawrence Inquiry, confrontation with and criminalisation by the police has remained a long-standing, all too regular experience of black youth. This incident was a frequently familiar, almost normalised interaction which informs the statistics that tell us that in 2011 black people were 30 times more likely to be stopped and searched than whites under Section 60 of the Criminal Justice Public Order Act 1994, up from an 11 to 1 ratio in 2009 (Delsol 2012). The increasing use of the notorious Section 60, which permits police officers to stop and search without reasonable suspicion, was a reminder that racial injustices are ever present and, indeed, on the rise. While powers to assist and arm the police have reached hitherto unprecedented levels and granted them exceptional liberties, the racial pathologisation of black youth as 'folk devils', gangsters, and drug dealers, and, generally, as culturally degenerate, was as evident in the popular and media narration of the 2011 riots which followed as it was in the 1980s.

In the year following the riots, another repetition of popular racist sentiment took hold of public discourse. In May 2012, when nine Asian men from Rochdale were found guilty of a variety of offences relating to child sexual exploitation, a huge national debate was prompted concerned with 'Asian grooming', reviving the colonial dichotomy of effeminate/ hyper-sexual Asian males (Kalra 2009). Spurred on by both the extreme-right British National Party (BNP) and the English Defence League (EDL), who protested that 'Our Children are not Halal Meat', and by the more liberal voice of the former head of Barnardo's, Martin Narey, who had pointed out that the street grooming of teenage girls in northern towns was overwhelmingly carried out by Asian men, the national press were forthright in posing key questions, such as 'are there more Asians involved in this kind of crime than might be expected, as a proportion of the population?' And, if so, 'are there any cultural factors that would account for it?' (Vallely 2012). A clear pathologisation of Asian men as sexually deviant with little respect for women went hand in hand with the denunciation of Asian women as submissive, veiled and abject, who were silenced in the debate which centred on the honour of white women. The current conjuncture reminds us that demeaning and degrading cultural representations of the racial outcast are alive and well.

Race in the current conjucture

Stuart Hall noted in the 1970s that 'Racism is always historically specific...Though it may draw on the cultural and ideological traces which are deposited in a society by previous historical phases, it always assumes specific forms which arise out of the present – not the past – conditions and organisation of society' (1978, p. 26). The present moment finds us under the radar of what has been termed 'advanced' neoliberalism, the neoliberal crises 'several stages further on' (Hall 2011). If neoliberalism's main objective was to reduce barriers to global flows of capital so that it could roam freely across borders, finding new work-forces, new markets, new resources to exploit, as David Theo Goldberg (2009) has noted, it also required greater security from perceived threats (racially perceived and defined) both within and outside the state. The central role of the state was thus restructured from welfarism to secu-ritism, or as Goldberg has articulated, from that of 'caretaker' to 'traffic cop' (2009, p. 334), where we witness the rapid erosion and/or milita-risation of all social welfare arms of the state. Consequently, while race remains a key structuring condition of state formation – now driving the neoliberalism of the late-modern capitalist state, just as it organ-ised modern state formation – the level at which it operates has altered significantly. In yet another moment of deep structural adjustment and economic stagnation, the realities of high unemployment, cuts to the welfare system, and the erosion of higher education, a time period char-acterised by austerity, we find the British state increasingly withdrawing from all aspects of social provision whilst ring-fencing and bolstering counter-terrorism budgets.

Yet, just as the state has shifted the way in which it packages and employs racisms, there prevails an oppressive and suffocating discourse which states that race is no longer relevant, that we are 'post-race' in a similar fashion to being 'post-colonial' and 'post-apartheid'. In September 2010, *Prospect Magazine*, for example, published a dossier entitled 'Rethinking Race' which consisted of articles by four 'postrace' Asian and black professionals. All four argued that racism was no longer so salient, but that the increase in monitoring required under the Race Relations (Amendment) Act 2000 had promoted a climate of suspicion and fear wherein racism was arising from its mere endorsement as a discourse; that is, through the state's encouragement to name racism, racism was being created. While the limited articulation of racism as an individual act or attitude was nothing new, the significance of this publication was its reflection of a much wider discourse on race and racism that has come to dominate and characterise the first decade of the twenty-first century. David Cameron, echoing this sentiment, appeared outside Downing Street in the aftermath of the 2011 riots, clearly stating that they were not race riots or a reflection of prevailing racial injustice and inequality, but an example of moral breakdown and criminality.

While the discourse of postraciality has received increasing attention in US popular, political and intellectual circles, this framing has to date been granted much less focus in British scholarly work, despite the fact that it is being increasingly adopted as political rhetoric to describe the contemporary moment. The problematic of the 'postrace' discourse comes to light when one considers the large discrepancies between racial rhetoric and racial experience, where for many racialised minorities ongoing racial stratification and injustice mean that conditions have largely remained unaltered or have worsened under present systems. It is this dichotomy which has been defined as the present racial crisis (Winant 2004), and a situation which remains unexamined. This collection seeks to address the gap in the literature by offering insightful theoretical and empirical contributions largely focusing on the British context. While there is a need to be alert to the nuances between the different racial state projects, this collection offers an important contribution to the international 'postrace' debate from a British perspective.

Aims of the book

The aim of this collection is to bring together a series of responses and reflections that provide a counterweight to this 'end of racism' agenda, and to make a much-needed intervention into the plethora of identity work which has largely come to dominate intellectual approaches to race in Britain. Almost nurturing the postrace mentality, the pervasiveness of identity politics as a means of addressing race foregoes the much deeper, entrenched forms of state racism which continue to inform the lived realities of many. At times, it could be characterised as a 'cultural studies lost', both from its roots and in terms of its future direction. Countering the reductionist tendency to see folks as the product of their position in the racial hierarchy – over-determined as victims and partial people – the necessity of the cultural turn formed part of the need for redress, to be addressed as fully human. Potent critiques of the nation emerged from this demand to be recognised, and race talk punctured settled notions of belonging, indicating some possibilities of a planetary humanism (Gilroy 2000). In the meantime, the inexorable inertia of state racism pushed on but with a more subtle veneer, and the presence of brown and black bodies, space invaders, lent the core institutions valuable cover stories (Puwar 2004). But as 'race-as-identity' work pushed towards achieving recognition and equality of representation, academic discourse caught in the necessity of producing innovation and novelty, at times of an ever-irrelevant kind, has been unable to catch up with the rampant exertion of state intervention in its punitive and coercive capacities that has come to mark the contemporary period. The continuing necessity of tackling the vicissitudes of the nation, should not mean a neglect of the role of the state. And it is in this vein that this volume is produced; it is primarily concerned with articulating race as it works in the discursive and material terrain of the state and its particular institutions. Its mission is thus to reflect upon and critique the contemporary 'state of race'.

A number of topics which have forefronted the politics of race in Britain over the last decade occupy these reflections. Since the election of New Labour in 1997, we have witnessed one of the most turbulent periods for the politics of race in the UK. The 9/11 and 7/7 attacks, continued urban unrest, the rise of the BNP and the EDL, the War on Terror, the politics of asylum, and the 'crisis of multiculturalism', all represent the reconfiguration of the politics of race and are discussed within our narratives of the racial present. The particularity of the cases is punctuated by an understanding that European-wide policy on integration and cohesion is often informed by the supposed 'progressive' stance of the UK. Mirza and Sirryeh's chapters address this wider context in relation to Muslim women and asylum seekers. The presence of the European court and the wider integration of individual states into extradition processes also frames the debate in Kapoor's chapter. This international comparative dimension is also present in Rhodes, who looks at the discourse of whiteness across the Atlantic. Indeed, the collection begins with Goldberg's reflections of the postracial in the USA and how this can be refracted into the European context.

David Theo Goldberg's work has been influential and instrumental in asserting the role of the state in creating and maintaining racial difference. His opening chapter considers some of the shifting contours of the 'postrace' debate in the USA, discussing how it reflects upon, but also alters and shapes, the neoliberal order. In particular, the election of Barack Obama in 2008 has led to what Goldberg has deemed the 'postracial', a mash-up of the hitherto known racial order, where public discourse has become much more explicitly racist compared with the 1960s, yet where the presence of racism is routinely denied, disavowed and deflected. In keeping with the neoliberalisation of the state and the subsequent individualisation of the social, the postracial creates epistemological and ontological confusions. Goldberg illustrates this schematic with examples from the USA, Europe and elsewhere, setting a larger frame for the subsequent chapters, which are mainly focused on Britain. Indeed, the second chapter, penned by Gargi Bhattacharyya, takes up some of the key insights into postracial neoliberalism and questions their applicability to the British context. Crucially, the usefulness of these concepts is tested on the ground of the rhetoric of austerity and a massive withdrawal of state funding from the provision of social goods. It is the presence of a welfare state that perhaps most distinctly marks the UK from the USA, and it is to the dismantling and reorienting towards the free market of institutions such as the National Health Service (NHS) that so marks the contemporary period for Bhattacharyya. There is, then, the reappearance in economically difficult times of what are termed older forms of racism, the crass division between insider and outsider rendered in popular culture through issues of criminality and immigration. This sits alongside newer forms of racism targeted at the alien patriarchal cultures of terrorists within, where the state's only role is that of increasing policing and surveillance. This division is necessarily heuristic, and is an attempt to disaggregate the ongoing impact of the War on Terror and the more recent 'austerity'. It is an analysis, in part, offered to consider how the objects of these discourses might find themselves able to respond. Bhattacharyya is interested in the way that racialised groups respond to the neoliberalisation of state services in an ambivalent manner, reflecting their previous experiences of poor treatment and racist exclusion. It could be argued that this ambivalence towards 'austerity' and the drastic reduction in welfare is a point of connection with the white population, but as James Rhodes articulates in his chapter, the construction of the white underclass through a range of popular and media techniques has become one element of the deflection of race onto a particular group rather than a point of recognition of the role of state racism.

In Chapter 3 Rhodes outlines the way in which the discourse of whiteness became embroiled in the politics of blame following the urban disturbances in the UK in 2001. The caricatured figure of the white working class has reappeared in the 'chav' and in the representation of a 'feral underclass'. In the postracial landscape, then, it is this group that carries the burden of the racists, whilst the tolerant, respectable middle class carry out a double disavowal of race and class. The endemically racist white working class service a number of political projects. They allow the state to represent itself as absolved of the responsibility of advocating equality, as some racialised minority groups have achieved economic success and the existence of poor whites means that all is well in the meritocratic society. Secondly, the core values of the middle class become universalised in a non-racist consensus. Ultimately, the white working class become available as a minority group in their own right, and the fear of a 'white backlash' allows politicians of the right and left to make arguments against multiculturalism as the process by which whites have been left out of state resources.

It is an in-depth analysis of multiculturalism that forms the core of Sivamohan Valluvan's Chapter 4. Whilst recognising the multiple ways in which the term has been used and abused, Valluvan wishes to recapture it from the critique that has rendered multiculturalism as only representing 'tolerance' of the cultural other. This is what he terms a 'mischaracterisation', a 'thinning' of a concept which still has much purchase as a site of critique of the nation, as well as pointing towards what is the only way of formulating a contemporary society. The critical edge that multiculturalism offers is demonstrated via the re-staging of a debate between Slavoj Žižek, political philosopher/commentator, and Sara Ahmed, feminist/ race theorist. Valluvan insightfully demonstrates how the 'illusion' of multiculturalism as the hegemonic tolerant is deployed by Žižek without being alert to the mirage-like status of the concept. In one sense, Žižek and Ahmed give too much power to the notion of multiculturalism. Rather than being focused on group rights or on the question of tolerance, multiculturalism can do better with more modest aspirations of causing disturbance to the neutrality of the nation-state in its treatment of racial difference. In sum, a robust multiculturalism (perhaps the opposite of a robust liberalism) enables the recognition of difference and an interrogation of misrecognition, not just at the level of an abstracted culture, but at the very heart of the way the state exerts biopolitical power. Mirza takes up the issue of multiculturalism but with the inflection of gender, in the last chapter of this section. By taking on the binary heroine/ victim, Mirza traces the representations of Muslim women in public and media discourse. To some extent there is no possibility of representation outside of this binary, there is no outside of these representations, as the Muslim women's body becomes the site upon which European racial discourse plays out its most virulent Islamaphobia. State multiculturalism, in its most illusory form, fosters and promotes a victimised Muslim woman terrorised at the hands of an equally imaginary community. Mirza offers the corrective to these circulating deceptions by alerting us to the multiple contexts in which women are exploited, abused and oppressed. The possibility of escape from the heroine/ victim dichotomy is represented in the actions of campaigning groups in the UK who struggle for women's rights in the context of state racism.

Whereas the first section of this volume embarks on an investigation into the conceptual terrain of the state of race, the second section encompasses five chapters which look in detail at a number of substantive issues that illustrate various aspects of the racial state. Opening with what is a rarely spoken about issue, Vron Ware asks the pointed question 'Can you have Muslim soldiers?' Her chapter takes us on a detailed tour of the British army's various attempts to deal with issues of equality, diversity and multiculturalism. To some extent, despite the army carrying some aura of special status due to its role in national defence, the examples given in the chapter demonstrate numerous continuities with other institutions, such as the NHS, in the difficulties faced in addressing racism. By bringing the army into the remit of a state public service there is the danger of perhaps over-normalising what is the ultimate tool of violence available to the state. However, Ware is constantly aware of the multiple levels at which the army uses the rhetoric of diversity and develops an interplay between the obvious colonial continuities and the current demands of the US/UK wars in Afghanistan and Iraq. It is this interplay between international issues and their impact on local institutions that is taken up by Shamim Miah looking at the experiences of Muslim parents and school children. Drawing on interview material, this chapter poignantly articulates the way in which the War on Terror conjoins with local issues of Islamophobia and general school-level racism. The specific manner in which anti-terror initiatives of the British state, such as CONTEST and Prevent, directly impact on the schooling of Muslim children is highlighted. It becomes apparent that there are direct continuities between the securitisation of education and the securitisation of community life more generally, demonstrated by the consideration of these policy frameworks in the following chapter by Virinder Kalra and Tariq Mehmood. The manner in which the dividing lines between the police and intelligence agencies coalesce is explored here through the example of the Birmingham spy cameras. Following the placement of surveillance technology in predominantly Muslim areas of Birmingham to track and monitor all those entering and leaving, a successful, locally led campaign resulted in the removal of CCTV cameras. However, in the process the deep complicity between hard (counter-terrorism) and soft (community-oriented) forms of policing was revealed, and it is this increasing racial securitisation of the British state that Chapter 9 exposes. In a detailed reading of the debate on the extradition treaty between the US and the UK that took place in the House of Commons in December 2011, Nisha Kapoor reveals the racist distinctions that were central to determining who was worthy of support and who was not. The clear divide between those who were deemed worthy of extradition (Babar Ahmed and Talha Ahsan) and those who ought to be protected (Gary Mackinnon), reveals the ongoing racial stratification of British justice but with new levels of racist technologies to hand. In this analysis of the British state in its current conjuncture, Kapoor points to Britain's leading position in the War on Terror and its increasing implementation of the exception as routine. The final chapter of the book returns us to the 'older racisms' theme developed by Bhattacharyya, addressing the hostility faced by asylum seekers. Ala Sirriyeh draws on interviews with groups of refugees and asylum seekers to examine the way in which the immigration system has come to increasingly merge with the ever-intrusive securitisation agenda. Using the notion of domopolitics, the way in which the concept of home becomes a site of struggle for those wanting to make a new life in the UK, and for those institutions seeking to keep them out, is a central narrative in the chapter. In a similar manner to the chapters on surveillance and extradition, Sirriyeh draws on campaigning bodies that are trying to challenge and address the increasingly punitive regimes that asylum seekers and refugees face.

If the issues highlighted in the last five chapters make for grim reading, it is only a small indication of the manner in which the British state has become increasingly punitive when dealing with issues of law and order. Our aim here is not merely to offer a pessimistic view for pessimism's sake but to draw attention to the ongoing realities of racial persecution that reach new heights in current times, making the claims to 'the end of racism' difficult to tolerate. As we narrate here some of the continuing practices of state racism, we anticipate a call for the re-mobilisation of an anti-racist lobby that unites against all dimensions and targets of racism in order to continue the fight for its redress.

References

Delsol, R. (2012) 'London Police Rethinks Stop and Search Tactics', *Open Society Voices*, 24 January 2012 http://www.soros.org/voices/london-s-police-rethinks-stop-and-search-tactics

Gilroy, P. (2000) *Between Camps. Nations, Cultures and the Allure of Race* (London: Penguin Books).

Goldberg, D. T. (2009) *The Threat of Race. Reflections on Racial Neoliberalism* (Malden, MA: Blackwell).

Hall, S., Critcher, C., Jefferson, T., Clarke, J. and Roberts, B. (1978) *Policing the Crisis* (London: Macmillan).

Hall, S. (2011) 'The March of the Neoliberals', *The Guardian*, 12 September 2011, http://www.guardian.co.uk/politics/2011/sep/12/march-of-the-neoliberals

Kalra, V. S. (2009) 'Between Emasculation and Hypermasculinity: Theorizing British South Asian Masculinities', *South Asian Popular Culture*, 7(2), 113–25.

Kundnani, A. (2007) *The End of Tolerance: Racism in 21st Century Britain* (London: Pluto Press).

Puwar, N. (2004) *Space Invaders. Race, Gender and Bodies out of Place* (Oxford: Berg).

Vallely, P. (2012) 'Child Sex Grooming: The Asian Question', *The Independent*, 10 May 2012 http://www.independent.co.uk/news/uk/crime/child-sex-grooming-the-asian-question-7729068.html

Winant, H. (2004) *The New Politics of Race. Globalism, Difference, Justice* (Minneapolis: University of Minnesota Press).

Part I

1
The Postracial Contemporary

David Theo Goldberg

The postracial is upon us.

It was born – or rather raciality was born again, anew – when Barack Obama got elected. Postraciality went public, declared itself the state of being, at least aspirationally. There quickly followed a frenzied media discussion about whether America had become postracial. It takes one presumptively black man to get elected president for a self-presumed white country's racial history to be wiped clean, apparently. The Great Man version of history takes a new turn on stage.

Even the critical response – Kim Crenshaw, Sumi Cho, CNN, and Tim Wise perhaps most subtly and insightfully, among others – became beholden to the logic, if in denial: not so fast, not yet, here the counter-evidence. In the US, the family wealth gap between whites and blacks and whites and Latinos, respectively, has spiralled to the highest since records were first compiled in 1984, now 20:1 (from 12:1) for the former, and 18:1 for the latter. Resegregation in schooling and housing has expanded in the past 30 years, faster this decade than before. Republicans have engaged in a variety of questionable tactics to discourage, if not prevent, people of colour from voting in districts where they have higher representation because they are more likely to vote for Democrats. A slew of politicians and media commentators, harsh conservative critics of Obama and his presumptive friends, have revealed in slips, innuendo, and outright vicious characterisation how unprepared Americans have been to deal with what Fanon called 'the fact of blackness.' The viciousness of mash-up internet images of the President and First Lady, from witch doctors to baboons, evidence of the ghost of racism shadowing the postracial.

In South Africa, the supposed model of a state transitioning to postraciality, racial animosities and structural inequities remain extensive. White wealth and black poverty have remained the structural default, notwithstanding a small burgeoning black bourgeoisie and the re-emergence of white poverty. White students at the University of the Free State urinated in a pot of soup and then gave it to a black cleaning woman to eat. Recently, a photograph was posted to a Facebook page of a grinning young Afrikaner in a military fatigue bush shirt, holding a rifle and kneeling over the dead body of a young black boy as if over the carcass of his dead prey. The Facebook page quickly generated nearly 600 'friends'. Authorities were investigating the commission of various crimes, whether or not the image was doctored (see Swart 2011's article in *Times Live*). At the same time, black nationalisms rival white paranoias.

In Europe, racial discrimination in policing and migration restrictions has been demonstrably on the rise against blacks and Muslims, not to mention the license given to public figures like Geert Wilders in the Netherlands to speak in racist ways about people of colour. Four young people of colour peacefully wearing T-shirts protesting that "Zwarte Piet is racist" at a Sinterklaas parade in a rural town in the Netherlands were beaten up by white policemen for challenging what effectively is the national mascot. In the wake of the London looting by youths after a young black man was shot by police in August 2011, historian David Starkey, interviewed on BBC, pompously pronounced that rioting white youth had come to 'act black'.

Are we postracial yet? Hell, no, the evidence screams back.

All of this, it seems to me, is the obvious response, much as I hate to put it thus. Less obviously, Harvard critical race legal scholar Charles Ogletree (2012) has suggested that the response 'depends' on the evidence one looks to: in some respects America is postracist, in others not. The affirming or negating responses nevertheless give in to the question, they presuppose its credibility, assume its seriousness. They take for granted a conception of 'the postracial condition' widely ascribed to, about which there has been all too little critical public discussion.

There is another, if related, line of questioning necessary here, suggesting a different trajectory of analysis. What work is the 'postracial' doing, as conception and claim? What is the recourse to postraciality producing socially, by design and/or implication, as social conception and ordering? In short, as racial articulation? And posed in this way, why now? Why the popularity of the 'postracial,' and not just in America but pretty much wherever race has (had) significant resonance? (Parts of Latin America, most notably Brazil, may be interesting, if telling, exceptions.) Why is it that public racist expression has become far more virile and vicious in the name of the postracial than it had been since the 1960s. What (and who), it might be asked in the face of this fact, is the postracial for?

I

The notion of 'the postracial' can be traced genealogically and interactively to conceptions of 'colourblindness' and the US civil rights movement, to anti-apartheid's 'nonracialism' (as articulated most clearly, for example, in the mid-1950s Freedom Charter), and broadly to the post World War II romance with racelessness. More deeply, immediately, and directly, 'the postracial' resonates conceptually and temporally, culturally and politically, with neoliberalism. The postracial, in good neoliberal spirit, is committed to individualising responsibility. First, it renders individuals accountable for their own actions and expressions, not for their 'group's'. By the same token, it supposedly does not ascribe responsibility to one's racial group for the actions and expressions of the supposed group's individual members. In this latter sense, the neoliberal's scepticism about the agency of social groups generally could be claimed to encourage the erosion of racial connectivity and, by extension perhaps, of any ontological claim to racial groups more broadly.

If liberalism's economic anthropology is centred around *homo oeconomicus*, neoliberal anthropology, as Foucault (2008) suggests, rests squarely on the heroic Man of Enterprise: he who makes and makes it up, the man adept at managing, if not manipulating, mixture, social intercourse, and mash-up. Committed to innovation and design, he works at opening up, prising open, entry for the sake in the end of nothing else but self-advantage, self-possibility, self-profit. If there is social benefit as a result, it would be a fortuitous value added, but that cannot be the goal or mandate. Looking good and looking cool. Self-minded in his hipsterdom, flaunting prowess and profit, but also projecting braggadocio and whatever can be gotten away with. Seemingly in full control even as he borders on being out of control, he networks only with the like-minded and like-looking. He makes things on the basis of innovative design, making things happen by making things up. Fabrication and self-making, creation and recreation as the presiding sensibility of the time. This makes evident too why recreational activity – extreme sports, extensive game playing, and so on – has been transformed, literally re-created, from what we do occasionally or on the side, a hobby, to a prevailing mode of profitable capitalisation and professionalising practice.

In keeping with the neoliberalising thrusts of individualisation and self-making, the postracial condition doubles racial response. On one hand, responsibility for racist expression is reduced to individualised account, to a bad apple, a rogue element, denying responsibility to structural conditions or larger social forces. For neoliberalising postraciality, racism is anomaly, the mark of a past historical moment, an irritating residue to be gotten over as quickly as possible, or even simply recreational ('I was just kidding'). It remains merely a stain on the social fabric now, to be washed away as quickly as possible, simply with a wave of the magic wand.

On the other hand, self-production apparently applies as much to the making of racial identity and self-expression as it does to any other mode of expression or product(ion). So one is licensed to make up one's personal racial life story and social identity for the sake of self-advantage. Virtual possibilities such as avatar identities obviously expand and elasticise the reach while multiplying the range of this self-making. And in doing so individualised responsibility is instantaneously magnified while its importance, its seriousness, is discounted, especially in moments when one might be called to defend one's choices. Social life takes on a game-like quality with all the implications thus entailed.

II

The presumption that race is no longer socially relevant plays out in a variety of ways, all coagulating in increasingly unspecifiable because unnameable conditions disadvantaging people of colour in general. So there is now intense resistance from whites generally to any social amelioration (let alone social benefits) accruing to anyone from a disadvantaged racial group in virtue of their ongoing racially identifiable social disadvantage.

In general, then, the postracial era we apparently are now taken collectively to inhabit is shorthand for the state of generalised social equality of opportunity supposedly marking contemporary social arrangements. Equal opportunity is the characterisation of conditions from which overt impediments to entry and competition have nominally been removed. Far from equality of outcomes, no longer is the pressing criterion for equality of opportunity the preparedness to compete – for places at university, or employment – but simply the minimal barrier to apply and be considered. That anyone can apply, no matter their racial characterisation, level of preparedness, or professional qualifications, suffices to meet the bar of postraciality. This is a long drop from the standard liberal commitment to an equality of opportunity as sharing a baseline level of preparedness; and any commitment expressed to an even more robust equity in outcome or distribution is quickly dismissed as socialist. While this way of expressing the commitment is now especially explicit in the US, that it is an entailment of central neoliberal presumptions suggests that it holds far more broadly, if less explicitly, even in states with more robust egalitarian histories.

In turn, this has opened up another less predicted effect. The removal of formal racial barriers to competition, discriminatory or affirming, has signalled a license of, even an insistence on, the erosion of barriers to free expression in racial terms. This has prompted white people to feel free to say almost anything crossing their minds about folks of colour, reiterating and reinforcing the most pernicious of stereotyping. Living in a postracial state seems to have entailed the possibility of expressing oneself in ways as blatantly and explicitly racist as one chooses without running the risk of being called on it, or if and when called to task being easily able to swat away the charge as unintended, misperceived, or simply silly.

The postracial accordingly empties out the racial conventionally conceived of its 'classic' meanings, thus opening the racial (in its empty silences) to be filled with any meanings chosen, at hand, fabricated. This 'filling' becomes a 'fulfilling' – of prophecy, prediction, of what is divined, always already known – of history, personality, productivity, national character (in a sense, national personality): they are not ready to live among us, for advancement, for democracy, and so on. Here Glen Beck's (2011) history lessons are exemplary, as are his make-believe claims about Egyptian events in Tahrir Square at the beginning of 2011 (in Beck's muddled mind, the popular uprising was fashioned by 'socialists and Islamists' looking to establish a caliphate throughout the Middle East). The postracial, in short, reinscribes destiny in the name of its supposed denial.

It follows that postraciality is pure political theology. It manifests as it transcendentally (re)inscribes unchallengeable belief, what Thomas Blom Hansen (2009) properly calls conviction: the racial silent, the silently racial – its ghostly presence burying alive racial histories – is the perfect medium for what I call 'make believe': of compelling belief in the unbelievable, the unseen 'truth' inscribed yet again in socialities of the skin, now presumed without naming (because they no longer have to be), evidenced experientially (as communities of experience) but lacking independent warrant. These commitments can now be asserted shamelessly because absent the apparent cover of classic racial terms.

Absent the terms, intentionality no longer has to be denied; it simply can be said never to have crossed my mind.

Postraciality proceeds, then, by way of *deflection* from attending to racial disparity: Invisible Man becomes Invisible Condition, the condition of Preferred Invisibility lost in the fog of social spectacularity. In more intimate settings I am simply co-existing with those like me, in looks and likes, means and manageability. In matters of individual racist expression, the apology is invariably for the offense taken ('I am sorry if you are offended'), almost never for causing harm or hurt. Indeed, this is tantamount to no apology at all. I feel bad – well, at least rhetorically – that you feel bad because of what I have done or said but don't for a moment think I am going to undo the deed or expression. The problem, really, is all yours; or even more insidiously, if only by implication, it is you who are in fact the problem.

This deflection enables the assertion of the racial in its social conditions and conditionality without calling attention to the raciality of its condition. Israel in Palestine offers the perfect case in point. So racism expresses itself in the extreme because it is de-linked from the constraints of its being named as racial injustice. The avoidances of racial reference, of being named in and on these terms – being named as pariah condition – evidences the lengths to which folks, folk history, privileged folks, folks asserting privilege while claiming disprivilege, ruling folks will go to purge itself, themselves to deflect the taint: I don't have a racist bone in my body, I didn't intend it, we are a nation of laws, we stand for justice, given our history how dare you suggest. David Starkey (2011) denied that his blackening of white London looters was *racial* stereotyping by insisting that he was characterising culture not biology, in immediate self-denial about the long and deep histories of racial culturalisation and culturalising modalities of racial expression and racist exclusion, ridicule, and rationalisation. The blissful state of ignorance, beyond and beside belief.

So the postracial is not simply a racism without race or a 'racism without racists', as Eduardo Bonilla-Silva (2003) has put it. Rather, and as I write in *The Threat of Race*, it amounts to 'racisms without racism'. This is the enigmatic condition of the circulation of racisms, renewed, reinvented, resurrected, born again though never dead, without the terms to name it as such, to identify, comprehend, condemn. We could even call this racisms' avatar condition. Reducing to singularity what is plural, poly-expressive and pluri-conditional, *the* postracial – substantivisation registered in the definitive article – homogenises raciality to the monotony of mono-expression, the more readily to dismiss.

III

The postracial, in some ways, is to the racial as the postcolonial is to the colonial: not the end of race, just as the postcolonial indicated not the end of colonial effects, but a different mode or set of modes in which the racial is instantiated, lived, lived out. Anne McClintock (1992) remarked that the shift from the colonial to the postcolonial signals a shift from relations of power (the coloniser and colonised) to the linearity of time (progress from the before to the after, the worse to the better off). This sort of shift covers over or draws attention away from those who continue to benefit and suffer from the postcolonial condition (the 'ex-colonisers' and their 'casualties'). Something like this logic marks the postracial condition too. Racisms reprise at the very moment of racial erasure – only now unmarked, unrecognisable, unseen.

So just as the 'post' in the postcolonial is not the end but the after-life of the colonial, so too, the 'post' in the postracial: the afterlife, the ghostly haunting by the racial of the social supposedly rid of the racial. To be postracial, just as to be postcolonial, is to imply, if not to admit, that the society in question must have been racial (just as it once engaged in colonial practice). But the implication of raciality is not quite admission, indeed is implicatively a denial of its once and present racism. The postracial, then, is racial as spirit condition of the social, sociality's unnamed because unnameable spirit, its shadow being. The postracial is another modality of racially marked and racially exclusionary sociality.

Structurally, postraciality is committed to expanding new markets and the new identities to support them emanating from but exceeding any traditional mode or expression of raciality. As a means to expansive marketisation, postraciality assumes a master thread in the social fabric of neoliberalisation. Markets are encouraged or expanded by seeking out new mixtures and what Stuart Hall (2011) calls 'the middle ground' that they presuppose and (re-)produce. Neoliberalising postraciality's 'meeting in the middle' extends renewed energy to integration as postracial expression, effectively leaving in place long-established hierarchies of racial articulation.

Postraciality, then, remains enigmatically a raciality. It is a raciality that in its enigmatic drive to exceed the bounds and bonds of race, to multiply or proliferate the inputs in capital's ever-expansive quest for profit and power, does so through denial. This denial is not just of historical conditions but of the contemporary constraints – the legacy of racially driven inequalities – structured by those historical conditions

reproduced across time. The postracial buries, alive, those very conditions that are the grounds of its own making. Buried alive, those conditions continue to constitute a hold, a handicap, a disability at the
intersection of race and class on those still forced to bear their load.
Class standing mitigates and mediates the load, admitting some into a
register of the privileges of whiteness, without dissolving or compen-
sating (completely) for the accumulated disadvantages.

A Tea Party group in Kansas, the Patriot Freedom Alliance, depicted
President Obama on its website in the figure of a skunk (Associated Press,
2011). The accompanying text rationalises that 'Skunks are half black,
half white, and almost everything it does stinks.' In the face of criticism,
a group spokesman simply denied the claim is racist. No explanation
needed because, divorced from any racial legacy in which it stands, the
charge of racism makes no sense. The nominalism of just calling a skunk
a skunk is divided by the firewall of denial from calling a monkey a
monkey, or a 'n – – r' a 'n – – r.'

But the postracial is not just the denial of lingering racial conditionality, its discarding of the racial to the past of history. It is more than that:
the 'post-' in the 'postracial' is the denial also about postracial *denial*,
deniability's recursive refusal. I assert my (non-)racial, my postracial
innocence not just by denying that I any longer, or ever, make (or made)
a racial reference or mobilised racist exclusion; I now further deny that I
am in denial. I can't possibly be racist now because I never was then. My
tolerance now – my openness to all otherness, or even more strongly to
all *my* otherness – is evidence of my characteristic tolerance. So I couldn't
have been racist then too. I can't be in denial because – tolerant then,
as now – denial was never an issue. So postraciality reaches also for the
denial of denial. I have turned my historical past into an empty white
canvas, perhaps even a canvas of whiteness. Or better yet a canvassing
of whiteness. The postracial is nothing less than the vanishing point of
race, and the supposedly fading pinprick of racism.

In the name of postraciality, political and demographic exclusions
become – as Saree Makdisi (2010, pp. 554–5) puts it in the case of excising
Palestinians from any consideration in siting Jerusalem's Museum of
Tolerance, just as they have been systematically excised from Israel
and to increasing degrees from Palestine more broadly – erased from
consciousness and consideration. These erasures become, in Makdisi's
terms, so 'clean, pure and total' as to cease being 'recognisable' as such at
all. They become the erasure of erasure itself, leaving in place consideration only of those who define and determine the terms of consideration
to begin with.

The postracial thus is also a passage to reversals: reversals of who gets charged with racism, of privilege charging the relatively disprivileged or the insurgent with racisms: whites calling blacks, or Muslims racist; Israelis condemning Palestinians; the Democratic Alliance Party in South Africa pointing fingers at the African National Congress (ANC); the Republicans in America charging the Democrats or claiming historical credit for ending slavery as a way of denying their own implication in the institution (cf. David Barton's historical revisionism), and so on. But the reversals sought also target longstanding civil rights laws: if the nation has elected a black president it no longer needs racially directed voting rights legislation or affirmative action programs, for its racist history is now behind it.

So the historical inheritance of racial privilege denies both its racist expression, but for its individualisation to a bad apple here or there, while insisting that the morally rejected behaviour of the racially disprivileged is the expression of group culture. Turnaround, it seems, is fair play. But it is also in keeping with the political right's tactic to take over the terms of progressive critique and turn them against the commitments for which they have long been taken to stand.

So the postracial is the predictable elaboration of the neoliberal – or, as I put it, the hyper-extentuation that is the neo-neoliberal – through the mimetic mixtures and mixings of unleashed and unlicensed social intercourse. Almost but not quite anything and everything goes. The mimetic here is the insistence that the standards, values, and social conditions to be aspired to and emulated are those of the racial dominant, of whiteness as see-through condition, as social transparency itself. A transparency that allows the thick traces of racial privilege to be reached only by tracing – mimicking – dominant sensibilities. And where mimetic mixing breaks down, where rogues and rogue states break the boundaries and erase the edges of socially acceptable mixture, institutionally mandated violence is invoked.

Neoliberalism – and the neo-neoliberal, by way of hyper-extension – serves to drive a wedge between the state and the economic (and civil society more generally). The economic and civic emphases on a robust economic deregulation and privatisation, combined with intensified social re-regulation and the independence of an expansive private sphere, are deployed to produce multiple effects. They seek to curtail the impact of the state and those aspects of its regulatory apparatus designed to expand equity, and to shrink the power of the state over matters economic and social. These emphases have been coterminous with the perception that government and its apparatuses have become increasingly diverse, if not black, less controllable as a consequence by traditional (and overwhelmingly white) elites. So such thrusts in the name of negative freedom have managed to delimit the impacts of the inversion of racially inflected power. Political power is either ceded or redirected in favour of extending economic power and social capital. The sort of impacts registered here are obviously played out differently in different state formations, a fact belied by reducing them variously to postraciality (as Ella Shohat (1992) remarks with respect to the 'postcolonial'), though the general logic nevertheless has broad applicability.

The Postracial Contemporary, then, is the instantiation – the instancing of and instant recourse to – the racial while denying that it adds up to racism or indeed that racial characterisation is being invoked. And denying the denial. It has become – it has been made – the default mode of globalisation's neoliberalising political rationality, the seams of its social logic.

IV

The postracial thus cuts away or undercuts the language for identifying, analysing, and addressing racially charged distinctions, discrepancies, divisions, disqualifications, disturbances, discreditations, disdain, indifference, and disingenuousness. In short, it increasingly removes or erodes the possibility of identifying racisms and their underpinnings, their structures, effects and affects, their implications.

So the postracial ends the possibility of *seeing* racisms and their structures of enablement, their conditions of possibility. The postracial blinds us to the racial, to racisms, their materialisations and traces. Barack Obama, Republican Senator Tom Coburn says, is 'a wonderful man...I just have a lot of admiration for him.' But as 'an African American male', Coburn continues, Barack Obama 'received "tremendous advantage" from government programs. His intent is to create dependency because it worked so well for him.' Here is the postracial president: marked with racism in the name of friendship ('some of my best friends are') while explicitly invoking race (African Americans, affirmative action) and yet, silencing the possibility of calling it for what it is. As friend he is like me, only not. Distantiation by subtle disadequation. (Political) death by dislikening in the name of liking. (Even more recently, Tea Party Republican Congressman Joe Walsh, characterising President Obama as 'idiotic' – a comment for which he later apologised – insisted that 'Obama was elected because he is black...I think we elected this president because of who he was...He was a historic figure. He's our first

African American president. The country voted for him because of that. It made us feel good about [our]self').

Newt Gingrich, front runner for the Republican presidential election nomination in 2012 at the time he uttered these words, declared Palestinians to be 'an invented people'. Lacking a state, they are generic Arabs, who could and do live anywhere. Of course, if statehood is a condition of peoplehood, pretty much every 'people' is invented at some point on these grounds. Defending this claim against the properly predictable criticism, Gingrich further demonised the Palestinian people as being politically fabricated only in 1977: 'They are all terrorists' he declared in an Iowa primary debate (10 December 2011). Judging from the (lack of) reaction, almost no one noticed.

These reversals – no longer the domain of the white privileged and powerful but of the black and brown (unfairly) advantaged – have a more general resonance underpinning them. Racism loses its historical legacy; anyone can now be racist. Writing about the popular American television program *30 Rock*, philosopher J. Jeremy Wisnewski declares that 'As hard as we try to avoid it, we may harbor racist assumptions – no matter what color we are' (2010, p. 58). Formal equality trumps even the deepest (and formally produced) substantive inequality. And if the historically disadvantaged and disenfranchised today are readily racist too, it follows that racism is no more than the sort of traffic infraction we all engage in pretty much all the time and no one bothers to call out. Call this driving while texting (in contrast, perhaps, to texting while driving).

The postracial accordingly inures us to how racisms feel, to the affective implications of racisms' expressions. Self- and socially licensed to say publicly anything that comes to mind about blacks or immigrants or Muslims, public figures in North America and Europe have expressed themselves openly in perniciously prejudicial terms indifferent to the harm their contempt may cause or, especially, to the violence or discriminatory exclusions to members of the targeted racial groups they may encourage. In Orange County, California, white Christians have made Muslim women and children run a gauntlet of ugly crowd epithets just to shop at the supermarket or visit the doctor. And Dutch parliamentarian Wilders, who is renowned for his insults of Muslims, has repeatedly equated the Koran with *Mein Kampf*.

The postracial makes it possible, accordingly, to ignore, avoid, or fail to attend to the spiralling disparities between the deraced privileged and the racially de-faulted disprivileged (or in short, the racial default). So the postracial becomes not just the cover up – the ideological 'racialisation' after the fact – but the constitutive ordering that enables, if it doesn't directly produce, the extension of the disparities from the racial default. Not only do blacks remain poor, but the poor are made to be black (as David Starkey remarked, 'Britain's white looters became black'). The postracial reinforces through extending the racial ontological by rendering race itself ontological, the unremarked and unmarked given of Being, of nature, simply a fact of life.

From which there is then no escape because the postracial is not just the denial of racism but the denial of the denial of racism.

The postracial accordingly embeds an epistemology of deception. Things are not as they appear to be. The non-racial, to which postraciality is conceptually wedded and out of which it historically has grown, is the refusal to acknowledge the structures of race ordering the social. In denying racial structures, in assigning them to an unreachable past, postraciality fails – really, refuses – to comply or to live up to pre-ordained expectations about how racial configuration and racist expression are manifest (slavery's emancipation was brought about by Republicans; the black US president is committed to enlarging racial dependency for African Americans; profiling Muslims as potential terrorists is demanded by state security; Muslim American students peacefully disrupting the Israeli ambassador's rationalisation of Gaza's invasion turn out to be violating the ambassador's free speech rights). It is not postraciality that reshuffles the structural deck, but the modes of articulation, expression, rationalisation, and explanation of extended racialities, their effects and refusals.

At the heart of postraciality's condition of deception is what Ackbar Abbas in a more generalised mode calls a state of *dis*-appointment (2010, p. 174). *Dis*-appointments fail to conform to their appointed places, to appointed modes of being and doing, to conventional (in this case, raced) sociality. At once states of ordinariness with recognisable everyday markers – residential, recreational, resourceful, socially containable, exploitable – they nevertheless are out of the ordinary, refusing their *appointed* and so anticipated sites or roles, unrecognisable as and in their everyday-ness. They are dis-locations and in a sense dis-locutions, appearing where least anticipated and expressing themselves in unexpected and unpredictable ways. They accordingly lack location, or more precisely locatedness, in terms of their comprehensibility.

A state's or social condition's *dis*-appointedness is the source and manifestation of its at least partial illegibility, spawning perhaps a crisis of social representation and control. The social conditions of everyday life here can no longer be taken for granted, assumed to deliver or underwrite or guarantee – as the state once did – the baseline daily conditions of existence, The postracial helps to make less or illegible the generalised condition today of racially expanding precarity, the proliferation of the conditions of precarious possibility, even as it helps to reproduce the very condition it refuses by withholding the terms of recognition. A precarity that is both epistemological and ontological, though the former is not simply epiphenomenal of the latter.

'Deception' in this account paradoxically constitutes modes both of being and (analytic) knowing, the latter reflecting on (not reflective of) the former. Knowing at an angle, obliquely, a kind of – if inadvertent – revelation. A seeing not just behind and beneath in those older structural models, but providing insight into the ontological condition of the behind and the underneath. A knowing not just in but through the misdirections and denials.

In short, the challenge here is to read deceptions as a way around the analytic and conceptual inadequations of the critical terms currently available to us: what are the significance and value of the misdirections in this case regarding race? Through deceptions, the misdirections to which the postracial in denial (of the denial) of its raciality gives life, an other history, other ways of being, their readings and meanings come into view, become socially compelling, those that may otherwise remain indiscernible.

If living in a critical condition opens up the recognition that there is no (longer a) future, as once we knew or had come to expect it, this non-future – the generalised state of precariousness – is ordered through race. Race not only identifies who is subject(ed) to a futureless precarity; one's proximity to precarity ascribes to one a raciality otherwise less ontologically binding. The proliferating – endless? eternal? – repetitions dis-appoint, not only in dashing the prediction of the yet to come, but also in the sense of spawning the refusals of the deadening drudgery, invigorating spaces, however fleeting, not reducible to the assimilative.

Thinking in terms of an epistemology of deception implies a modernity not as progress but as the social folding in on itself to stave off the polluting if ceaselessly fascinating and so enticing horrors of what Philip K. Dick (1954) famously called 'dust people'. This relation between deception and the dissolution of subjecthood suggested by Dick's notion of 'dust people' conjures a rethinking of race as modes of deception rather than as the theological creation of peoplehood and its evolution. Race can be conceived in terms rather of the secreting of identity, in this doubled and ambiguous sense, as seeping into and molding personal, social, and political formation while also conjuring (public) secrets, even banalities, of belonging, banishment, beleaguerement, and belligerence.

The postracial then, in the final analysis, is a mode of social magic, the alchemy of racism into nonracialism, its etherealisation, the ghosts of racisms past dissolved into the indiscernible pixels making them up. Dust people, confined to memorialisation on the History Channel, are variously disappeared, otherwise invisible and illegible to the socially (and racially) dominant.

V

Recourse to the postracial holds at arm's length the threat of conceptual confusion: con-fusion, the conflation/mixing of categories that has come with the massive demographic movements of globalisation and the associated stress on mixtures, commercially and recreationally, aesthetically and culturally. Mixture and mash-ups are now the objects of contemporary desire. The postracial is the refusal of the world's dissolving mixings, the fear of being confused, of mixing one's metaphors, of misstating because misreading who one is speaking to, for, about, and against. Call this, following Alex Abramovich, the fear of being 'phenomenologically fucked'. The postracial seeks to stave off the conditions of being conceptually confused – is she, isn't she? – and of being phenomenologically screwed.

Obama is the outcome – the symbol, the avatar – of the postracial, not the prompt or the cause. Many thought, perhaps over-optimistically, that Barack Obama's election to the US presidency would signal that racism, and perhaps racially produced disposability, was now an historical relic in America, the American example for the world to emulate, just as the end of apartheid – 'racism's last word' – might signal to the world that the relic of race had finally been put to rest.

Far from being a thing of the past, however, racism has become reanimated as a key instrument of the political, only now in new ways and to new purpose. That the notion of race can be so easily filled with new political purpose, alas, is basic to its chameleonic and politically instrumental nature. A strategy of raciality is to extend suspicion to anything marked by its terms, effectively to erode the standing of those racially inscribed by innuendo or explicitation.

Thus, longstanding if subtly transmuting racial orders invariably shadow the postracial, delimiting its possibilities and constraining its reach. Structurally, postraciality keeps in place prevailing conditions of historically produced racial arrangement and power, both domestically and globally, now stripped of their historically inherited terms of recognisability. Ideologically, postracialism does not solely absolve whites of guilt for past racisms. Rather, it erases the very histories producing the formations of racial power and privilege, burying them alive but out of recognisable reach, thus wiping away the very conditions out of which guilt could arise. That denial of denial: no guilt because there is nothing recognisable to be guilty about. Postracialism is the uncanny feeling that there but for good fortune or God's will go I. The uncanniness concerns the hint of misfortune while denying its possibility, or at least denying any responsibility for it structurally, causally, or morally. That I go there not suggests I have done something right, recognised in my earthly or heavenly reward. The force of sustained and sustaining historical subjection is reduced to the personalising roulette of misfortune or bad decision-making.

Postracialism is reduced, then, to reinstating a sociality of commercial mixing and social segregation only now superficially scrubbed of its explicitly pernicious terms of articulation. To promote tourism, the State of Mississippi has established the 'Mississippi Freedom Trail' alongside the 'Mississippi Blues Trail' and the 'Mississippi Country Music Trail' (the equivalences themselves are staggering). The 'Freedom Trail' identifies for tourists about 30 key sites in the civil rights struggle, from the Greyhound bus station that formed a key stop on the Freedom Rides in 1963, at which civil rights activists were so brutally beaten by bigots as Mississippi police idly watched; the driveway of his home in which Medgar Evers was shot to death by Klansmen in 1963; and the firebombed tomb of NAACP leader Vernon Dahmer. Then Mississippi Governor Haley Barbour, one time Republican presidential candidate and vocal supporter of the Citizen's Councils, he expressly whitewashed of their racist past, appropriated $20 m, to establish a civil rights museum to attract tourist dollars to a severely under-employed state. At the same time, in indices regarding employment, education, living standards, and the criminalisation of black Mississippians, the state continues to rank as or among the worst in the US (Trillin, 2011, pp. 36–42).

In the name of postraciality, racisms are manufactured and manifested more silently, informally, expressions of private preference schemes rather than of formalised state policy, reproducing the given and seemingly gone. Mississippi's Citizen's Councils, for example, were established in the 1960s expressly to delimit desegregation, a commitment they continue now silently to enact. Postracialism denies just how conceptually confused we have increasingly become, and how phenomenologically impoverished it actually leaves us. Postraciality distressingly leaves us phenomenologically challenged, twice over.

References

Abbas, A. (2010) '"Thinking through Images: Turkishness and Its Discontents": A Commentary', *New Perspectives on Turkey*, 43 (Fall 2010), 163–74.

Abramovich, A. (2009) 'Phenomenologically Fucked', *London Review of Books*, 31, 19 November 2009, http://www.lrb.co.uk/v31/n22/alexabramovich/phenomenologically-fucked

Associated Press (2011) 'Kansas Tea Party Illustration Draws Racism Claims', *Yahoo News*, 11 December 2011, http://news.yahoo.com/kansas-tea-party-illustration-draws-racism-claims-012650692.html

Barton, D. (2011) 'The Founding Fathers and Slavery', *Wallbuilders*, July 2011, http://www.wallbuilders.com/LIBissuesArticles.asp?id=122

Bonilla-Silva, E. (2003) *Racism without Racists: Colorblind Racism and the Persistence of Inequality in the United States* (New York: Rowman and Littlefield).

Dick, P. K. (1954 [1992]) 'The Adjustment Team', in *The Collected Stories of Philip K. Dick. Vol. II: We Can Remember It for You Wholesale* (Secaucas, NJ: Carol Publishing).

Foucault, M. (2008) *The Birth of Biopolitics: Lectures at the College de France 1978–9* (New York: Picador), pp. 147–50.

Hall, S. (2011) 'The Neoliberal Revolution: Thatcher, Blair, Cameron; the Long March of Neoliberalism Continues', *Soundings*, 48 (summer 2011), 9–27.

Hansen, T. B. (2009) *Cool Passions: The Political Theology of Conviction* (Amsterdam: Amsterdam University Press).

Makdisi, S. (2010) 'The Architecture of Erasure', *Critical Inquiry*, 36(3), 519–59.

McClintock, A. (1992) 'The Angel of Progress: Pitfalls of the Term "Post-Colonialism"' *Social Text*, 31/32, 84–98.

Ogletree, C. (2012) 'President Obama's Election and Pursuit of a Post-Racial America', Al Meyerhoff Public Interest Lecture, University of California, Irvine, Law School, 15 February 2012.

Rowley, J. (2011) 'Coburn Says Obama Pushes Reliance on Programs That Aided Him', *Bloomberg News*, 18 August 2011, http://www.bloomberg.com/news/2011-08-18/obama-fosters-program-dependency-coburn.html

Shohat, E. (1992) 'Notes on the "Postcolonial"', *Social Text*, 31/32, 99–113.

Starkey, D. (2011) 'White Rioters in London in August 2011 Were "Acting Black": This Not a "Racial" Characterization but a "Cultural" One', *Newsnight*, 11 August 2011, http://www.youtube.com/watch?v=bAGTE_RGN4c

Swart, W. (2011) 'Wanted: Facebook Racist', *Times Live*, 28 August 2011, http://www.timeslive.co.za/local/2011/08/28/wanted-facebook-racist

Trillin, C. (2011) 'Back on the Bus: Remembering the Freedom Riders', the *New Yorker*, 25 July 2011, pp. 36–42.

Walsh, J. (2012) 'Obama Was Elected Because He Is Black', *Huffington Post*, 30 April 2012, http://www.huffingtonpost.com/2012/04/30/joe-walsh-obama-was-elect_n_1465964.html

Wisnewski, J. J. (2010) 'Race at the Rock: Race Cards, White Myths and Postracial America', in J. J. Wisnewski (ed.), *30 Rock and Philosophy: We Want to Go to There* (New York: Wiley-Blackwell), pp. 57–74.

2
Racial Neoliberal Britain?

Gargi Bhattacharyya

The rush to label all recent social, economic and political phenomena as neoliberal is reminiscent of discussions of postmodernism – sometimes particular terms seep between sub-disciplines and are exchanged as a kind of cipher for a broader sensibility, in this case, the suspicion that economics might matter after all. However, as with previous catch-all terms, the explanatory value of the term may be limited or so expansive that it is hard for us to speak meaningfully to each other (see Ferguson 2009). If we are to take neoliberalism as a frame through which to understand the remaking of global racism but with local configurations, then there may be some value in considering again what we mean when we name our neoliberal times. After all, the point of sharing these catch-all terms is to enhance our shared understanding, even if we may continue to disagree on the details of what is happening and why it matters. As a result, what follows is largely an exercise in clarification, to try to think again about the term 'neoliberalism' and what it might signify in the concept 'racial neoliberalism'. I use this discussion to consider the suggestion that neoliberalism is in crisis and perhaps has been for some time, and how plausible such a suggestion is in relation to racial neoliberalism in Britain. This leads to a reconsideration of the definition of racial neoliberalism and its applicability to Britain, and of the impact of austerity measures on these patterns of racism. Consequently, I argue that we need to adopt some flexibility in our use of the concept of racial neoliberalism and, in particular, in our attitude to its relation to securitisation. Perhaps we have lived through a time where heightened state coercion runs alongside claims of economic liberalisation, but perhaps also, other circumstances might throw up alternate configurations of this relationship. Parallel to this uncertainty is a question about the reach of neoliberalism and whether there is a subject of racial neoliberalism in the mould of the much discussed neoliberal subject. I end without firm conclusions about the existence of racial neoliberalism in Britain but with the suggestion that a serious interrogation of the claims made for this concept allows us to focus and reflect on the challenges before us. After all, aren't we discussing this thing, racial neoliberalism, only in order to resist racial injustice?

Thinking through 'neoliberalism'

The debates about postmodernism share some of the difficulties with defining neoliberalism – in particular, the tension between viewing postmodernism as a philosophy (perhaps even a politics) and the adaptation of 'postmodernity' that sought to transform the term into a description of our age, not a celebration of the alleged death of grand narrative and the democratic potential of fragmentation and surface, but an account of how the overall structure of feeling of a time can be remade. For neoliberalism, there is a similar uncertainty – is it a culture or a technique? David Harvey (2005) splits the concept in two thereby addressing both aspects – so when we consider neoliberalism, then what is evoked is hegemonic project, ideological stance, perhaps zeitgeist, whereas with neoliberalisation, technique and process come to the fore. There are clear benefits to this division which for our purposes enable us to consider the discursive narratives of racial neoliberalism; postrace, meritocracy, opportunity, security to protect our way of life, and the governmental techniques associated with neoliberalisation: restructuring public services, punitive approaches to welfare, and military occupation. The question that remains, however, is the extent to which these two aspects and the variations within each aspect can be understood usefully as one entity. Temporarily giving up the term neoliberalism as a catch-all would lead to a double focus on racial neoliberalism (ideas and propaganda) and racial neoliberalisation (the emerging techniques of racism in a neoliberal world).

Even with this clarification of focus, is it asking too much for this conceptual framework to identify all problems associated with racism and racial structuration. Stuart Hall (2011) argues that neoliberalism should be understood as a hegemonic project, splicing together contradictory elements to link the imagery and logic of popular common sense to the highly interested project of enabling and protecting the class interests lurking behind neoliberalism's supposed freedoms. For Hall, the cheerleaders of neoliberalism have been winning the ideas war, even as the practices of neoliberalisation fail in some instances to deliver or to be developed in any meaningful sense. The barely planned reforms of British state social welfare provision, such as the reorganisation of the National Health Service or the complete overhaul and potential dismantling of higher education, could be regarded as examples of neoliberal rhetoric outrunning neoliberalising technique. Similarly, perhaps the ideas war of racial neoliberalism has had greater impact (so far) than the practices of racial neoliberalisation.

If neoliberalism is understood as a particular fixing mechanism employed by the international institutions of global capitalism in the late twentieth and early twenty-first centuries, then by implication, the debt-laden events of recent years demand another adaptation. Whatever the debates about the strange death or even stranger resurrection of neoliberalism (Peck, Theodore and Brenner 2009; Crouch 2011) as an approach to economics and some aspects of government, for us the question must be the extent to which the mutation, racial neoliberalism, also adapts or dies as a result of economic crisis. For Britain, there are signs of an escalation of some themes of racial neoliberalism, for example, in official assertions that racism is in the past, as seen in the response to the summer riots of 2011 (Stratton 2011). Numerous media commentaries sought to compare the disturbances of 1980s Britain and the events of 2011, noting the parallels of economic downturn and recently elected Tory (-led) governments, but asserting that in the 1980s racism constituted a legitimate grievance and gave a political coherence that could not be claimed for the events of 2011. Now, it was argued, things were much better, and racism had been all but eradicated from British life. A discourse which continued the concerted silencing of race and discussion of racism in recent popular debate, racism was yet again described as an unfortunate but long-gone aspect of Britain's past. The response was another example of Britain's self-congratulatory moment of the postracial, shaped by the assertion that the Stephen Lawrence Inquiry had represented an acknowledgement of and coming to terms with racism, which meant the job was done. Despite the reminders of Doreen Lawrence, among others, that racism remains a significant and sometimes violent barrier in British life,[1] there is a continuation of more celebratory 'postracialism', not least through the emergence of a (still limited) group of ethnically diverse emissaries of official institutions and mainstream political parties, in part presented as an answer to the often-asked question (in 2008/9): where is the British Obama?[2]

This skirmish over the speakability of race in popular discourse comes at a time when the formal institutions of anti-racism are in flux. The restructuring of official bodies, such as the Commission for Racial

Equality, to form the umbrella body, that is, the Equality and Human Rights Commission, which is now responsible for overseeing adherence to anti-discrimination legislation on the grounds of not only race, but gender, age, sexual orientation, disability and religion or belief, echoes changes in equality legislation and the bringing together of previous law into the single Equality Act. All of this has taken place in a manner that moves away from conceptions of structural inequality. Although the push to enable consideration of multiple discriminations has been welcome, the parallel consequence has been a silencing of hard-fought-for recognition of the historical specificity and reach of racism in favour of a model of inequality that places different aspects of inequality as equivalent and, to an extent, interchangeable. Inevitably, this encourages the increasingly prevalent view that the experience of discrimination is a result of unfortunate interpersonal relations, with little or no connection to wider context or history. Linked to the restructuring of equality legislation, there has been a conflation of equality with human rights in both the institutional response and in popular discourse, with human rights then derided as an expression of excessive individualism, which may also cause looting (according to some of the official pronouncements in the aftermath of the 2011 riots), a weakness requiring containment by state enforcement of responsibility (Stratton 2011). This echoes the push to construct a willing subject of neoliberalism who pursues self-government and self-interest through the post-welfare framework of personal responsibility, as opposed to any idea of universal entitlements described in accounts of the neoliberalisation of social life (Wacquant 2009; 2010). As Wacquant argues, such a self-understanding serves to legitimate the move from welfare state to penal state – because the unlucky citizens seeking to survive this punitive regime have only themselves to blame.

However, there are also areas where other aspects of racial neoliberalism appear to be changing. After a decade of highly publicised and celebrated erosions of civil liberties in the name of security, the 'new' racism of anti-terrorism initiatives seems to reassert the 'old' racism of law and order. In part, I suggest, this is a response to the difficulty of maintaining a sense of emergency over a long period of time. The continual assertion that anti-terror measures have averted possible attacks and confounded terrorist conspiracies relies too heavily on the goodwill and credibility of an electorate who express a general distrust of officialdom and politicians. Old-fashioned racism that presents some as subhuman, violent, disorderly and unable to become like 'us' is more reliable, more deeply embedded in popular culture and consciousness, and more available as a familiar explanation in economically difficult times. In fact, both narratives have intertwined in recent years, with law and order narratives about the grooming of children for sexual exploitation, organised crime, and illegal immigration all reworked to reference such security-coded tropes as political Islam, transnational networks among migrants and among Muslims, the alleged failure of multiculturalism and/or integration, and the dangerous incursion of alien beliefs and cultures. This recognition that apparently new forms of racism often rework older tropes has become another banality of the field. The racist narratives of the War on Terror owe something (clearly, explicitly, and sometimes too proudly) to earlier imperial adventures, with the endlessly repeated implications of clashing civilisations and moral crusades; but, equally, War on Terror racism creates some quite new demons, transnational networks that inhabit migrant diasporas and exploit new communication technologies and the widespread access to cross-border mobility in our time. The central racist fantasies of the War on Terror are rooted in both the specificity of our historical moment, where the rich fear the consequences of transnationalism, mobility and technology in the hands of others, and the recurrent racist fear that others remain pre-modern, unchanging, vengeful and beyond the constraining influence of reason. This imagining is not only a replaying of older colonial forms of racism, although it may include aspects of these older forms. As a consequence, racism in our time veers between the fear that others have never changed and will never change and are destined to be dangerous natives for all eternity, and the fear that the natives have learned more extreme ways to be dangerous as a result of immersion in our contemporary world and its possibilities. It is not that either fear supersedes the other, only that there is an ebb and flow between older and newer racist mythologies and that this movement indicates something about the wider context of racism.

Despite the continuing occupation of Afghanistan, what is arguably occupation by corporation in Iraq, and the still to be fully revealed actions in Libya, there has been a rhetorical move away from the logic of the War on Terror on the part of government (Milliband 2009). Now the Iraq war is presented, at the very least, and including by leading proponents of this endeavour, as problematic – and more widely, as a disastrous mistake that will continue to overshadow international politics for a generation. Although it is clear that much of the machinery of the War on Terror continues – including Guantanamo, secret prisons, extradition agreements that favour the US, a panoply of anti-terrorist legislation, and the emergence of extensive if changeable programmes to address so-called domestic extremism – official rhetoric from all parties indicates that the logic of the War on Terror – us and them, war without end, a continuum between radicalisation at home and military choices abroad, and the wholehearted and resource-intensive propagation of so-called humanitarian intervention as a cover for pre-emptive strikes – must be disavowed. Similar practices continue, not least in the ongoing killings of civilians in Afghanistan and Pakistan. In fact, intervention in Libya has been presented as a rehabilitation of military intervention legitimated by diplomacy, in contrast to the debacle of Iraq, while Iran and Syria await their turn. Nonetheless, the Bush-Blair crusade of reshaping the world through military might and moral conviction has for the moment rescinded, a sign of austere times, perhaps.

It is through more local violence that the emerging face of a postracial Britain might be signified. In the aftermath of the 2011 urban disturbances, and in a context of official vilification of anyone in need of state assistance, which works to foster further division and a sense among citizens that we are competing for scarce resources, we appear to be in a period of rapid reassertion of where racial danger lies: with a normalising of recent anti-Muslim rhetoric in official statements and even in the popular media and a resurrection of old-fashioned demonisations of 'black youth' and all others who imbibe black cultural influences through urban culture.[3] Stuart Hall (2011) suggests that the project of neoliberalism benefits from harnessing the post-imperial melancholia of popular racism, even though this nostalgia is in contradiction to the destruction in the name of markets celebrated by other (more central) aspects of neoliberal thought. Hall describes this as using appeals to popular common sense, referencing familiar aspects of popular belief to add emotional pull to the more innovative elements of the neoliberal narrative. It doesn't matter that these elements are in contradiction, what matters is that the overall narrative appears to appeal to commonsensical beliefs. Old-fashioned law and order racism fulfils this need, whereas the less established claims of War on Terror racism require more work, more explanation, and, potentially, a new repertoire of racist language and concepts.

This is not to suggest that War on Terror racism has disappeared – and by this I mean the particular escalation and re-articulation of anti-Muslim racism that constantly references security, civilisation and national allegiances – only that the articulation of popular racism adapts, returning to longstanding tropes of the subhuman, the irrational, those beyond civilisation. Of course, these representations do refer to Muslims as well as to 'black youth'. My point is only that the more complex and convoluted racist narrative of the War on Terror – that they hate our freedoms; that they have come to inhabit the networks of modernity for anti-modern aims; that the new demons are engaged in a secret war against 'us' that is motivated by ancient hatreds but enabled by the newest technologies; that the offspring of migrants affect integration in order to destroy our way of life from within – has become more muted in favour of more old-fashioned forms of racism. This is well illustrated by the way in which the issue of grooming young white females for sex has mutated into an issue of Muslim sexual deviancy (Vallely 2012). If racial neoliberalism is adapting in the face of economic crisis, this adaptation appears to combine a refocusing of varieties of postracialism to legitimate and veil the uneven impact of austerity, with a pulling away from, perhaps even a normalisation of, recent innovations in state racism through security in favour of older forms of state racism through law and order.

Racial neoliberalism and the British State

The gains of welfarism have always been won through a combination of resistance, organisation and, alongside this, a particular understanding of what makes a stable environment for capital accumulation. The threat of industrial disruption and the power of working-class political organisations, which at times have participated and been influential in the central operations of government, has previously created a space in some locations where 'welfare' is an acceptable compromise to enable economic business as usual (De Angelis 2000). At the same time, a workforce that is not impoverished, even if the aspiration for affluence is no longer spoken, is as useful and necessary as a local market, not least for the celebrated 'services' that were seen to offer clean and medium-status (neither 'low' nor threateningly 'high') work for all. The attacks on gains in welfare and employment protection only, following the 2008 debt crises, amplify a tendency that has been present in earlier incarnations of the modern state. Previous accommodations between welfare and impoverishment have inhabited, or perhaps created, divisions within the workforce and population. In Britain, these are often racialised and have led to a highly segmented labour market, not least during so-called boom times, and a variety of barriers (formal and informal) to the benefits of welfare provision (see Willis 1986; Li 2010). It is important to remember that the high points of welfarism also included entrenched poverty for particular sections of society. As the availability of social welfare provision gets worse for society as a whole, we might remind ourselves not to begin to mourn a lost golden age that for many never existed.

The usual response to this is agreement that this process, which could be seen to signal the beginning of a certain kind of immiserating neoliberal experience for some, started some years ago (perhaps as early as the disruptions of the oil crisis of 1973). Though if this periodisation is also related to the way in which we can construct a history of race, then this time period also encompasses the passing of key anti-discrimination legislation in Britain in the mid-seventies, even if, arguably, this legislation could also be framed as enabling individuals to gain rights over the collective demand of anti-racist justice. Indeed, this is an example of what Goldberg (2008) terms 'racism cordiale', a system of hierarchy that maintains both good manners and longstanding injustices, while at the same time utilising the logic of occupation to maintain everyday practices of racist exclusion and humiliation. However, the concept of racial neoliberalism suggests that racial politics is remade in particular ways in the time of neoliberal economics and state practices – yet key aspects of this racial neoliberalism predate the ascent of neoliberal economics. These ideas about economics and politics may trace back to the innovations of the economists of the Chicago school, but the historical particularity of neoliberalism as a period or set of events comes about only with the expansion of financial speculation (Coyle 2000). Without this link to a particular expression of global capitalism, it is not clear what is gained by trying to trace the racial dynamics arising from neoliberalism.

Racial neoliberalism is based on an account of global capitalism of a variety, until recently, created and sustained through an extreme privileging of financial speculation. This includes a shift of influence and authority from individual states and their internally defined interests to an endless promotion of what is demanded by the (international) market, thus inhabiting and exacerbating local patterns of inequality and, in this process, remaking racism as, again, a simultaneously local and global process. In *The Threat of Race*, Goldberg (2008) outlines the particular incarnations of these themes in a range of settings, providing a suggestive framework through which to consider global racisms in a manner that is attentive to regional histories. The apparent crisis in this phase of neoliberalism has brought about a range of responses, including quite contradictory actions. In addition, the majority of commentary has focused on state actions; so, despite the claims by both celebrants and critics of neoliberalism that the corporation has overtaken and/or infiltrated the state, the financial crisis has initiated an intensive re-evaluation of the responsibilities and possibilities of states. What has shifted is a move away from (or perhaps a tactical silencing/forgetting of) any suggestion that the state might intervene to improve the lives of the less enfranchised, the vulnerable or the poor, or seek to equalise social and economic outcomes. Instead, the central duty of the state becomes that of enabling/regulating economic activity and growth. As we have seen in recent scuffles around the Euro, a government's ability to achieve any other social goal is seen to rely on its ability to achieve this one underlying aim – to show economic competence and, through this, to ensure that the nation can participate in the global economy.

There is not much space for the pursuit of racial justice in this story. Along with other laudable but, apparently, too-expensive endeavours, these niceties are consigned to the ever-growing list of things that we can no longer afford. A few brave or bullish souls suggest that, anyway, it has been wrong-headed to believe that state intervention can change social outcomes, and that this is another wasteful activity (and perhaps corrupt and corrupting – as it allows the distribution of state resources for political favour) that should be stripped out of government (see Cai and Treisman 2005 for a review of some of these ideas). Unsurprisingly, the challenges that arise with economic crisis have led to a hardening of disadvantage for black communities, even while racism is disallowed as an explanatory term (McQuaid et al. 2010). In an echo of Goldberg's (2008) account, this denial of the impact of racism on social and economic outcomes can be presented as arising from an understanding that race is a fiction and that, of course, it is an economic disadvantage that is deepened by economic crisis, with the already vulnerable suffering the most. Within this account, there is no room to consider the impact of the fiction of race across time and the legacy of such histories of persecution or discrimination.

The texture of state racism in a time of austerity seems less easily deciphered. Yes, the cutting and stripping back of welfare hardens existing patterns of disadvantage, but this is a result of withdrawing positive assistance and losing jobs in areas that have employed groups who have faced barriers in other parts of the labour market. The more interesting and confusing question is how more-active and resource-hungry forms of state racism adapt to the constraints of austerity – after all, repression does not come cheap. This is not to disregard the claims that racial neoliberalism can, and does in many contexts, encompass both marketisation and authoritarianism, or that the claim of austerity is no more than another rhetorical ploy to re-allocate resources for other ends or to other friends. However, it is to raise the question of whether the contradiction between celebrations of small state, big market and intrusive and resource-hungry low-level (and not so low-level) repression is a constitutive contradiction or a historical peculiarity of our time.

Securitisation as an aspect of neoliberalisation

Some have argued that neoliberal economics does, in fact, require a certain level of state coercion – to protect the interests of corporations and a corporate class that are increasingly at odds with the experience and interests of the rest of the population; to limit the impact of any resistance to the rolling back of public services and the impoverishment of the wider population; and to ensure the continuation of a 'business-friendly' environment at the expense of other more widely distributed social goods (Wacquant 2009; Springer 2012).[4] Some or all of these goals may be reached through indirect actions, perhaps through the continuing confirmation to the public that the state has the means and the will to repress dissidence and disorder. If we accept this account, then the continuing investment in expensive but theatrical displays of repressive capability makes tactical sense. Both the articulation to the wider population that the threat to our way of life is embodied by small groups of dangerous men, as opposed to such threats as the dismantling of welfare systems, and the reminder that the state retains the capacity and will to persecute those who are identified as sources of social disorder, can be used to confirm that the state has a role if only as dispenser of coercion. I take it that Springer (2012) is referring to something like this in his account of the move from the violence of exception to the violence of example. The extreme theatricality of anti-terror measures, including both the combination of ineptitude and brutality of highly publicised arrests, and the open secret of human rights violations (something that, sadly, appears to garner significant support among some of the British public), echo other displays of state power, such as disproportionate violence in the policing of protesters – all with the message that acquiescence and quiet dissatisfaction is a safer option than dissent.

As a result of various aspects of 'post-democracy' (Crouch 2004), such as scepticism about the effectivity of the state or the political class in terms of its ability to identify potential threats, let alone address them, and the increasingly vocal distrust of political authorities which considers most, if not all, pronouncements of authority as no more than electioneering by another name, the difficulty for liberal democracies is that the wider population may also take a sceptical view of the theatrical repression of dangerous dissidence. The downgrading of government authority in popular consciousness, described by some as a characteristic of neoliberalism, undermines the authority of both official warnings of terrorist threats and public attentiveness to displays of coercive power.[5] There may be popular support for particular actions (such as the attempt to deport Abu Qatada, despite the prohibitions on the use of evidence obtained through torture), but these also are shaped by the fleeting interests of celebrity culture. Do you support the deportation of this cartoon villain today – despite the risk of torture and death? By the following day, such concerns are overtaken by new scandals – the latest celebrity death or footballing love-rat – and this passing interest in displays of repressive power blurs into the endless stream of expressions of outrage in response to the titillating triggers of popular media. In a time when the state is portrayed as representing bossiness without authority, constantly telling us what to eat, how to live, or how to avoid risk, but with no ability to influence events in any meaningful way, highly staged demonstrations of coercive power or assertions of the need for coercive power (and continuing fear) may be viewed with suspicion or indifference.

The various activities of the War on Terror fit into this requirement of state coercive power and intensification of marketisation. Goldberg (2008) argues that the repressive arm of neoliberalism is deployed against those who are deemed to be beyond the salvation of the market. Certainly, Iraq has demonstrated the macabre ability of corporate capital to transform all human suffering into a business opportunity. Afghanistan seems less decided, perhaps because the militarised fix has had less success there. The inclusion of economic opportunity as one of the positive goals of war has become an open objective of military intervention, as respectable, it seems, as national security. Other elements of the War on Terror, however, do not fit so easily into this narrative of forcing disaster to enable capitalism (Klein 2008). Considerations of the coercive function of the state as it is remade to serve neoliberal ends identify two key moments of activity. One is the penalisation of social provision, through an extension of the role of prisons, a reworking of welfare to enable punitive measures against the needy and a reframing of the needy as imaginatively linked with the criminal. This is the account that has been proposed, forcefully, by Wacquant (2009). The other is the shock-doctrine assessment of Naomi Klein (2008) – the process by which military occupation and destruction or natural disasters becomes an opportunity to remake economic relations, to dispossess previous inhabitants and to pursue the experiment of neoliberal economics full throttle, in spaces where the local population has few options and little leverage. In both accounts, coercion enables profit making for some; yet there seems to be a clear distinction between the violent remaking of economic life in the disaster zone and the more creeping penalisation of social provision in spaces which were until recently still characterised by welfarism. It is not at all clear where the assorted innovations of the War on Terror at home – that space of domestic security as opposed to military occupation – fit into these accounts of coercion for neoliberal ends.

In Britain a renewal of practices of state racism, including some innovations in law such as the introduction of indefinite detention without trial (transformed through legal challenge to house arrest), confirmed in the public imagination that some groups merited such repression. This did seem to enable an imaginative linking between the less-than-human at home and the less-than-human abroad – so that the logic of a realm beyond the law for some became an accepted component of security for the rest of us. However, although such practices appeared to achieve consent, in that protest was limited, the efficacy of proclamations of perpetual danger is less clear. Perhaps the general British public might, on the whole, be indifferent or moderately enthusiastic about the abandonment of legal process for some demonised groups, but sceptical about both the nature and extent of terrorist threat. And, more importantly, dubious about the ability of discredited institutions of government to protect anyone (Archetti and Taylor 2003). This reinvigorated racism at home was accompanied by a range of semi-covert practices designed to facilitate transnational cooperation in human rights violations in the name of security. It formed another aspect of the reinscription of race as a category signalling danger to civilisation, and meriting any amount of violence in order to curtail such a threat. Sometimes this has led to cooperation to safeguard markets or businesses, but sometimes this cooperation seems tied to more old-fashioned aspirations to regional influence. The repressive practices of the War on Terror may have become intertwined with the propagation of the idea of the market as saviour, but this seems to have been an accidental coalition. More likely, and as usual, the proclamation of participation in the War on Terror in different parts of the world reflects the longer-running political battles of those locations. This can be seen in Israel's attempts to rebrand an occupation that is more than six decades old or India's desire to reframe a seemingly endless border dispute with Pakistan or in President Assad's attempt to portray Syrian democracy protesters as a terrorist fringe that must be met with violent repression. In these examples, and many others, the securitisation practices of the War on Terror have a complex, varied and sometimes tenuous relation to the goals of neoliberal economics.

The easy claiming of torture and other forms of violence as necessary techniques for protecting national interests harks back to much older traditions of displaying power – through ravaged bodies and demonstrations of iron will. Not only is this a celebration of a certain kind of state power, it is an ongoing assertion of the necessity of the most brutal forms of power politics and the extensive and expensive governmental machinery that this requires. Not power exercised in order to safeguard markets, but power exercised in the name of the necessity of power. Significant changes have occurred in the way states legitimise their military activity. These include the least imaginative and sometimes frighteningly direct linking of racialised communities at home and occupied populations abroad; the apparent acceptance that legal process can be elided if national security (and perhaps economic security) is deemed to be under threat; and the development of a range of practices of surveillance, penalisation and exclusion designed to divide the human from the less-than-human. However, I am not at all sure whether any of this is an outcome of neoliberalism. Though it may be useful to coin broad and elastic concepts, such as neoliberalism, it is also important to remind ourselves that not all events can be encompassed by one overarching conceptual frame. If neoliberalism really is all-encompassing, a new meta-narrative that can bring together and legitimise so many disparate elements in the pursuit of consolidating class interests, then it becomes difficult to imagine points of intervention or resistance. This is something like Barnett's (2005) argument that if neoliberalism comes to be described as everything everywhere, with every inconsistency waved away with the assertion that we acknowledge contradiction, then there seems little benefit to this analytic process. It might be more useful, more attentive to particular histories and more open to imagining alternatives or points of intervention, to think about why some things look like neoliberalism, but perhaps are not.

Are all 'neoliberal subjects' really an outcome of neoliberalism?

> Stories about 'neoliberalism' thereby succeed only in finessing a set of interminable conflicts between equally compelling values of individualism and collectivism, autonomy and responsibility, freedom and obligation (Barnett 2005, p. 8).

A significant theme in the discussion of neoliberalism is the creation of the self-disciplining neoliberal subject who internalises what Wacquant terms 'the cultural trope of individual responsibility' (2010, p. 213). For some of those who tend towards big *N* accounts of neoliberalism – as the overarching narrative of our time and the texture of all our everydays – the manifestation of neoliberal logics in the self-governance of individual subjects has been of central interest (see, for example, Rose 1999). The neoliberal subject is the key to understanding the transformative impact of neoliberalism, but it is also one of the constructions that appears to render neoliberalism inescapable, a meta-narrative of our time that seeps into every corner of existence. Such all-encompassing accounts bring the consolation of providing a catch-all narrative to frame our world but, as Clive Barnett (2005) argues, granting such omnipotence to this concept limits our understanding of more varied and unpredictable events on the ground, and with that, limits our ability to imagine points of intervention or alternative. Forgetting neoliberalism, as Barnett suggests, may allow a greater acknowledgement that the restructuring of public services is shaped by a variety of forces, including popular forces that resist, in various ways and for various reasons, the logic and authority of the state. Thinking of racial neoliberalism in Britain, we might consider how and why some of those suffering racism also appear to embrace the logic and practices of neoliberal living.

What indications are there that racialised groups are enthusiastic supporters and participants in state-delivered welfare? Being a recipient does not mean that this is your chosen model of citizenship. There are plenty of indications that versions of populist anti-statism inform the views and political formations of racialised minorities. For example, the recent innovation of the 'free school', another Tory wheeze to enable various groups to set up schools and bypass the bureaucracy/regulation of the local education authority, has been embraced enthusiastically by communities suffering racism – as an opportunity to establish faith schools or to assert parental influence over the curriculum or to offer local schooling in areas without a nearby school (see Vasagar and Walker 2011; Wadsworth 2012). Over the last number of decades, again predating the emergence of an unregulated financial market, black politics has championed community organisation, including as providers of key services that the state appears unable or unwilling to offer or to offer effectively. While we may condemn Cameron's self-serving propagation of the 'big society', the celebration of community cooperation because state-provision is disappearing, this rhetoric echoes many favoured themes of community and anti-racist politics. Plenty of those raised in black politics or anti-racist campaigning believe, quietly, that we (the people; the community; black, self-organised groups) can do things better than the (racist) state.

At the same time, there is a well-founded scepticism, and not only in black and minority communities, about mainstream party politics, the operation of state bureaucracies at local and national levels, and the role of officialdom in all its forms (see Stoker 2006 for a discussion of these issues). Attempts to argue for the defence of the role of the state and of state-provision are hampered by this popular dissatisfaction. It seems to me that dark-skinned folk of varying hues have embraced the promise of neoliberal subject-hood with enthusiasm, despite the real threat of even greater impoverishment as a result of a rolling back of the state in the name of the market. Our communities look set to lose out as a range of social gains are threatened. These include public-sector jobs, the benefits brought by public services, the partial regulation of some parts of the labour market and the protections this offers workers, the remains of public housing, and welfare benefits which are now under extreme attack. All of this is framed by explicit plans to render those on benefits destitute in order to motivate them into work. Yet, despite all this, there appears to be little love for the state in popular consciousness.

In part, this arises from a sense in recent years that the state is constantly failing, a sense that it promises welfare but is unable or unwilling to include all in its reach. This disappointment or scepticism towards the role of the state creates a climate where many are open to looking elsewhere for solutions to addressing social need. However, although there are social rewards for those willing and able to perform particular versions of neoliberal subjectivity, such as celebrating the irrelevance of race, the end of racism and the ascendance of meritocracy (a performance which may appear to be linked to a gain in social status for some), much of the suspicion or indifference or inattention towards state-based solutions makes no reference to the supposedly greater benefits of market-based interventions. Instead, any consideration of non-state or anti-state initiatives among minority communities needs to account for a number of experience specific effects. Firstly, of course, one of the main areas of mobilisation of minority groups has occurred in relation to the failure of public services, and specifically the experience of racism and exclusion when accessing these services. Coupled with the increasing knowledge of possible alternatives such as peer support in illness or community-based schooling, it is not surprising that there is widespread cynicism towards official solutions. This is present amongst all communities, often expressed as a distrust of politics and any initiative seen to be linked to political institutions and/or goals. Secondly, one needs to consider the migrant belief in self-reliance. The pursuit of individual goals, the role of successful individuals in assisting/raising the community, and a widespread celebration of the pursuit of wealth as a version of undoing or escaping racism has come to shape whole communities many generations after that moment of arrival. Thirdly, poor knowledge about the role of the state as service-provider or regulator and a resulting indifference to changes in state practices means that community institutions, particularly those that are religious based, come to form alternative sources of support. This includes as providers of extensive charitable activity, as arenas for social networking, and as alternative institutional spaces that may make no reference to the state or the market. These and other important factors (including those identified by Barnett such as the death of deference, the rise of consumer-based democracy, and the influence of community-based sources of knowledge that critique official services) may, taken together, give some insight into the apparent embrace of so-called neoliberal subjectivities by those who seem to lose most from the impact of neoliberal economics.

Despite the targeting of old-fashioned and newfangled state racisms on these same groups, this is not occupation/repression of those who are not market-ready or willing. If anything, there is more vocal enthusiasm for some kinds of markets among black and minority populations. Equally, we should remember that the compromise of Keynesian-enabled economic and social policy, despite the many gains for ordinary people, did not deliver in an equitable fashion. Even the most significant gains by black and minority communities were experienced simultaneously with further racist barriers – public-sector employment, but not at representative proportions or higher grades; access to important public services, but of a lesser quality or less effective delivery than that offered to much of the white population; the safety net of welfare provision, but greater barriers to accessing entitlements; and a relegation of significant sections of our communities to perpetual poverty, in times of boom as well as bust.

Given all of this, it is unsurprising that the ideas of neoliberalism and racial neoliberalism have some popular attraction, including for those with most to lose from neoliberal practices. As always, and I think very much in the spirit of Goldberg's provocation and Hall's call to engage with a hegemonic project in movement, the best overarching stories (always necessarily incomplete and imperfect) are those that force you to reconsider the local detail of your situation. It may be difficult to fully equate Britain to a space of racial neoliberalism, but the questions raised by an engagement with racial neoliberalism certainly provide ample space from which to dissect the contemporary in the hope of finding methods to resist.

Notes

1. http://www.guardian.co.uk/uk/2012/jan/04/lawrence-verdict-racism-britain
2. For example, the Discrimination Law Association held an event entitled 'Where is the British Obama?' in January 2009, with high-profile speakers including Diane Abbott MP, Simon Woolley (Operation Black Vote), Sunder Katwala (General Secretary of the Fabian Society) and Rabinder Singh QC.
3. See the most outrageous example of historian David Starkey alleging that 'The whites have turned black,' http://www.bbc.co.uk/news/uk-14513517
4. Although Hilgers (2012) suggests that there are other experiences of neoliberalisation that do not display this particular configuration of economic liberalisation and penalisation of social provision.
5. See Swyngedouw (1991) for a discussion of how neoliberal innovation in forms of governance can empower some and exclude others.

References

Archetti, C. and Taylor, P. M. (2003) *Managing Terrorism after 9/11: The War on Terror, the Media, and the Imagined Threat*, http://ics-www.leeds.ac.uk/papers/pmt/exhibits/2846/Final%2520Report.pdf

Barnett C. (2005) 'The Consolation of "Neoliberalism"', *Geoforum*, 36(1), 7–12.

Barnett, C., Cloke, P., Clarke, N. and Malpass, A. (2008) The Elusive Subjects of Neoliberalism: Beyond the Analytics of Governmentality, *Cultural Studies* 22(5), 624–53.

Cai, H. and Treisman, D. (2005) 'Does Competition for Capital Discipline Governments? Decentralization, Globalization, and Public Policy', *American Economic Review*, 95(3), 817–30.

Coyle, D. (2000) *Governing the Global Economy* (Cambridge: Polity).

Crouch, C. (2004) *Post-Democracy* (Cambridge: Polity).

Crouch, C. (2011) *The Strange Non-Death of Neoliberalism* (Cambridge: Polity).

De Angelis, M. (ed.) (2000) *Keynesianism Social Conflict and Political Economy* (Basingstoke: Palgrave).

Ferguson, James (2009) 'The Uses of Neoliberalism', *Antipode* 41(1), 166–84.

Goldberg, D. T. (2008) *The Threat of Race: Reflections on Racial Neoliberalism* (Oxford: Wiley-Blackwell).

Hall, S. (2011) 'The Neoliberal Revolution', *Soundings*, 48(summer 2011), 9–27.

Harvey, D. (2005) *A Brief History of Neoliberalism* (Oxford: Oxford University Press).

Hilgers, M. (2012) 'The Historicity of the Neoliberal State', *Social Anthropology*, 20(1), 80–94.

Klein, N. (2008) *The Shock Doctrine* (Harmondsworth: Penguin).

Li, Y. (2010) 'The Labour Market Situation of Minority Ethnic Groups in Britain and the US: An Analysis of Employment Status and Class Position, 1990/1–2000/1', Working Paper 2010–01 (Manchester, Institute for Social Change).

McQuaid, R., Egdell, V. and Hollywood, E. (2010) 'The Impact of Reduced Public Services Spending on Vulnerable Groups: Review of UK and International Evidence', 12 July 2010 (Edinburgh Napier University: Employment Research Institute).

Milliband, D . (2009) '"War on Terror" Was Wrong: The Phrase Gives a False Idea of a Unified Global Enemy, and Encourages a Primarily Military Reply', Comment Is Free, *The Guardian*, 15 January 2009, http://www.guardian.co.uk/commentisfree/2009/jan/15/david-miliband-war-terror

Peck, J., Theodore, N. and Brenner, N. (2009) 'Postneoliberalism and its Malcontents', *Antipode*, 41(1), 94–116.

Rose, N . (1999) *Powers of Freedom: Reframing Political Thought* (Cambridge: Cambridge University Press).

Sassen, S. (2007) 'Globalisation, the State and the Democratic Deficit', *Open Democracy*, 18 July 2007, http://www.opendemocracy.net/article/globalisation_liberal_state_democratic_deficit

Springer, S. (2012) 'Neoliberalising Violence: of the Exceptional and the Exemplary in Coalescing Moments', *Area*, 44(2), 136–43.

Stoker, G. (2006) *Why Politics Matters: Making Democracy Work* (Basingstoke: Palgrave).

Stratton, A. (2011) 'David Cameron on Riots: Broken Society Is Top of My Political Agenda', *The Guardian*, 15 August 2011, http://www.guardian.co.uk/uk/2011/aug/15/david-cameron-riots-broken-society.

Swyngedouw, E. (2005) 'Governance Innovation and the Citizen: The Janus Face of Governance-beyond-the-State', *Urban Studies,* 42(11), 1991–2006.

Topping, A. and Dodd, V. (2012) 'Doreen Lawrence: Britain Still Blighted by Racism', *The Guardian,* 3 January 2012, http://www.guardian.co.uk/uk/2012/jan/03/doreen-lawrence-britain-blighted-racism.

Vasagar, J. and Walker, P . (2011) 'The 24 Pioneering Free Schools', *The Guardian,* 29 August 2011, http://www.guardian.co.uk/education/2011/aug/29/24-pioneering-free-schools

Vallely, P. (2012) 'Child Sex Grooming: The Asian Question', *The Independent,* 10 May 2012, http://www.independent.co.uk/news/uk/crime/child-sex-grooming-the-asian-question-7729068.html

Wacquant, L. (2009) *Punishing the Poor: The Neoliberal Government of Social Insecurity* (Durham, NC: Duke University Press).

Wacquant, L. (2010) 'Crafting the Neoliberal State: Workfare, Prisonfare, and Social Insecurity', *Sociological Forum*, 25(2), 197–220.

Wadsworth, Marc (2012) 'Bid for Black "Free School" Launched,' *The Voice*, 6 January 2012, http://voice-online.co.uk/article/bid-black-free-school-launched

Willis, P. (1986) 'Unemployment: The Final Inequality', *British Journal of Sociology of Education*, 7(2), 155–69.

3
Remaking Whiteness in the 'Postracial' UK

James Rhodes

The riots of August 2011 that swept through London, spreading to cities across the UK, including Manchester and Birmingham, marked the latest episode of urban unrest, following on from serious disturbances in 1981, 1985 and 2001. Having been triggered by the fatal shooting of Mark Duggan, a black British man in Tottenham, the riots reveal the enduring racialisation of crime and disorder, antagonism between black communities and the police, as well as enduring patterns of racial disadvantage (Solomos 2011). Well-worn narratives of family breakdown, welfare dependency, gang culture, criminality, cultural dysfunction and moral degeneracy that have historically been attributed to both black and South Asian populations in the wake of prior incidences of urban unrest, featured heavily in the media coverage of the riots. Max Hastings (2011), writing in the *Daily Mail*, declared those involved to be 'wild beasts', symptomatic of the emergence of a 'large, amoral, brutalized sub-culture of young British people who lack education because they have no will to learn, and skills which might make them employable ... They have no code of values to dissuade them from behaving anti-socially or, indeed, criminally.' The Justice Secretary, Ken Clarke MP, agreed, declaring the riots to be the result of the unruly behaviours and cultural practices of a 'feral underclass, cut off from the mainstream in everything but its materialism.' (Lewis et al. 2011). While the emphasis on materialism and consumer culture, as well as the influence of social media represented newer features of these discourses (Solomos 2011), so too did the explicit recognition that the rioters were multiracial in their composition. Despite the involvement of white rioters being an omnipresent feature of urban unrest over the last few decades, this has generally been deemphasised within the accounts of both the media and politicians. However, the coverage of the riots of August 2011 frequently referenced the 'whiteness' of many of the protagonists involved. Writing in *The Independent,* Michael McCarthy (2011) concluded that, 'This was a multiracial phenomenon. There were plenty of black rioters and plenty of white rioters, too. But what united them was the abandonment of all restraint and that the cultural norms which had once been so powerful in British society were irrelevant to them.' Writing in the Australian *Herald Sun*, Andrew Bolt (2011) saw the riots as highlighting that, 'Britain has a white underclass, too, and one dangerously loosened from the soft ties of tradition, religion, and class'. On 12 August 2011, the historian David Starkey appeared on the BBC programme *Newsnight*, as part of a panel discussion about the riots. Starkey stated his belief that the events demonstrated how sections of the white population 'have become black' as, 'a particular sort of violent, destructive, nihilistic gangster culture has become the fashion' (cited in O'Carroll 2011). In a subsequent newspaper article, Starkey (2011, p. 17) reasserted these points claiming that,

> It is the white lumpen proletariat, cruelly known as the "chavs" who have integrated into the pervasive black "gangsta" culture: they wear the same clothes; they talk and text in the same Jamaican patois; and, as their participation in recent events shows, they have become as disaffected and riotous (Starkey 2011, p. 17).

This invocation of the role of 'chavs' and the 'white underclass' in the 2011 riots was the latest manifestation of increasing anxiety about a loss of 'respectability' of swathes of the 'white working-classes', and their replacement by an apparently dysfunctional, socially redundant and morally unrestrained section of society (Haylett 2001; Nayak 2006, 2009; Garner 2007; Webster 2008; Gillborn 2010; Jones 2011). Simon Heffer, writing in the *Daily Telegraph* in 2007, stated that 'Something called the white working class has almost died out. What sociologists used to call the working class does not now usually work at all, but is sustained by the welfare state.' Instead, this group has given way to a 'feral underclass' (cited in Jones 2011, p. 7). Indeed, the way in which terms such as 'chav', and 'white underclass' are often used synonymously with 'white working class', reflects this perceived social, cultural and moral disintegration. The term 'chav' attempts to capture this asserted loss of class 'respectability', and names a stigmatised grouping of poor whites who fail to adhere to dominant values, norms and practices. This chapter is interested in the impact that these representations of a 'white working class', and a purported 'white underclass' or 'chavs', has on conceptions of whiteness more broadly. The 'chav' caricature maps onto existing conceptions of the 'white working-class' who are often cast as endemically racist, backward and lacking in a form of 'multicultural' literacy. These concerns have escalated in the wake of the rise of far-right groups such as the British National Party (BNP) and the English Defence League (EDL). The rise of these forms of representation has occurred as the UK has experienced de-industrialisation, economic restructuring, the retreat of the welfare state and the rise of neoliberalism. At the same time, the UK has also experienced increasing ethnic diversity, as well as shifts in racial governance, and anti-racism legislation. Winant (1997, p. 34) suggests that similar transformations in the US have meant 'An unprecedented period of racial anxiety has resulted, in which competing racial projects struggle to reinterpret the meaning of race and to redefine racial identity. A crucial theme in these struggles has turned out to be the identity of whites, and the meaning of whiteness.' It seems that a parallel process of racial anxiety is currently occurring in the UK, where the increased scrutiny of whiteness has occurred within the context of 'postracial' and 'colour-blind' racial discourses which seek to denounce the enduring significance of 'race' and racism as key structuring technologies of contemporary society (Lentin 2008; Goldberg 2009; Rhodes 2009; Lentin and Titley 2011). This does not mean that whiteness or white identities are declining in significance; rather, its borders and content are changing. As Lewis (2004, p. 66) rightly states, 'Racial discourses, ideologies, and structural arrangements shift over time', and the rise of 'colour-blind discourses' suggests that 'Expressions of racial sentiments and preferences may well have shifted such that whiteness functions in new ways.' This chapter focuses upon how the symbolic construction of the 'white underclass' represents part of a broader reconfiguration of 'whiteness' as its boundaries are being redrawn and its associated values and practices reoriented within the context of purported moves towards a 'post-racial' society.

The centre and peripheries of whiteness

The development of 'whiteness studies' as a field of academic inquiry has led to important advances in how 'whiteness' is conceptualised. There has been a move away from viewing whiteness as invisible, static, homogeneous and unmarked, with a greater emphasis being placed on its instabilities, its contradictions and its heterogeneous nature (Roediger 1991; Bonnett 2000; Hartigan 1997a, 2003, 2005; Frankenberg 2001; Doane 2003; Byrne 2006; Wray 2006; Garner 2007). Whereas previously whiteness was seen as both invisible and normative, as being a state of 'racelessness', this is increasingly recognised as only *appearing* to be the case, as 'It is only the specificity of white as linked to power that enables it to imagine that it is of so little importance as an identity' (Garner 2007, p. 46). Investigations aimed at understanding whiteness must bear in mind that it still operates as a position of privilege, offering resources – both material and symbolic – to those it deems fully or contingent members. The precarious positioning historically of various class, ethnic and religious communities within the connotative range of 'whiteness' in both the UK and the US (Roediger 1999; Bonnett 2000; Haylett 2001; Hartigan 2005; Wray 2006; Garner 2007; Nayak 2009), has led to a growing recognition that whiteness is not simply about pheno-type, but is instead a symbolic form of identification rooted in economi-cally, socially, and culturally conditioned sets of values and practices that change in relation to broader transformations within 'racialized social systems' (Doane 2003). Whiteness is increasingly recognised as a relational identity that constructs both a centre and peripheries on the basis of 'interracial' and 'intra-racial' distinctions (Hartigan 1997; Byrne 2006; Wray 2006; Garner 2007). Indeed, the asserted existence of a 'white underclass' demonstrates that 'gaps occur between whiteness and whites, so that white groups sharing the same skin colour are not "equally white"' (Haylett 2001, p. 355). Garner suggests that while not losing sight of the dominance of white racial identity and its historic functions as an identity rooted in ideas of racial supremacy (2006, p. 262), there is also a need to recognise the 'plural trajectories of white-ness' (Garner 2007, p. 75). For instance, it is clear that the privileges whiteness affords cannot be equally claimed; in the context of economic restructuring, welfare reform and the neoliberal political trajectories of the US and the UK, for those exhibiting peripheral forms of white iden-tities there is an increasing 'perception of diminishing funds' (Garner 2006, p. 265). In an attempt to capture these ambivalences and frac-tures, Garner advocates a conception of whiteness which views it as 'a contingent social hierarchy granting differential access to economic and cultural capital, intersecting with, and overlaying, class and ethnicity' (Garner 2006, p. 264).

The contingency of these claims to whiteness are clearly illustrated in the discursive construct of the chav (and its regional variations) and the white underclass in the UK. Those marked by these forms of categorisa-tion occupy the peripheral spaces of whiteness, residing at its borders, positioned somewhere in between dominant white identities and the spectre of blackness – similar to the symbolic functions that 'white trash' serves in the US (Newitz and Wray 1997; Hartigan 2005; Wray 2006; Garner 2007; Webster 2008). These terms are used to designate an apparently distinctive, dysfunctional section of the white population. Those labelled with these epithets are seen to be characterised by unemployment, welfare dependency, drug and alcohol abuse, criminality, promiscuity, family breakdown, poor consumptive tastes, high rates of illegitimacy, racism, and moral and embodied degeneracy (Murray 1996; Newitz and Wray 1997; Hartigan 1997a, 2003; Nayak 2006; Wray 2006; Tyler 2008; Webster 2008; Gillborn 2010; Jones 2011). They provide a symbolic formation that explains the declining strength of the nation and the fragmentation of the 'white working-class', or at least it's less 'aspirational' and 'respectable' elements (Murray 1996; Haylett 2001; Wray 2006; Webster 2008; Gillborn 2010; Jones 2011). In many ways, these terms serve a similar symbolic function to the types of pathologies ascribed to the black and 'non-white' populations of the 'underclass'. They are employed to negate from structural explanations of poverty, inequality, stigmatisation and marginalisation, focusing instead upon individualised accounts of cultural and moral degeneracy. These narratives also then serve to reject the idea that forms of economic redistribution can address what are essentially 'cultural' problems. It is clear, however, that, these terms are not simply an expression of class disgust and distancing; just as underclass discourses have served to produce and reproduce notions of the racial 'otherness' of non-whites, so too terms such as 'white trash' and 'chav', are also 'racial epithets' (Newitz and Wray 1997; Hartigan 2003, 2005; Wray 2006). They name the apparent existence of social groupings which 'fit insecurely within the body of whiteness as a hegemonic order of political power and social privilege' (Hartigan 1997a, p. 319). Hartigan observes how in the US terms such as 'white trash' are

> used to name those bodies that exceed the class and racial etiquettes required of Whites if they are to preserve the powers and privileges that accrue to them as members of the dominant racial order...White trash is also applied to Whites whose lifestyles, speech, and behaviours too closely match the 'marked' cultural forms associated with blackness or other symbolically informed forms of racial identity and difference (2005, p. 115).

In the UK too, both Nayak (2006) and Haylett (2001) reveal the ways in which the identities of poor whites are seen as being compromised by their apparent economic insecurity, immorality, and their cultural degradation, and the resultant ability of this group to challenge dominant conceptions of whiteness that construct it as a virtuous and 'justifiably' dominant form of identification. Nayak observes that this 'darkened underclass' of 'chavs', 'like many minority ethnic groups before them ... [are] associated with street crime, disease, drugs, overbreeding ... and the seedy underbelly of the "black economy"' (2006, p. 824). Haylett, too, recognises that 'Where "black" was the originary signifier of the abject, a residual matter, defilement, and disorder, "white" embodied in degenerate working-class "others" comes to share the symbolic register' (2001, p. 361).

Of course, there is nothing necessarily new about this. In the UK historically, those of white skin have not always been viewed as 'white'. Jewish and Irish populations occupied similarly liminal spaces between blackness and whiteness – a trend that is also evident in the contemporary positioning of poorer Eastern European white migrants and Gypsy/ Traveller communities. Similarly, whites of lower social and economic positions have also been placed at the margins of whiteness, at its intersections with blackness. In the UK, the 'non-respectable' white working classes have also historically been seen as a 'race apart'. This 'refusal of authentic whiteness to the working class' operated through two representational strategies: 'imaginatively aligning them with nonwhites, and by asserting that they are literally racially distinct from the middle and upper classes' (Bonnett 2000, p. 33; see also, Nayak 2009). Bonnett argues that it was only within the context of the advent of welfare capitalism, and the incorporation of the white working classes into conceptions of the nation that there occurred, 'a shift in emphasis from whiteness as a bourgeois identity, connoting extraordinary qualities, to whiteness as a popularist identity connoting superiority but also ordinariness, nation and community' (Bonnett 2000, p. 30).

What differs in terms of the contemporary symbolic significance of the purported existence of a white underclass and its related slurs, is the social, economic and political context in which these debates are occurring. Racial identities are not fixed but in a constant process of reproduction, contestation, and transformation in relation to broader societal and structural changes (Doane 2003; Lewis 2004; Garner 2006, 2007). Tied to significant changes in the nature of capitalism and state approaches to economic redistribution, there have also been transformations within the politics of 'race'. While previous debates regarding poor and ethnically 'other' whites as the embodiment of marginal forms of whiteness in the UK marked the narration of a process of *becoming* white, now they are concerned with *remaining* white. As Webster (2008, p. 295) states, whiteness, 'is about becoming, being and staying "white"'. What also appears to be distinct is the discursive emphasis placed on the *whiteness* of 'white trash', 'chavs', and the 'white underclass'; while themes of interracial contamination and racial degeneracy remain central to such representations, it seems that this symbolic 'darkening' used to taint the 'whiteness' of those it targets, is not accompanied by a de-emphasis of their white racial identities; instead it is placed at the very foreground of these discourses, as this supposed social category are 'marked as excessively white – *offensively and embarrassingly white.*' (Haylett 2001, p. 355; emphasis added). It is this emphasis that is the object of inquiry for the remainder of this chapter: what kind of symbolic work does the *white* in 'chavs', and the 'white underclass' perform in the context of contemporary 'postracial' claims? After all, as Bottero (2009, p. 14) recognises, 'Before we straightforwardly accept the existence of the "white working class" [or chavs or white underclass] as a clear-cut social group we need to remember that such class labels are part of campaigning strategies, as much an attempt to *create* social and political constituencies as to *represent* them.' The remainder of this chapter, then, considers how such categories are constructed and deployed in relation to dominant conceptions of whiteness.

Reconfiguring whiteness

In the wake of the introduction of anti-racist legislation in the UK as well as the increasing social unacceptability of overt expressions of racism, it has been argued by many, from across the political spectrum, that we have seen the advent of a 'postracial era'. Here, 'contemporary, western, postcolonial societies are imbricated in an idea of their constitutive nature as tolerant and democratic and, by association, non-racist or indeed anti-racist.' (Lentin 2008, p. 488). Within this conception, the machinations of the state and of systemic processes that generate material, economic, political, and cultural inequalities are dismissed as racism and racist exclusion are individualised, 'by reducing the social to the preferential, the state to (in)civil society' (Goldberg 2009, p. 77). As Goldberg states, in this age of what he terms 'racial neoliberalism', 'Race disappears into the seams of sociality together even as it tears it apart' (ibid: 157). In this era of purported 'racelessness' it therefore appears strange that the 'whiteness' of 'chavs' and the 'white underclass' should be so overtly explicated. However, central to the increasing attention that has come to be placed on whiteness as a racialised system of categorisation and identification in itself, is its increasing inability to maintain its status as unmarked, invisible, and normative (Winant 1997). Of course, it is those possessing the most marginal forms of whiteness who are most likely to have their 'whiteness' marked and scrutinised. In both the US and the UK, it is the lower classes of white society that are most commonly represented with the prefix 'white'. Hartigan states how terms such as 'white trash',

> Are deployed and projected in order to maintain the unmarked status of whiteness. In each instance of these labelling practices, a normative status of whiteness is affirmed, one that is free from the blemish of poverty and protected from the ruptures of decorum that might undermine its hegemonic status... Each of these epithets hence assembles a host of stigmatized "traits" that can be mobilized either to assert distance from this disparaged social condition or to affirm one's position squarely within it. (2003, p. 110)

While it is clear that discourses pertaining to a white underclass serve to produce boundaries and what Dyer terms 'gradations of whiteness' (1997, p. 12), Carroll questions, in relation to white masculinity, whether the central strategy within white privilege is 'not to be unmarked, universal, or invisible (although it is sometimes one or all of these), but to be mobile and mutable' (2011, pp. 9–10). He argues that it is important that we recognise the 'reactive' nature of whiteness, 'to see how it *responds* to sociopolitical transformations' (Carroll 2011, p. 10). The symbolic marginalisation of the whiteness of the 'white underclass' is part of this process of reformation, as the values, norms and practices are, at least symbolically, being reformulated in response to the contemporary 'post-racial' landscape.

It is the changes in the social, economic and political landscape that inform shifts in the nature and boundaries of whiteness. Lewis argues that 'In any particular historical moment... certain forms of whiteness become dominant... Hegemonic whiteness thus is a shifting configuration of practices and meanings that occupy the dominant position in a particular racial formation and that successfully manage to occupy the empty spaces of "normality" in our culture' (2004, p. 634). In relation to whiteness, the explicit racial markings of its peripheries and the traits assigned to those occupying these marginal spaces become a way in which the normative and the dominant are re-composed. In the contemporary period, it appears that there is a move towards a dominant form of white identity that overtly rejects the significance of phenotype, instead casting itself as 'non-racial' – a progressive, metropolitan, and multicultural form of whiteness, particularly inhabited by more affluent, educated whites who see 'race' as an irrelevance, and instead seek out a controlled exposure to 'difference' (Haylett 2001; Byrne 2006; Reay et al. 2007; Goldberg 2009; Nayak 2009; Bush 2011). As Nayak observes, 'In contrast to the parochial whiteness thought to be inhabited by sections of the white working class, the bourgeoisie tend to be envisaged as mobile, cosmopolitan citizens no longer rooted to archaic images of whiteness' (2009, p. 29; see also Beider 2011, p. 19). Within these conceptions, it is poorer whites who are deemed unwilling and unable to relinquish their attachments to a retrogressive form of white racial identity. The irony of this is that the political silencing of class-based rhetoric and the rise of identity politics and multiculturalism has encouraged marginal white groups to identify in racialised terms in competition for political, material, and cultural resources (Haylett 2001; Webster 2008; Bottero 2009; Gillborn 2010; Jones 2011). This marks part of a broader shift within the era of 'racial neoliberalism' as it is minority ethnic groups – but also poor whites – who are charged with ensuring that race remains significant through their enduring attachments to such forms of identification:

> Racism is redirected to malign those who invoke race, implicitly or explicitly, but now to undo the historical legacies of racisms even modestly to redress its effects. Here racism is reduced in its supposed singularity to *invoking* race, not to its debilitating structural effects or the legacy of its ongoing unfair impacts. (Goldberg 2009, p. 360)

Within this process of white – and national – reorientation, groups such as 'chavs', the 'white working-class', and the 'white underclass', come to be constructed as nativist, backward, and intrinsically racist. Indeed, a key way in which this group is distinguished is through associations with racism (Haylett 2001; Webster 2008; Gillborn 2010; Beider 2011; Jones 2011; Rhodes 2011). Within these discourses, 'The unifying theme is of the "atavistic backwardness of the white working-class as a burdensome barrier to a modern "multicultural" nation' (Webster 2008, p. 307), as they are charged with being the key constituency – and often the only one – prone to overt racism and racist violence. These critiques have been articulated particularly forcefully by liberals. Writing in the *Independent,* Alibhai-Brown (2009) attacked what she saw as a growing sense of 'victimhood' amongst poor whites, with recourse to the supposed endemic racism of this section of British society. She argued that it was, 'Working-class white men [who] provoked race riots through the Fifties and Sixties; they kept "darkies" out of pubs and clubs and work canteens' (also cited in Jones 2011, p. 118). David Goodhart (2012), reflecting on the convictions of Gary Dobson and David Norris for the murder of Stephen Lawrence in 1993, stated how, 'I can't help feeling that the Lawrence case...highlights new divisions between a minority-friendly elite liberalism and the disaffected white working class of south London and north Kent.' Such portraits of the 'white working class' as endemically racist have gained increasing symbolic currency with the rise of far-right political organisations such as the BNP and the EDL. Politicians and the media have frequently categorised this as a 'white working class' problem, as support for the party has become associated with the poorest strata of this group in particular (Rhodes 2011). Writing in the *Daily Telegraph*, Simon Heffer (2007) stated that,

> The white underclass will simply complain about resources and time being spent on an ethnic minority, while it is allowed to stew in its own juice and continue its precipitate decline. Should you doubt this, simply look at why the BNP does so well in white working-class areas: the doctrine of the evil of preferential treatment for others has done so much to strengthen that party.

This process of casting marginal whites as the constituency of racist attitudes and violence again is part of a broader representational strategy within the 'postracial' project as understandings of racism are shifted away from systemic processes and instead located as the atypical actions of various marginal individuals and groups (Doane 2003; Lentin 2008; Goldberg 2009).

This reconfiguration of whiteness, however, remains characterised by ambivalences (Hage 1998). For instance, the increasing promotion of a form of whiteness that is literate, competent, and open to the consumption and 'appropriation' (Reay et al. 2007) of ethnic and racial difference, has been opposed by groups across the political spectrum. These sentiments have been seen as part of a 'rising white backlash' against multicultural and race equality policies (Hewitt 2005; Cowles et al. 2009; Gillborn 2010; Rhodes 2010; Beider 2011). Here there has emerged a perception within the field of multiculturalism that it is whites – particularly poorer, working-class whites – who are seen as suffering from a perceived cultural disenfranchisement. Hewitt (2005, p. 69), for instance, states that 'White working-class groups...see themselves as being invisible in the ideological marketplace and see instead a multicultural discourse that validates the very groups that appear to threaten them.' Indeed, in the wake of the rise of the far right, the 2001 riots, as well as the 9/11 and 7/7 terror attacks, there has been a move away from an explicit celebration of state multiculturalism, towards greater emphasis on social cohesion and the integration of black and minority ethnic groups. Here, 'white backlash' sentiments, and the supposed endemic racism of poorer whites has become a way through which state multiculturalism has been critiqued, and through which the broader, cross-class perceptions of white cultural disenfranchisement identified by Hewitt, are instead displaced onto peripheral whites. Here, it is often argued that multiculturalism poses a threat to the development of a raceless society, as it is deemed to promote difference over commonality. The 'resentment' of peripheral whites is seen as being in need of management, through an emphasis on integration into what is constructed as a 'non-racial' imagining of nation and community (Rhodes 2009). While 'state multiculturalism' itself is deemed to be the centre of such claims, Lentin and Titley (2011) reject this. They argue that these anxieties are less about state approaches to ethnic and racial diversity, and are indicative of broader fears over the very existence of 'multiculture' itself. It is clear that even where an asserted form of progressive, multicultural whiteness and nation is still widely promoted, this brings with it its own anxieties about the future of whiteness as a foundational pillar of both nation and privilege. As Ware argues elsewhere in this volume in relation to the armed forces, while ethnic and racial diversity is advocated as central to a healthy institution, society and nation, such ideas are founded upon an idea of *appropriate exposure* and *balance* (see also Byrne 2006; Reay et al. 2007). Reay et al in their study of the educational choices of the middle classes also question just how progressive this emergent form of identity truly is, and whether it really destabilises white hegemony. They argue that the apparent value placed on ethnic and racial difference,

> Is mostly a partial and narcissistic valuing; one that is primarily about recognising a more colourful self in the ethnic other in a process that both residualizes both a hyper-whitened working class identity and an excessively black black working class who come to share the same symbolic register in the white middle-class imaginary. (2007, p. 1054)

Where ethnic and racial diversity is deemed to threaten the dominant position of whiteness these claims to a postracial whiteness begin to reveal their superficiality. While the idea of a 'postracial' society is forwarded, where this is seen to potentially lead to a 'post-white' society, this then becomes more problematic. The symbolic power of the categorisations 'chav', 'abject whites', and 'white underclass' and the emphasis placed on the 'whiteness' of these groups betrays the ongoing normative associations between unmarked forms of whiteness and virtue, morality, and respectability.

Hage, in his study of whiteness, racism and multiculturalism in Australia, argues that positions which alternatively seek to oppose or accommodate racial and ethnic difference are ultimately both expressions of white privilege and dominance, representing 'fantasies' of the power to either tolerate, to incorporate, or to exclude; both of these positions 'work at *containing* the increasingly active role of non-White' populations (Hage 1998, p. 19; emphasis in original). In both positions outlined above, those that reject multiculturalism or embrace it as a constituent element of whiteness, nation and identity, reveal an enduring projection of white power and dominance. While for some, the resentment and racism of peripheral whites leads to calls for state multiculturalism to be abandoned and for this perceived cultural disenfranchisement to be addressed, for others, the reconfiguration of whiteness as 'raceless', progressive, and multicultural sees marginal whites cast as collateral damage in this process. In both instances, the boundaries of whiteness itself are being redrawn. The symbolic construction of the racial and class 'otherness' of purported groups such as 'chavs', 'white 'working class', and the 'white underclass', are key to this 'recuperative' project (Carroll 2011), whereby attempts are made to reconfigure dominant and normative (and more affluent) forms of whiteness as progressive, raceless, and post-racial. For Carroll, debates that focus upon the peripheries of whiteness can be seen as a location where 'Identity formation maintains privilege through a process of disavowal and transformation' (Carroll 2011, p. 7). Here, attempts to cleanse normative whiteness of its racist and supremacist features are occurring. Within this project, poor whites are marginalised, constructed as the obstinate barrier in the remaking of a non-racial, benign form of whiteness. At the same time, the incorporation of assimilable and 'model minorities' is also used to denounce the exclusionary basis of whiteness and its symbolic range. Newitz (1997, p. 139) views this intraracial disciplining of 'white trash', as evidence of contemporary 'fantasies about whites resolving their racial problems without ever having to deal with people of colour'. The production of peripheral forms of whiteness outlined above then can be seen as part of a broader reconfiguration of whiteness-as-'non-', or 'postracial'.

Unmaking and remaking white privilege

While it is not clear that there exists a distinct 'white underclass', it is apparent that de-industrialisation and the decline of manufacturing, economic restructuring, and the shift away from policies of economic redistribution in favour of cultural recognition in the UK, mean that increasingly white skin itself does not afford the same material privileges as it previously has done. Many poorer whites (and the poorest groups across UK society more broadly) have seen their median incomes and lifestyles decline over recent decades. Similarly, the rise of multiculturalism, identity politics and the enacting of anti-racist policies has led to a broad perception that there has been a marginalisation of whiteness within politics, the economy, and popular culture (Hewitt 2005; Dench et al. 2006; Garner 2007; Webster 2008; Cowles et al. 2009; Rhodes 2010; Beider 2011). Here, whites, particularly poor whites, are often cast as the 'true' casualties of the development of global capitalism, the rise of multiculturalism and immigration, race equality policies, and political correctness. This is not only a position adopted by organisations such as the BNP; it has also found a range of support from the political mainstream. The cultural categories of 'chav', 'poor whites', the 'white working class', and 'white underclass' play an important symbolic role here. In 2006, the Labour Member of Parliament (MP) for Barking, Margaret Hodge, responded to an increased BNP presence in her constituency by vocalising what she saw as the frustrations of her 'white working class' constituents:

> They can't get a home for their children, they see black and minority families moving in and they are angry ... Nowhere else has changed so fast. When I arrived in 1994, it was a predominantly white, working class area. Now, go through the middle of Barking and you could be in Camden or Brixton. That is the thing that has created the environment the BNP has sought to exploit (cited in Kite 2006, p. 1).

Similarly, in justifying the BBC series *White Season,* shown during 2008, the commissioning editor Richard Klein stated that the aim of it was to address the feelings of 'abandonment' and 'neglect' felt by the 'white working class', many of whom, he argued, 'see themselves as an oppressed ethnic minority too, and lower down the ladder than other groups on the hierarchy of victimhood' (cited in Ware 2008, p. 25). More recently, in January 2009, a report carried out by the National Community Forum (NCF) and the Department for Communities and Local Government

(DCLG) uncovered the sense of resentment felt towards immigrants and minority ethnic groups by 'poor whites' living in social housing (Cowles et al. 2009). Also, in January 2009, speaking at the launch of the Connecting Communities initiative – aimed primarily at addressing the perceived neglect of amongst poor whites and the 'white working-class', John Denham (2009) stated that, 'It is not surprising that they may question whether they are being treated unfairly and to worry that others are, unfairly, doing better.' As Ware (2008) recognises, there are dangers in the political promotion and legitimisation of such ideas.

While the focus on marginal forms of whiteness can be seen as a way of deconstructing simplistic notions of white homogeneity and uniformity, Wiegman argues that there is an implicit danger in this political, media, and academic attention on 'injured' forms of whiteness – whether as a means of leftist deconstruction of whiteness or as part of a more conservative form of racial redress. She argues that in assuming that,

> The power of whiteness arises from its appropriation of the universal and that the universal is opposed to and hence devoid of the particular, we have failed to interpret the tension between particularity and universality that characterises not simply the legal discourse of race...but also the changing contours of white power and privilege (1999, p. 117).

Wiegman asserts then that, rather than seeing the peripheral (or the particular) as working against the centre (or the universality) of whiteness and white privilege, the former actually is both an aspect and a driver of the reproduction and endurance of the latter – a key aspect of 'the contradictory formation of white racial power that has enabled its historical elasticity and contemporary transformations' (Wiegman 1999, p. 118; see also Carroll 2011). Indeed, Wiegman argues that, 'The split in the white racial subject – between disaffiliation from white suprema-cist practices and disavowal of the ongoing reformation of white power and one's benefit from it – is constitutive of contemporary white racial formation.' (Weigman 1999, p. 120). This is a phenomenon that Winant (1997, p. 75) labels 'racial dualism' as whiteness has been reinterpreted as 'both egalitarian and privileged, individualistic and "normalized", "colour-blind" and besieged'. In both the US and the UK, authors have recognised this tendency within the trajectories of whiteness and white privilege in the contemporary era (Winant 1997; Wiegman 1999; Doane 2003; Lewis 2004; Gillborn 2010; Bush 2011; Carroll 2011). Indeed, it is in the construction of 'white victimhood' – as well as the remaking of 'liberal whiteness' (Wiegman 1999) as a progressive, multicultural and postracial identity – that this form of 'dualism' becomes most apparent.

The identification of certain whites as peripheral and victimised serves to both shore up, and simultaneously disavow, white privilege. Perhaps most obviously, it enables a rejection of the privileges that whiteness affords, as the existence of 'poor whites' is used to deny the ongoing racial stratification of the UK. An article that appeared in *The Economist* in 2006 stated that poor whites increasingly represented a 'forgotten underclass', as 'Muslims and blacks get more attention. But poor whites are in a worse state.' The piece went on to claim that 'The nation's most troubled group, in both relative and absolute terms, is poor, white and British-born.' David Goodhart (2011), in an essay which revisited Oldham, Bradford, and Burnley a decade on from the 2001 riots, concluded that in Bradford, 'The white schools have some of the worst results in the country (though improving), and the white underclass is probably in a worse state than its Asian counterpart.' Similarly, Trevor Phillips (cited in Brogan 2008), the head of the Commission for Equality and Human Rights (CEHR), called for more political attention to be paid to a rising 'white underclass' in the context of escalating economic recession. Phillips stated that 'In some parts of the country, it is clear that what defines disadvantage won't be black or brown. It will be white. And we will have to take positive action to help some white groups, what we might call the white underclass.' Indeed, *Prospect Magazine* in its 2011 'Rethinking Race' issue, as well as the CEHR (2010) Report, 'How Fair is Britain?' emphasised the significance of class over 'race', downplaying 'the ethnically specific statistics which defy the simple class-based analysis' (Alexander 2011). This is reflective of similar arguments currently being advanced in the US. Charles Murray (2012, p. 12), for instance, has argued that the existence of a 'white underclass' points to how 'America is coming apart at the seams – not seams of race or ethnicity, but of class'. Here, Murray denies the endurance of systemic racism, instead presenting the US as a 'class-ridden' but fundamentally 'raceless' society. Ignoring discrepancies in the dispersal of inequalities across various racialised groups, Murray concludes that an emphasis on the 'decline' in the socio-economic position of many whites necessitates a paradigm shift in the conceptualisation of contemporary social divisions, away from race to class.

There are a number of troubling aspects of these arguments cited above; firstly, they serve to negate from the idea that the UK continues to be stratified by 'race' as well as class. Such arguments serve to reinforce white privilege in a number of ways. In pointing to the existence of 'poor' or 'failing' whites, the notion of a meritocratic society – free from the destructive influence of racism – is insinuated. The fact that 'whites' can also be poor, while minority ethnic groups can succeed, is used to point to the lessened social impact of racism and ideas of racial difference. The construction of white disadvantage is used to diminish the significance of racial stratification, obscuring the disproportionate rates of white poverty in comparison to that of black and minority ethnic groups (Alexander 2011). These 'raceless' accounts in shifting emphasis onto 'class', also place 'race' and class as distinct variables locked in a struggle of legitimacy as explanations for social, economic, and cultural marginalisation. Pitting race and class as binary opposites leads to a failure to see that 'Race interacts with class [and] enhances and modifies its impact' (Bourne 2011), and a denial of the ways in which interlocking systems of difference produce complex forms of inequality that are irreducible to an unending zero-sum game of either/or. Here racism is reduced simply to class exclusion, which is then used to reject the necessity, even the efficacy, of measures aimed at addressing racialised disadvantage. In the US, for instance, Murray (2012, p. 13) points to what he sees as the futility of pursuing race equality legislation. He urges readers considering the contemporary divisions in US society, not to 'kid yourselves that we are looking at stresses that can be remedied by attacking the legacy of racism'. In the UK, Munira Mirza (2010) has made similar assertions stating that 'Race is no longer the disadvantage it is often portrayed to be.' Here, the invocations of marginal white racial identities are paradoxically used as evidence of the existence of a raceless society, or at least a society where the significance of 'race' is declining. However, despite claims to 'racelessness', such invocations simultaneously serve to reinforce notions of 'race' as representing the grounds upon which difference is to be identified and measured; even if as mentioned in the previous section, it is only those poorest whites that are seen as clinging stubbornly to the 'whiteness' of their identities. Such discourses reassert ideas of immutability and distinction and 'exaggerate the difference between ethnic groups and masks what they hold in common.' (Bottero 2009, p. 7). Within these notions, the 'white underclass' or the 'white working-class' and 'its members are believed to have separate values, needs and motivations to working-class people who aren't white' (Hanley 2008, p. 36; see also Hartigan 1997, p. 356).

Some of the arguments deployed in defence of white privilege go even further, through assertions that whiteness itself represents a form of ethnic or racial 'penalty'. While this is a perspective forwarded by far-right organisations, it is also evident within more mainstream political, media, and cultural representations. During 2008, for instance, the low educational attainment of poorer white boys received significant media attention in the UK. Gillborn (2010, pp. 9–10) notes the emphasis placed within these accounts on the ethnicity of white students as an explanatory factor for poor educational attainment, when actually most groups in poverty achieve relatively poor results, regardless of the ethnicity. The danger inherent in these arguments is that they present disadvantage as an outcome of being 'white'; it is asserted that it is *because* poor whites are 'white' that they are marginalised. Within the coverage of the issue of poor white educational attainment, Gillborn (2010, p. 13) argues that this was precisely the picture presented as 'media and political commentators...repeat a view of White "working-class" boys as a racially victimized group.' Such arguments are then used to cite, not only the futility of race equality measures, but also their inherent 'unfairness' as 'Those arguing for greater race equality in education find themselves rendered silent by a discourse that rewrites reality; if White children are racial victims, then moves to address race inequity for minoritized groups are not only redundant but dangerous. Antiracist and multicultural education initiatives are positioned as a problem, their funding threatened, and a new focus on White students is promoted' (Gillborn 2010, p. 13). Indeed, in the midst of these debates, Trevor Phillips called for the introduction of 'positive action' programmes directly targeting white males in school (Brogan 2008). Goldberg (2009, p. 92) identifies such sentiments as a key component of contemporary racial politics where, 'whites are projected as the real victims of antiracist excess (of leftist antiracist racism, of political correctness, of liberal soft-headedness, of the ideology of egalitarianism).'

The denial of 'white privilege' and the move towards a 'postracial' form of dominant whiteness through the invocation of marked and marginal white identities may seem counter-intuitive. However, as argued in the previous section, dominant discursive constructions of whiteness seek to displace racism and enduring attachments to nativist forms of racial identity from the centre to the peripheries of whiteness. In doing this dominant forms of whiteness are presented as modern, multicultural, and even 'postracial'. This status is maintained despite the construction of 'white victimhood', by displacing these sentiments onto marginal white groups, who are simultaneously invoked as 'victimised' but also 'degenerate' due to the perceived threat of racism and racist violence that this victimisation 'fosters' (Gillborn 2010, p. 7). This is a position regularly adopted by both New Labour and the Conservatives within the UK in the wake of an increased backlash towards state multiculturalism, and the rise of far-right groups such as the BNP and the EDL. Here, very 'perceptions' of 'unfairness' towards whites are legitimated, while movement away from race equality programmes of action is cast as being done in the name of combating racism and potential threats to social cohesion. As Gillborn (2010, p. 8) observes, 'typically this line of argument is used to promote both more restrictions on the number of migrants able to enter the UK in the future, and to justify greater surveillance and/or control of minoritised people already in the population.' The comments of Trevor Phillips again exemplify these views when he warned that failure to control immigration in the context of recession risked leading to a 'surge' in support for far-right parties (Brogan 2008). Both New Labour and Conservatives have also called – on 'behalf' of the 'white working class' for tighter controls to be placed on immigration. In January 2009 for instance, Labour MP Frank Field stated that, 'If Labour wants to influence the outcome of the next general election, it had better start addressing white working-class concern about immigration.' (cited in Summers 2009). Gillborn (2010, p. 9) identifies such claims as threads of a 'familiar racist argument of previous decades (and centuries) where a perceived threat to White interest is used to discipline minority groups: by warning of the danger of inflaming support for racist parties, politicians and commentators invoke the threat of racist violence as a means of re-centring White interests and rejecting calls for greater race equality'. Indeed, as Bottero (2009, p. 7) observes, anxieties about the social positions (or perceived social positions) of minority ethnic groups exceeding those of 'poor whites' is based on a premise 'of some sort of priority citizenship', in which it is assumed that groups such as the 'white working class', 'should be doing better'.

The 're-centring' of white interests that Gillborn refers to reflects anxieties over the lived realities of multiculture, as well as state multiculturalism itself (Lentin and Titley 2011). The advancement of global capitalism and the banishing of racism in its more overt forms as permissible or acceptable constituent elements of personhood, collectivity, and of nation inform a 'crisis of whiteness', as there exist clear concerns regarding loss of white privilege. Indeed, Goldberg (2009, p. 337) states how 'racial neoliberalism' and its attendant reductionist view of racism and racial inequality 'can be read as a response to this concern about the impending impotence of whiteness.' In framing the concerns of the 'white underclass' and the 'white working-class' as being primarily addressed through a reorientation of immigration and multicultural policies, it betrays not only a political unwillingness to engage with material inequalities (Ware 2008) but is also a way through which racial anxieties are displaced from the centre to the peripheries; on the one hand cultural categories such as the 'white underclass' are used both to reconfigure the centre of whiteness as progressive, multicultural, and 'raceless'; however, simultaneously they are invoked as evidence rejecting the racial stratification of UK society and as a justification of a retreat from state policies to directly address racism and racialised inequalities. This again demonstrates the way in which rather than seeing the mobilisation of sentiments of 'white victimhood' as emblematic of declining white racial power, it may be more expedient to instead think about how whiteness and white privilege is being both secured and reconfigured.

Conclusion

In the context of contemporary economic recession, the apparent advent of a 'postracial' era, and a perceived 'crisis of whiteness', the purported existence of a 'white underclass' has come to be symbolically deployed in the remaking of whiteness and white privilege. In constructing centres and peripheries of whiteness, claims of the enduring significance of 'race' as a basis for a system of privilege or of disadvantage are disavowed. Within this the cultural categories of 'chavs', 'white underclass', and the 'white working-class' serve multifarious and ambivalent ends; they are the constructs through which intraracial borders are policed, serving as conspicuous markers of whiteness, as white racial identities and racism itself are deemed constitutive only to the identity of peripheral whites. Opposed to this, the symbolic centre of whiteness and its norms, values and practices, are reconfigured as essentially progressive, multicultural, and 'postracial' in its composition. After criticising the 'white underclass' in the name of reconfiguring whiteness, they are then cast as the bearers of 'resentful' – but increasingly *legitimate* and *understandable* – sentiments of dispossession and anger which are then used to bolster white privilege. Here, the deprivations experienced by increasing numbers of poor whites are used to reject claims of enduring white privilege – providing the basis for claims to the essentially 'raceless' nature of contemporary society as well as the grounds on which the need for measures to address race equality are deemed both unnecessary and potentially damaging to the cohesion of society itself. This represents a process through which poor whites are simultaneously cast as collateral damage in a reassembling of whiteness and the reproduction of white privilege: their apparent peripheral form of whiteness – articulated through languages of moral degeneracy and racial contamination – is used as an explanation as to why greater numbers are increasingly struggling to retain the material rewards that whiteness has traditionally granted; however, on the other hand, while there is increasing competition for scant resources marginalised whites, 'know that their interests will be secure against those of minoritized groups', as 'they are beneficiaries of whiteness (seen clearly in the 'Victim' discourse) but also at times in a liminal position when necessary or useful.' (Gillborn 2010, pp. 22–3). It is in this ambivalent treatment of 'chavs', 'white underclass', and the 'white working class' that this liminality reveals itself. While often chastised for their apparent backwardness, social, cultural and moral degeneration, state dependency, racism, and attachment to traditional racial identities, they are also constructed as a grouping that must be placated in order to avoid the asserted threats of political extremism, violence and declining social cohesion.

References

Alexander, C. (2011) 'Rethinking Race or Denying Racism?' 15 June 2011, http://soundings.mcb.org.uk/?p=76

Alibhai-Brown, Y. (2009) 'Spare Me the Tears over the White Working-Class', *Independent,* 5 January 2009, http://www.independent.co.uk/opinion/commentators/yasmin-alibhai-brown/yasmin-alibhaibrown-spare-me-the-tears-over-the-white-working-class-1225824.html#

Beider, H. (2011) *Community Cohesion: The Views of White Working-Class Communities* (York: Joseph Rowntree Foundation).

Bolt, A. (2011) 'Riots Are the Result of a Class Chasm', *Herald Sun,* 10 August 2011, http://www.heraldsun.com.au/opinion/riots-are-the-result-of-a-class-chasm/story-e6frfifx-1226111972605

Bonnett, A. (2000) *White Identities: Historical and International Perspectives* (Harlow: Prentice Hall).

Bottero, W. (2009) 'Class in the 21st Century', in K. P. Sveinsson (ed.), *Who Cares about the White Working Class?* (London: Runnymede Trust), pp. 7–15.

Bourne, J. (2011) 'Both Class and Race', Soundings. *Policy matters for Muslims in Britain* http://soundings.mcb.org.uk/?p=72

Brogan, B. (2008) 'Help the White Working Class or Risk Surge in Far-Right Extremists, Says Equalities Chief', *Daily Mail,* 28 October 2008, http://www.dailymail.co.uk/news/article-1081125/Help-white-working-class-risk-surge-far-Right-extremists-says-equalities-chief-Trevor-Phillips.html

Bush, M. (2011) *Everyday Forms of Whiteness: Understanding Race in a 'Post-Racial' World,* 2nd edn (Lanham, MD: Rowman and Littlefield).

Byrne, B. (2006) *White Lives: The Interplay of 'Race', Class and Gender in Everyday Life* (London: Routledge).

Carroll, H. (2011) *Affirmative Reaction: New Formations of White Masculinity* (Durham, NC, and London: Duke University Press).

Commission for Equality and Human Rights (CEHR) (2010) 'How Fair Is Britain?' (London: CEHR).

Cowles, J., Garner, S., Lung, B. and Stott, S. (2009) *Sources of Resentment, and Perceptions of Ethnic Minorities among Poor White People in England* (London: National Community Forum/Department for Communities and Local Government).

Dench, G., Gavron, K. and Young, M. (2006) *The New East End: Kinship, Race and Conflict* (London: Profile Books).

Denham, J. (2009) 'Connecting Communities', speech given at the Institute for Community Cohesion, 14 October 2009, http://www.communities.gov.uk/speeches/corporate/connectingcommunities

Doane, A. (2003) 'Rethinking Whiteness Studies', in A. Doane and E. Bonilla-Silva (eds), *White Out: The Continuing Significance of Racism*, (New York and London: Routledge), pp. 3–18.

Dyer, R. (1997) *White: Essays on Race and Culture* (London and New York: Routledge).

Economist, The (2006) 'Poor Whites: The Forgotten Underclass', *The Economist*, 26 October 2006, http://www.economist.com/node/8089315

Frankenberg, R. (2001) 'The Mirage of an Unmarked Whiteness', in B. R. Rasmussen, E. Klinenberg, I. J. Nexica and M. Wray (eds), *The Making and Unmaking of Whiteness*, (Durham, NC, and London: Duke University Press), pp. 72–96.

Garner, S. (2006) 'The Uses of Whiteness: What Sociologists Working on Europe Can Draw from US Research on Whiteness', *Sociology*, 40(2), 257–75.

Garner, S. (2007) *Whiteness: An Introduction* (London and New York: Routledge).

Gillborn, D. (2010) 'The White Working Class, Racism and Respectability: Victims, Degenerates and Interest-Convergence', *British Journal of Educational Studies*, 58(1), 3–25.

Goldberg, D. T. (2009) *The Threat of Race: Reflections on Racial Neoliberalism* (Oxford: Wiley-Blackwell).

Goodhart, D. (2011) 'A Tale of Three Cities', *Prospect*, 22 June 2011.

Goodhart, D. (2012) 'Stephen Lawrence and the Politics of Race', *Prospect*, 4 January 2012.

Hage, G. (1998) *White Nation: Fantasies of White Supremacy in a Multicultural Society* (Annandale: Pluto Press).

Hanley, L. (2008) 'This White Working Class Stuff Is a Media Invention', *The Guardian*, 30 May 2008, p. 36.

Hartigan, J. (1997) 'Green Ghettos and the White Underclass', *Social Research*, 64(2), 339–65.

Hartigan, J. (1997a) 'Unpopular Culture: The Case of "White Trash"', *Cultural Studies*, 11(2), 316–43.

Hartigan, J. (2003) 'Who Are These White People? "Rednecks", "Hilbillies", and "White Trash" as Marked Racial Subjects', in A. Doane and E. Bonilla-Silva (eds), *White Out: The Continuing Significance of Racism* (New York and London: Routledge), pp. 95–111.

Hartigan, J. (2005) *Odd Tribes: Towards a Cultural Analysis of White People* (Durham, NC, and London: Duke University Press).

Hastings, M. (2011) 'UK Riots 2011: Liberal Dogma Has Spawned a Generation of Brutalised Youths', *Daily Mail*, 12 August 2011, http://www.dailymail.co.uk/debate/article-2024284/UK-riots-2011-Liberal-dogma-spawned-generation-brutalised-youths.html

Haylett, C. (2001) 'Illegitimate Subjects? Abject Whites, Neoliberal Modernisation, and Middle-Class Multiculturalism', *Environment and Planning D: Society and Space*, 19(3), 351–70.

Heffer, S. (2007) 'The Underclass Must Be Helped to Help Itself', *Daily Telegraph*, 11 August 2007, http://www.telegraph.co.uk/comment/personal-view/3641888/The-underclass-must-be-helped-to-help-itself.html

Hewitt, R. (2005) *White Backlash and the Politics of Multiculturalism* (Cambridge: Cambridge University Press).

Jones, O. (2011) *Chavs: The Demonization of the Working Class* (London: Verso).

Kite, M. (2006) 'White Voters Are Deserting Us for the BNP', *Sunday Telegraph*, 16 April 2006, http://www.telegraph.co.uk/news/uknews/1515854/White-voters-are-deserting-us-for-BNP-says-Blair-ally.html

Lentin, A. (2008) 'Europe and the Silence about Race', *European Journal of Social Theory*, 11(4) 487–503.

Lentin, A. and Titley, G. (2011) *The Crises of Multiculturalism: Racism in a Neoliberal Age* (London and New York: Zed Books).

Lewis, A. E. (2004) '"What Group?" Studying Whites and Whiteness in the Era of "Color-Blindness"', *Sociological Theory*, 22(4), 623–46.

Lewis, P., Taylor, M. and Ball, J. (2011) 'Kenneth Clarke Blames English Riots on a "Broken Penal System"', *The Guardian*, 5 September 2011, http://www.guardian.co.uk/uk/2011/sep/05/kenneth-clarke-riots-penal-system

McCarthy, M. (2011) 'No Shame, No Limits: Has the Behaviour of the Mob Destroyed the Idea of British Civility For Ever?' *The Independent*, 10 August 2011, http://www.independent.co.uk/news/uk/crime/no-shame-no-limits-has-the-behaviour-of-the-mob-destroyed-the-idea-of-british-civility-for-ever-2334863.html

Mirza, M. (2010) 'Rethinking Race', *Prospect*, 22 September 2010.

Murray, C. (1996) 'The Emerging British Underclass', in R. Lister (ed.), *Charles Murray and the Underclass: The Developing Debate* (London: IEA Health and Welfare Unit), pp. 23–53.

Murray, C. (2012) *Coming Apart: The State of White America, 1960–2010* (New York: Crown Forum).

Nayak, A. (2006) 'Displaced Masculinities: Chavs, Youth and Class in the Post-industrial City', *Sociology*, 40(5), 813–31.

Nayak, A. (2009) 'Beyond the Pale: Chavs, Youth and Social Class', in K. P. Sveinsson (ed.), *Who Cares about the White Working Class?* (London: Runnymede Trust), pp. 28–35.

Newitz, A. (1997) 'White Savagery and Humiliation, or a New Racial Consciousness in the Media', in M. Wray and A. Newitz (eds), *White Trash: Race and Class in America* (London and New York: Routledge), pp. 131–54.

Newitz, A. and Wray, M. (1997) 'Introduction', in M. Wray and A. Newitz (eds) *White Trash: Race and Class in America* (London and New York: Routledge), pp. 1–12.

O' Carroll, L. (2011) 'David Starkey's Newsnight Race Remarks: Hundreds Complain to BBC', *The Guardian*, 15 August 2011, http://www.guardian.co.uk/media/2011/aug/15/david-starkey-newsinght-race-remarks

Reay, D., Hollingworth, S., Williams, K., Crozier, G., Jamieson, F., James, D., and Beedell, P. (2007) '"A Darker Shade of Pale?" Whiteness, the Middle Classes and Multi-Ethnic Inner-City Schooling', *Sociology*, 41(6), 1041–60.

Rhodes, J. (2009) 'Revisiting the 2001 Riots: New Labour and the Rise of "Colorblind" Racism', *Sociological Research Online*, 14(5).

Rhodes, J. (2010) 'White Backlash, "Unfairness" and Justifications of British National Party (BNP) Support', *Ethnicities*, 10(1), 77–99.

Rhodes, J. (2011) '"It's Not Just Them, It's Whites as Well": Whiteness, Class and BNP Support', *Sociology*, 45(1), 102–17.

Roediger, D. (1999) *The Wages of Whiteness: Race and the Making of the American Working Class*, revised edn (New York: Verso).

Solomos, J. (2011) 'Race, Rumours and Riots: Past, Present and Future', *Sociological Research Online*, 16(4), http://www.socresonline.org.uk

Summers, D. (2009) 'White Working Class Feels Ignored over Immigration, Says Blears', *Guardian*, 2 January 2009, http://www.guardian.co.uk/politics/2009/jan/02/immigration-working-class

Starkey, D. (2011) 'It's Not about Criminality and Cuts... It's about Culture', 20 August 2011, *Daily Telegraph*, p. 17.

Tyler, I. (2008) '"Chav Mum, Chav Scum": Class Disgust in Contemporary Britain', *Feminist Media Studies*, 8(1), 17–34.

Ware, V. (2008) 'Towards a Sociology of Resentment: A Debate on Class and Whiteness', *Sociological Research Online*, 13(5), http://www.socresonline.org.uk

Webster, C. (2008) 'Marginalized White Ethnicity, Race, and Crime', *Theoretical Criminology*, 12(3), 293–312.

Wiegman, R. (1999) 'Whiteness Studies and the Paradox of Particularity', *boundary*, 26(3), 115–150.

Winant, H. (1997) 'Behind Blue Eyes: Whiteness and Contemporary US Racial Politics', *New Left Review*, 225(September–October 1997), pp. 73–88.

Wray, M. (2006) *Not Quite White: White Trash and the Boundaries of Whiteness* (Durham, NC, and London: Duke University Press).

4

The Status of Multiculturalism and the Retreat from Difference

Sivamohan Valluvan

> The biggest cheer of the afternoon came when Mr Sarkozy defended what he called the values of the French Republic against multiculturalism.
>
> *(Financial Times* 2012)

Any collection which aspires to sketch the *state of race*, as particular to the contemporary British and European conjuncture, is necessarily compelled to grapple with the term *multiculturalism*. Multiculturalism has come to be the site at which much of the popular discussion concerning racialised ethnic diversity, whether accommodating or hostile, is hosted. The question that multiculturalism then raises vis-à-vis race is double pronged. It is about the state of race in society (the accommodation of difference racially and ethnically manifest) and the state as always-already racialised (the exclusions rationalised by normative narratives concerning racially construed ethnic difference). Multiculturalism is of course 'a deeply contested idea' (Hall 2000, p. 210) and thus, predictably polysemic. It can, for instance, be read as a state doctrine (insofar as, a government policy is no longer overtly assimilationist); a mere descriptive 'statement of fact' (Younge 2010, p.187) concerning some shared spaces (i.e. multiculture or diversity); or, as has been recently described by Lentin and Titley (2011, p. 2), just a messy 'patchwork of initiatives, rhetoric, and aspirations' broadly sympathetic in *tone* to the presence of ethnic difference in the public sphere. In spite of this expected range, it is adequate for the purposes of this chapter to distinguish between two chief strains: one possessing an ideologically symptomatic, anti-minority resonance whilst the other fosters an understanding of diversity consistent with a broader politics of ordinary multiculture (conducive to inclusive, cross-ethnic undertakings). Let me rename these two strains in the following fashion: multiculturalism as tolerance of the other as commonly represented, and multiculturalism as also involving the interrogation of that common representation.

In expanding on the perspectives which surface in this short debate, I will take care to dissociate myself from the formulation of multiculturalism which reads *only* as the 'tolerance of the other'. It will be suggested that such a prevalent 'thinning' of what multiculturalism entails is central to a broader repudiation of ethnic difference as a whole. In the following, this 'thin' understanding of multiculturalism will be termed synonymously as a 'mischaracterisation'. Whilst this is not meant to intimate notions of 'authentic' meanings, I believe the word apposite – insofar as the increasingly simplistic framing of multiculturalism rests heavily on a *characterisation* of the excluded minority (most notably Muslims) as both illiberal (read uncivilised) and trenchantly communalist. This characterisation plays all too neatly into the hands of mainstream voices nostalgic for a difference-free polity to be deemed credible. The minority presence, *precisely* due to their excessive attachment to an illiberal group 'culture', is ably situated at the explanatory centre of any number of social ills: be they security and crime (Bawer 2010); unemployment and welfare dependency (Sarrazin 2010); or even democratic deficits, the collapse of the welfare state and the alleged erosion of trust (Goodhart 2004; Putnam 2007). In parts I and II of this chapter, by way of parsing a recent debate between Slavoj Žižek and Sara Ahmed, I propose to unpack the way such discursive narratives are licensed by this thinning of what multiculturalism is said to stand for and, in turn, demonstrate how this mischaracterisation might be read as a 'laundering of racism' (Lentin and Titley 2011, p. 15) appropriate for contemporary times.

As many others have already argued – most notably Wendy Brown (2006) – any notion of tolerance rests on the necessary and thereby problematic marking of what it is that needs to be tolerated. It is rightly argued that such appeals to tolerance are disposed to preserving prevailing hierarchies of power. However, in building on this important line of critique, the question that needs to be asked is whether a bracketed appeal to tolerance is able to deliver even that minimal notion of tolerance, let alone advance an inclusive disposition towards racialised ethnic difference. Parts III and IV will hereby explore the manner in which this conception of multiculturalism, in practice, can seem to paradoxically further the cause of nation-state assimilationism. The case to be answered here is: how can any such thin version of the multicultural imperative lead to any other conclusion than the declaration of its own impossibility. After all, the multicultural call to tolerance – if only that – is evidently not about tolerance of others, for it only recognises such figures in the form that they are already intelligible: as members of dysfunctional foreign cultures which are, quite simply, *intolerable.*

Having established this context, I advance in part V of this chapter a modest defence of multiculturalism which retains its critical, pluralist thrust. I propose that it is the latter rendition (an interrogation of how difference is represented by the dominant gaze) that is able to harness the lived, mundane routines of metropolitan multiculture; what Paul Gilroy (2004, p. xiv) in his description of such encounters dubs the 'unkempt, unruly and unplanned' interactional fields where difference is neither elided nor an essentialised cumbrance.[1] In other words, an underlying critique of dominant representational standards must figure centrally (even when undemonstrative) in any variety of multiculturalism that is consistent with everyday articulations of ease with diversity. Of course, such a call to representational critique is neither novel nor dramatically radical. I do, however, think it worth revisiting in order to retrieve multiculturalism from the politically destructive caricature which currently holds sway. A multiculturalism which is better configured to tap into the energies of ordinary, intermeshed multiculture cannot afford to any longer leave undisturbed the representation of ethnic identities as foundationally tied to a particular monoculture, a single culture which is discrete, alien and constitutionally illiberal (uncivil).

I: Are we all multiculturalists now?

A recent exchange between Slavoj Žižek and Sara Ahmed ably exemplifies the tension between the two understandings and signals the manner in which a wilful mischaracterisation underpins even the best of critical theoretical undertakings (namely, Žižek) within the current discursive field concerning multiculturalism.[2] This revealing discussion around the status of the term was prompted by Žižek's charge during a plenary talk that 'Multiculturalism is hegemonic. It is an empirical fact.' Though he declined to expand on the claim during the talk itself, he has maintained in a number of short pieces elsewhere (Žižek 1997, 2011) that he reads a multiculturalist consensus – wherein the political centre adopts a platform which is tolerant of the other's difference (Žižek 2010) – as serving a hegemonic function.

Žižek is uninterested in multiculturalism as it simultaneously (i) dulls the subversive (radical) potential of minorities whilst preserving their status as awkwardly different; (ii) is anti-solidaristic through its stress on inviolable difference; and (iii) manages to goad 'liberals' into defending the indefensible – practices and values they would themselves reject as categorical wrongs – merely on account of the overriding *ought* injunction concerning the 'respect of the other'. Whilst the first statement is unique to Žižek's commendably impassioned agitation for a Universalist resistance, the other two are shared by many others across the political spectrum, such as Bruce Bawer and Pascal Bruckner; the latter having denounced it 'as the racism of the anti-racists [where] in the name of social cohesion, we are invited to give our roaring applause for the intolerance that these groups show for our laws' (Bruckner 2007). The underlying agreement here is that multiculturalism, as a principle of absolutist respect which difference of its own accord obtains for itself, is seen as having *successfully* embedded itself at the centre of European politics.

In contrast, Ahmed (2008) considers Žižek's sweeping read of multiculturalism's political status entirely misplaced: as it is, in actuality, 'the speech act that declares liberal multiculturalism hegemonic which is hegemonic'. Ahmed sees little empirical grounds to conclude that multiculturalism is in any way pervasive or politically centrist. Thus, in terms of reading the ideological moment, she thinks it of greater relevance to show who has most to gain when multiculturalism is popularly evoked as somehow being rampant, as somehow enjoying the consensus of the establishment. As echoed in Lentin and Titley's (2011) recent work, she concludes that it is through constructing an enemy daunting in its magnitude (i.e. consensus of the centre) that it is possible to endow one's own position (i.e. anti-multiculturalism), which is the actual majority position, with a sense of urgency as well as a righteous, dignified air; 'One suspects that hegemonies are often presented as minority positions, as defences against what are perceived to be hegemonic, which is how they can be presented as matter of life and death' (Ahmed 2008).

Ahmed incorporates into her response the concept of the 'non-performative' which she had developed earlier (2005) to characterise the inability of various white voices to convert their stated anti-racist credentials into tactile, material deed. The *action* of a non-performative lies in the persuasive declaration of a certain situation as such (e.g. multicultural or anti-racist), whilst no material change in the state of affairs transpires (2005, p. 3). Transposing this metaphor to the prevailing discourse of multiculturalism, Ahmed (2008) reads the establishment status of multiculturalism as a 'fantasy', seductive to those who are nostalgic for a re-purified, homogenous polity – a fantasy which places a mythical pro-difference agenda at the political centre and thereby galvanises resistance against it.

The above can be considered as revealing of the broader social debate. It is apparent that Žižek and Ahmed have two rather different conceptions of what multiculturalism entails. Furthermore, the promise of multiculturalism (however insufficient as an ultimate end) is something which Ahmed is seemingly wary of abandoning. To better handle how Ahmed might potentially expand upon a multicultural undertaking, and also to offer a primer of my own argument to follow, it is instructive to visit her development elsewhere of the term 'stickiness' – a term she uses to capture the texture of certain associations which are embedded in the popular imagery concerning a particular identity type. In *The Cultural Politics of Emotion* (2004), Ahmed encourages us to interrogate how words and the emotions they evoke (e.g. terror and fear or crime and distrust) enjoy a proximate relationship to certain identities (e.g. Muslim and black respectively): '[T]he work of emotions involves the sticking of signs to bodies' (2004, p. 13). It is the proximity of such associations which mobilises a politically violent indifference concerning the deprivations these communities often contend with. Multiculturalism, when routed through her parallel arguments concerning the non-performative and proximate attributions, steps beyond *mere* tolerance and presents itself as a critical exercise which the majority polity at large is invited to partake in. By disrupting these associations (e.g. Islamic terror), by disrupting this proximity that such adjectives enjoy, the majority is asked, in the phraseology of Gayatri Spivak (1988, p. 287), not simply to claim that they are committed to inclusion, but 'to unlearn [the] privilege' they obtain from the very way in which they *apprehend* the world around them.

The two positions can hereby be summarised in the following way. Multiculturalism as tolerance is indeed an ideological ruse, just not in the manner in which Žižek deems it to be. For Žižek, tolerance is hegemonic, as it is an ideologically centred co-option of minority dissent and undermines a Universalist resistance amongst the exploited, whilst for Ahmed, it is the *illusion* that we are tolerant that is hegemonic. Ahmed's short intervention suggests in turn that tolerance is worth pursuing and that it needs be anchored in something hitherto under-appreciated by the prevailing political culture. This 'something' might be phrased provisionally as a *critical or interrogative* tolerance. A tolerance which incorporates a semiotic literacy among majority and minorities alike concerning the 'regimes of representation' (Hall 1997, p. 232) which organise difference unequally along various normative indices.

II: To tolerate the intolerable?

Žižek issued a rejoinder, later reproduced in his *Living in End Times* (2011), whereby he clarified the nature of his reservations about multi-cultural politics (2011, pp. 39–48). Though for the most part compelling and in seeming agreement with Ahmed, he manages unwittingly through the course of his argumentation to further the purchase of the critical representational politics which Ahmed would consider propositional to any multiculturalism remotely worthy of its name. Similarly, the putatively 'hegemonic' multiculturalism which he ridicules seems identical to the one routinely *condemned* by *centrist* politicians when fumbling for electorially decisive political capital. As Lentin and Titley mention in passing:

> While Žižek's general argument about the cost-free politics of liberal multiculturalism is one that [we accept], what is of interest in his focus on the 'mask' of multiculturalism is the yawning gulf between his mapping of multicultural politics and the changed political coordinates and discourses now assembled through it. (2011, p. 5)

Žižek (2011, pp. 45–6) draws our attention to a Slovenian example when elaborating on the shortcomings of multiculturalism. He refers to a Roma settlement and the anxieties which emerged amongst the Slovenes of the nearby town; therein, he cites sympathetically the *fear* articulated by the Slovene residents concerning a wave of criminal activity attributed to various local Roma. Žižek mocks here the multicultural liberals who live far away in the comforts of metropolitan excess. They are laughable in their eagerness to denounce the concerned Slovenes as racist, urging the preservation of the Roma 'way of life' (201, pp. 39, 46). Though part of Žižek's point, with justification, is to draw attention to the liberal pretence of the urbanites, what is equally apparent here is the charge that multiculturalism has evidently led to this morass of relativistic ir-reason. As will be expanded below in some depth, this type of carica-ture, common as it is, reads multiculturalism as a series of imperatives which obliges, *ipso facto*, the unconditional tolerance of another ethnic-ity's way of being. No other concerns are any longer admissible. Or, as Bruckner (2007) puts it in more bellicose terms: 'Criteria of just and unjust, criminal and barbarian, disappear before the absolute criterion of respect for difference.'

Žižek has invited us to consider an example I am not wholly familiar with. My purpose is therefore to conjecture the context in a manner that is recognisable. Conveniently, the Sarkozy administration's move to evict, *en masse*, Roma settlements in France owing to a series of criminal incidents traced back to members of those communities is a useful analogue for the scene Žižek relates, given the widespread publicity it received. Some criticism of the move did transpire in certain quarters, most notably, and to her credit, from the EU Justice Commissioner (*The Guardian* 2010). The mooted policy was, however, seen to enjoy populist purchase, whereby 79 per cent of the public was approving (*Bloomberg* 2010). It can in turn be speculated that the discursive climate which licensed such an indiscriminate act of expulsion was the coupling in the popular imagination of Roma communities with criminality. A forum to consider the various structural and historical constraints which the multiculturalists pilloried by Žižek sought to underscore was largely absent in the discursive assemblage the French Right exploited for short-term political gain. Perhaps more importantly, the multiculturalist in both instances would also ask us to be wary of conflating Roma with crime: in other words, disrupt the ordinary attributions which such newsworthy incidents tend to revive. It is of course misleading of Žižek to imply that these voices believed that the police should not take action. Here, the conflation of multiculturalism with an element of lawlessness is baffling, yet all too familiar to those versed in anti-multiculturalism homilies.

> Predictably, Slovenian liberals condemned them as racists [...] When the TV reporters interviewed the 'racists' from the town, they were clearly seen to be a group of people frightened by the constant fighting and shooting in the Roma camp, by the constant theft of animals from their farms, and by other forms of small harassments from the Roma.[3] It is all too easy to say (as the liberals did) that the Roma way of life is (also) a consequence of the centuries of their exclusion and mistreatment, that the people in the nearby town should also open themselves more to the Roma, etc. – nobody clearly answered the local 'racists' what they should concretely do to solve the very real problems the Roma camp evidently was for them (Žižek 2011, p. 46).

Žižek also seems to suggest that the entire community is collectively responsible for this 'harassment'. The Roma camp is without hesitation marked as a *problematic* space (as is so often the case when spaces with a sizeable minority presence are discussed), posing a threat to the wronged farmer community. Why is Žižek so quick to adopt this conflict frame, why is the 'them and us', the culprits and the frightened, so uncritically assumed to be self-explanatory? Why are the townspeople's grievances accorded the emphasis of being *very* real? After all, it could equally be asked: What should be done to concretely solve the very real problems the Slovene town evidently was for *them* [the Roma]. The repetition of the adjective 'constant' further reveals his sense that the troubles of the townspeople are more immediate, requiring a response which multiculturalism cannot handle. Surprisingly, the same reasoning which allows for Sarkozy's posturing is latent here in Žižek's dismissal.

As foreshadowed, this straw-man multiculturalism (one which does not involve critique but simplistically accords difference an inviolable right) is the same conception favoured by a commentariat who style themselves as brave guardians of liberal and solidaristic values. Bruce Bawer (2008, p. 5), a self-declared 'centrist' essayist who authored a well-received call to arms concerning the increased profile of Islam in the West, makes a typically unsubtle claim in *Surrender*: '[T]he pernicious doctrine of multiculturalism which has asked free people to sacrifice their own liberties, while bending their knees to tyrants, has proven so useful to the new breed of cultural jihadists that it might have been invented by Osama bin Laden himself.' Not much is left to the imagination. We witness here the customary proximate fixing of an inherent, dysfunctional violence (i.e. bin Laden) onto the bearer of difference. Multiculturalism, as a broader political programme, is seen in turn as the sponsor of such pathology, automatically deferring to the authority of ethno-cultural difference.

For Žižek – despite his writing from the other end of the ideological spectrum – the political objective of multiculturalism is seemingly little different. The multiculturalist state commits to the tolerance of those who it otherwise dislikes. To transpose a characteristically elegant phrase of Adorno and Horkeimer[4]: *multiculturalism is the social bad conscience of nationalism*. The state does not care to address the processes by which it is exclusionary, but merely tries to grant a separate political and performative space to those whom they intend to continue excluding. Though Žižek's case is welcome in sentiment, and resembles the sharp commentary of Wendy Brown (2006) on the inadequacy of tolerance, it does maintain as operative the same conception of multiculturalism as paraded by the increasingly mainstream, nationalist guard in the course of their disparaging of ethnic diversity. During such harangues, multiculturalism is referenced as an extensive set of anti-liberal, anti-cohesive concessions a misguided establishment class makes due to the segregationist relativism supposedly made incumbent by multiculturalism.

Žižek is of course right to suggest, in agreement with Ahmed, that the 'general "civil racism" is rendered invisible' (2011, p. 45) when sentiments of tolerance are appealed to in the act of demonstratively rejecting a vulgar racism (e.g. Front National). The spectacle of nominal anti-racism allows for the understated routines of racial vilification practiced in everyday representations to obtain a further layer of obfuscation. This 'multiculturalism as tolerance' – where racism is individualised or re-narrated as only relevant to a fringe subculture – absolves what Anne-Marie Fortier (2008, p. 31) sardonically dubs the 'decent majority' of any complicity in racist discourses.

However, this rendition of multiculturalism is surely one which is, in the final reckoning, uninterested even in a nominal tolerance but rather aspires for assimilation. As will be argued below, I believe the distinction here to be crucial. To put it boldly, does the term 'tolerate' remain even intelligible if it concerns only the special interests of those subjects whose representational cues as fundamentalists, criminals and welfare dependents endure? Does the term remain applicable if multiculturalism comes to be framed as the accommodation of *illiberal* peoples and thereupon, necessitates the loss of 'our' most cherished political norms? Multicultural tolerance, if that alone, is evidently not about the recognition of others, as it only recognises such figures in the form that they are already intelligible; as others and the dysfunctional attributes the proximate imagery invokes.

III: Multiculturalism as relativistic, illiberal tolerance

If multiculturalism is to be peddled in this thin form, it is nothing but a convenient foil for what Back et al. (2002) identified as the New Labour retreat to assimilationism. It is this *instrumental* value of such a narration of multiculturalism for a nationalist cause, intensified by the fallout of 9/11, which Žižek, in a manner I consider symptomatic of the broader discursive moment, seems unable to recognise. Pathik Pathak's (2007) critique of the resurgent fashion for Left communitarianism – best exemplified by the ubiquity of David Goodhart[5] – is an instructive starting point in unpacking the service this distorted multiculturalism does in supporting an end which is, by the final reckoning, assimilationist.

Pathak suggests that there is little in *principle* to distinguish the liberal communitarians from the hollow multiculturalism which they denounce. Positing Bikhu Parekh as the foremost 'grandmaster' of an insular multiculturalism, Pathak (2007, pp. 263–4) argues that Parekh's 'a community of communities' vision is merely a synonym for 'plural monocultures'. By the same token, David Goodhart (2004) – despite having garnered great acclaim among a liberal Left fatigued by multiculturalism – himself is tempted by the allure of monoculture, but as a *singular, national* monoculture. The intimation of this Left-communitarian argument is that monoculture, and its unapologetic policing (Goodhart 2004, 2005), is the very basis for the affective solidarity needed for a coherent redistributive welfare state to function.

I contend that this symbiosis of assimilationism and multiculturalism is even more insidious than Pathak accounts for. Multiculturalism, portrayed as a programme to facilitate the tolerance of ethnically other 'monocultures', can be read as a *necessary* discursive prop to advance a rehabilitated assimilationist narrative. It acts as the obverse side of the assimilationist coin. While eschewing the overt summons to a homogenous ethnic polity (i.e. traditional assimilation), it suffices to engineer the same end by maintaining that racialised ethnic groups, unless reconstituted, pose a threat to the *democratic* conversation by virtue of the negative features which their 'cultures' espouse. The homogenous and hermetically sealed minority monoculture, when appraised by an unsympathetic symbolic standard, can only be deemed as being incompatible with the civilisational, civic values that the majority nation monopolistically appropriates for itself (e.g. freedom, civility, decency, enterprise) (McGhee 2009). Hereby, when multiculturalism is presented as the tolerance of such other monocultures, it is pitched as so dramatic an imposition that at stake in any significant concession to it is the irretrievable erosion of our prized liberal core.

There is, of course, *already* a well-recognised political conservatism to any simple appeal to tolerance in the sense that the prevailing political hierarchy is reinforced in the very act of distinguishing those who tolerate from those who are to be tolerated. This insight concerning the power relations which undergird acts of conditional tolerance has been made compellingly by both Wendy Brown (2004) and Jacques Derrida (2003, pp. 127–130). There is no dissolution of the distinction between insider and outsider, but instead, the outsider remains a negatively coded, undesirable entity, awaiting interrogation and verdict. In Derrida's argumentation, however, there lies a further implication apposite for the argument sketched above. The political logic of tolerance suggests not only that it is invariably an exercise of privilege, but more importantly, that there is in actuality a certain *impossibility* to tolerance itself. I rephrase his argument here as entailing that an appeal to tolerance, short of any other political undertaking (e.g. 'unconditional hospitality'), can only function negationally – as only a call for the 'reasonable amongst us' to be intolerant. In this sense tolerance cannot be seen as somehow hegemonic (in the sense that 'free will' or 'the American Dream' is), but rather, as a narrative reference which reminds the rational listener that the outside object *cannot* be tolerated or only be *partially or conditionally* tolerated. Any bracketed appeal to tolerance can seemingly only function in a negational narrative wherein the speaker cites the impossibility of 'us', the impartial adjudicators, to be tolerant of 'them', the ethnic, group-beholden others. Put bluntly, how is a positive appeal to tolerance concerning the fundamentalist-cum-terrorist ever to be advanced? The function of 'multiculturalism-as-tolerance' to a broader assimilationist project is I believe of the same negational sort. Multiculturalism phrased thus, as illiberal and relativistic, gives tolerance a viable narrative purchase *only* to those who wish to be seen as intolerant of the relevant others. It only appeals to those who wish to be seen as anti-multiculturalism – wherein they 'turn tolerance into a sign of the nation's weakness' (Fortier 2008, p. 6).

IV: Why multiculturalism?

The rest of this chapter will advance a more detailed rebuttal of 'the deformations, straw men [and] false alternatives' (Gaita 2010, p. 1) which abound in the brand of multiculturalism evoked by its detractors. When presented as 'tolerance politics' and by extension, a dilution of liberal principles, multiculturalism functions best as a compelling narrative trope for the popular discrediting of ethnic difference in general. In looking to advance a more practicable stance, one which is more sincere in its reception of difference, it will be necessary to unpick this false either/or concerning liberalism and ethnic diversity. Doing so will also bring to the fore the importance of a critical representational politics to any multicultural sensibility.

Before proceeding, however, it would be wise to sketch a few points which answer the question, Why multiculturalism in the first place? The touchstone for my argument here is *Multiculturalism without Culture*, the invaluable work of Anne Phillips (2006). Phillips isolates at one stage a few select observations when justifying her need to defend multiculturalism. First, the indelible currency of multiculturalism lies in its anti-nationalism, anti-majoritarianism and anti-homogeneity (2006, p. 71). This basic, canonical purpose should not be under-appreciated. Second, multiculturalism is already couched in a heuristic which recognises that minority and majority communities are *mutually constituted*. Though Phillips might be premature in reading cosmopolitanism as being relatively untouched by such considerations, the point stands that multiculturalism necessarily assumes that the quality of minority life is greatly determined by the treatment, both representational and material, it is subjected to by the majority polity (2006, p. 72). Both these points will feature in the discussion to follow.

It is, however, her third argument, a directly political (2006, p. 72) one, which is perhaps most crucial at this initial juncture. To retreat from multiculturalism, she intimates, shows a certain political naïveté and intellectual resignation. When multiculturalism is caricatured in the course of a broader 'return to narrower and more exclusionary notions of national identity' (2006, p. 72), it is imprudent to defer to the legitimacy of the very caricature. She argues that, given how much multiculturalism is already with us, 'This is not the moment for sounding the retreat from everything that multiculturalism implies' (2006, p. 72). To pursue this route amounts to an unwitting form of quietism. Not least, I might contend, because the darker denizens of the contemporary West themselves recognise that at stake in the struggle to define multiculturalism is the legitimacy of their own lives as denizens of multiculture – as denizens of those multiethnic spaces which resist any attempt at an uncomplicated, efficient narration of national identity.

It is in this context that a more able, politically competent multiculturalism is to be formulated. When caricatured, a series of dangerous false dichotomies gain traction. It is worth revisiting here David Cameron's 2011 Munich speech (*New Statesman* 2011a) in which it was declared that 'Multiculturalism has failed.' In opposition to the sins of multiculturalism, David Cameron made positive mention of the need to cultivate multiple identities: 'Yes, I am a Muslim, I am a Hindu, I am Christian, but I am also a Londoner or a Berliner too.' It is this regrettable state of affairs, where the celebration of multiple identities is rallied in the course of attributing pathologies to ethnic difference (recall that the context of the speech concerned terrorism and Muslims), that it becomes easier to grasp the discursive techniques by which multiculturalism is distorted in furthering an exclusionary end. This subscription of Cameron's to the rhetoric of multiple identities (which was, after all, so central to the multiculturalism of Bikhu Parekh 2000) is not one simply of convenience, but one that reveals a more complicated complicity between the rejection of multiculturalism and the way multiculturalism comes to be represented in these debates. Here, multiculturalism manages to stand in opposition to the ability to peddle multiple identities; whilst, as will be argued, it would seem that its purpose is to *de-problematise*, at the very least, some of those 'multiple' identities.

V: Multiculturalism and the Politics of Misrecognition

In the following I expand on the error of formulating multiculturalism as the tolerance of illiberal, special group rights. I also exemplify how such a framing is central to a rehabilitation of racialised exclusion palatable for modern sensibilities. In advancing this critique, the importance of an interrogative representational politics to any logically viable multiculturalism will hopefully become better apparent.

As prefaced at length, many critics of multiculturalism, regardless of political creed, have understood it as a political programme which promotes a particularly extensive mode of communal segregation. David Hollinger (2000), for instance, deems multiculturalism destructive for broader democratic deliberation as it promotes a retreat to the comforts of ethno-cultural particularities. Other critics, most notably Brian Barry (2001), understand multiculturalism as a policy and ethos which, in the name of cultural egalitarianism, begrudgingly tolerates the habits and values of certain minority communities despite their being in contravention to the normative standards (both ethically and aesthetically) particular to the majority community. In this sense, multiculturalism, as pictured by its critics, is seen as propagating a rationale of 'self-contained and radically incommensurable' (Bernstein 2010, p. 381) communities whose cultural properties are featured as homogenous and timeless, insomuch as they are seen as inherent to the integrity and substance of the respective group.

Part of the problem is, of course, that some prominent early proponents did engage with multiculturalism in this unhelpful 'cultural' mode. Kymlicka's (1995) canonical endorsement of multiculturalism was premised on the idea that certain groups should be afforded 'special rights' and other unique facilities which could allow them to pursue the types of lives which chimed with their culturally contingent understandings of value and integrity. For Kymlicka, the fullest remit of such rights only applies to 'national minorities' (as members of 'societal cultures' with territorial and historical integrity). Indeed, much has been made of how to extend Kymlicka's framework to immigrant communities: classed by him as 'voluntary' arrivals who expect to participate in dominant society. He does nonetheless develop a parallel cluster of 'polyethnic' rights which are suitable for immigrants; it is such rights, as opposed to those pertinent to 'societal cultures', which is the brand of multiculturalism most of us in Europe commonly recognise when the term is evoked. Whilst there is understandably no room for self-governance, ethnic minorities are granted certain exemptions and other privileges which might allow them to maintain the behavioural and value properties which constitute their sense of *cultural* particularity. David Miller, through less receptive to multiculturalism, commends a 'confirmation' of other cultures on a comparable basis that:

> [U]nless the ethnic group you belong to – ethnicity being a pervasive, visible phenomenon in the sense that it is something that a person carries with her wherever she goes – has its identity *confirmed* in symbolic and other ways by the relevant state, you are likely to feel vulnerable and demeaned. (1995, p. 122, emphasis added)

Both these positions apprehend multiculturalism as simply the facilitating of group rights to minorities who are otherwise deprived of such provisions. In short, a sensibility which chimes with the thin conception of tolerance critiqued previously, and one which I argue is politically quixotic. I mention here the influential work of Koopmans and Statham (2005), which claims to reject multiculturalism on the grounds that the more overt an official policy of multiculturalism (read simply as recognition of group rights), and the more generous the welfare state, the more likely it is to stunt social mobility for the various minority groupings. Apart from the dubious nature of this link, the authors themselves noted (2005, pp. 151–3) in their study of five European countries that the number of special group-rights 'demands' made (as reported in the 'mass print-media') in proportion to the total number of claims pertaining to 'immigration and ethnic relations' in general, were a paltry 1.2 to 7.7 per cent.[7] My purpose with this mention is not to trumpet its empirical validity but to lift forth its irony. Namely, a prominent work professedly hostile to multiculturalism, in the course of gathering empirical material, *itself* runs up against the fraudulence of the received conception of the term. Consequently, they themselves signal that the 'clash of civilisation' (2005, p. 152) thesis which maps onto the assimilation-multiculturalism dichotomy is simply a misnomer. Minority immigrants and their descendants are not concerned with multiculturalism when phrased as the right to specific special rights. It is less the demand for special rights and more the demand for corrective redress against mistreatment (e.g. police discrimination, lack of resources or negative public representations). The infatuation with multiculturalism as the politics of difference, speaking in terms of jurisprudence, appears a chimera largely tangential to the lived politics and activities of these actors.

Rather, with emphasis on what was previously signalled in the discussion of Ahmed, the priority of multiculturalism might be better understood as the urgent need to *undo* the pervasive discursive mechanisms which represent certain racialised actors as pathological and/or carriers of permanent and problematic cultural traits. This extended quote of Juliet Hooker is particularly helpful here in trying to think of multiculturalism beyond recognition.

> [T]he harms suffered by subordinated racialised groups are not reducible to the lack of recognition of their collective cultural identities by the state. [To be reduced thus] disregards the crucial ontological mechanism through which race is constituted as a basic feature of human existence, such as the visible markers of difference that immediately brand an individual as *both* "other" and inferior or threatening (Hooker 2009, p. 100, emphasis added).

Hooker, much like Phillips (2006) and Gooding-Williams (1998), proceeds to argue that the initial intervention of multiculturalists within political theory, even as formulated by Kymlicka, was invaluable in terms of their ability to convincingly posit as their central proposition that the state is not *neutral* in the values it espouses. The limitation of their subsequent deductive leaps, however, was that – though it was possible to demonstrate that the 'reality of ethnocultural injustice thoroughly disproves the premise that the state is neutral towards culture' (Hooker 2009, p. 14) – these early formulations of multiculturalism were remarkably uncomfortable with assessing how the semiotic situating of minority ethnic 'culture' in the inscriptions of *race* was central to such operations of normative civic exclusion (2009, pp. 98–105).

It might be ventured that the intertwining of race in the signification of ethnic culture (vis-à-vis a normative culture masquerading as neutral) results in a relational state of affairs far more debilitating than mere 'non-recognition' would analytically allow for. Rather, it actively situates the bearer of a certain ethnic culture as the embodiment of deprivation: deprivation as the absence of a multitude of liberal values which the hegemonic state confers, by positive relation to the negation, upon the privileged, non-racialised subject type. Put differently, the ethnic culture ascribed to the appropriately marked racial subject becomes the semiotic site of absence.

In light of such intersections of race and ethnicity in the contemporary European moment, a multiculturalism which is logically consistent with its foundational premise is the commitment to counteract these racial inscriptions. To rework Charles Taylor's (1994) famous heading, '*Multiculturalism is a politics of recognition which disturbs the politics of misrecognition*'. Or, with regard to Miller's phrasing, multiculturalism is not simply a matter of 'confirmation', but one of concomitant deconstruction, one that 'engages more ruthlessly with cultural stereotypes' (Phillips 2006, p. 72). As opposed to being a struggle for cultural withdrawal and seclusion, a multiculturalism which is 'race-conscious' (Hooker 2009, p. 15; Gooding-Williams 1998, p. 32) is a resistive undertaking which seeks to unwrite existing discursive scripts. Whilst it is certainly a critique of intolerance, constitutive of this critique is the *interrogation of the other as she is generally represented;* an interrogation of governing representational standards.

For instance, the recent furore around the right to build mosques (whether in Switzerland, Sandhurst and everywhere in between) is far less an appeal to special treatment on the part of the Muslim community than the desire to gain credibility by combating misrecognition. Its public rejection (of the right to worship which other religious groups already enjoy) relies on an intuitive understanding of the Muslim as a threat, as misogynistic, as undesirable. In that context, the right to build a mosque maps on to a larger, overarching struggle over representation. As opposed to any demand which tries to surreptitiously imagine a particular custom as essential, inherent and binding upon all those who have Muslim background, it merely tries to purge the image of the Muslim of its disabling, hostile negativity. The politics of this scenario does not appear to be an appeal to tolerance but an appeal to acceptance. In this distinction lies the caricature of multiculturalism and the multiculturalism, where difference garners an ordinary, quotidian legitimacy.

In turn, though it is a formidable disruption to any narration of a national collective (Hesse 1999, 2000), it is difficult to see how multiculturalism could be construed as an attempt to suspend the rule of law or the basic civic rights and protections which constitutes the core of a liberal state. As Gary Younge (2010, pp. 188–9) articulates with typical journalistic flair, it would be difficult to find many who might think that *forced* marriages and honour killings, two phenomena which are often said to be excused by multiculturalism, should not be seen as matter-of-fact criminal behaviour (kidnapping and murder respectively). David Cameron in a recent Hampshire speech (*New Statesman* 2011b) on immigration and multiculturalism suggested that we, freshly armed with a 'muscular liberalism', should be willing to condemn forced marriages. In doing so, he stated, 'I've got no time for those who say this is a culturally relative issue.' The bravado posturing masks the absurdity of the claim. To quote from a lead editorial piece in *The Independent* (2011): 'Yet he omitted to name these deluded individuals who believe that forced marriages are acceptable.' Such attempts to submit the commitment to salient expressions of diversity as incompatible with a liberal basis of individual rights is, however, a key trope through which assimilationism gains ground. It dismisses diversity, not through reference to it as undermining a unitary *nation*-state ideal, but rather, by perceiving diversity as breaching the basic juridical foundations of the *liberal* state. Crucial herein to any critique of contemporary European nationalisms is the troubling of those stereotypes which position certain groups – and at the broader level, multiculturalism – as being ill-suited to liberal ways.

It logically follows that enshrined in any viable multicultural ethos is the 'right of exit' (Kukathas 2003) – the right of members to associate and dissociate as they themselves see fit. I ignore, of course, whether this crucial clause in Kukathas' treatise is 'sociologically' possible, but as a political right particular to a liberal society, it enjoys first-order status. No person should be obliged to (as positive law, so to speak) partake in any custom. Equally so, no person should be prevented from partaking in any custom (negative law) unless it demonstrably contravenes the Millian harm-principle so sacrosanct to prominent liberal critics of multiculturalism such as Barry (2001, 2002, p. 206). This might seem a rather prosaic point but is all too often missed when it is being claimed that multiculturalism is somehow exogenous to liberalism. Indeed, 'extreme Liberalism' might be as apt a summation of Kukathas' defence of multiculturalism as can be mustered: 'Whilst [Barry] believes he is defending a liberal theory, in fact he is doing no such thing because he *dare not go* where his liberal premises take him' (Kukathas 2002, p. 195; emphasis added).

To consider one topical example, in the recent debates concerning the burka, apart from its negligible numerical presence (for instance, a maximum of 2000 women out of 4.9 million Muslims in France are estimated to wear it [Younge 2010, p. 176]), what is most puzzling is its condemnation in the name of *liberal* feminism. It is said that women, unaware of having internalised oppressive norms, should be shown a liberated path (Spivak's [1988, p. 297] memorable line: "White men saving brown women from brown men" could not be more timely). As Jasbir Puar (2007) intimates in her commentary on the unholy alliance between feminism and European nationalism, since when did liberalism assent to the theoretical legitimacy of 'false consciousness'?

Ultimately, a multicultural politics is rather more modest than the supposed exemption-oriented illiberalism of Liberal tolerance. It merely attempts to engender inclusion through troubling the pre-eminence of the nation-state ideal and the exclusions such ideals rationalise. This commitment is realised through the destabilising or supplanting of those discursive operations which reinforce the problematic imagery fixed to certain marginal ethnic identities (e.g. the *Hijabed*, Muslim woman). In this sense, it retains the thrust of the initial multicultural critique. Namely, the state shall be shed of its *neutral* veneer, and be asked in turn to confront the discursive mechanisms by which it delegitimises the concerns and difficulties of those citizens who are conspicuously marked as different.

The attempts to channel through popular media more variegated representations of the black male, in comparison to the narrow and repetitive fare of hip hop, sport and police mug-shots (whether on the evening news or fictionalised), appeals to another such multicultural sensibility. The pronounced presence the black male garners in the contemporary symbolic realm, as a body and image to be desired and emulated, is greatly ambivalent: whilst it posits the young black male at the centre of a spectacular, hyper-consumerism, it simultaneously ties him to a history of exuberant, 'innate naturalism' (St Louis 2000, p. 54). An amusing instance of the rigid representational cycle currently pervasive was the farcical practice of the BBC Newsnight team to invite Dizzee Rascal, the popular grime artist, to comment on race-worthy news events (most notably, Obama's presidential triumph). Apart from the comicality of a hapless, avuncular Jeremy Paxman sparring with a man noted for his MCing abilities, it reveals the deeply embedded association of the authentic black male voice, regardless of topic, with a non-intellectual 'street-culture'. More recently, the Tudor historian David Starkey, in a notorious rant against degenerate black culture, pointed to David Lammy, the black MP representing Tottenham, as a positive example of black mobility. After all, Starkey reasoned, by the way he 'sounds' Lammy 'could be white'. Apparent in such commonplace examples is the fact that a multiculturalism which is uninterested in the symbolic standards by which difference is apprehended cannot do much to further inclusion. The multicultural point is not to 'tolerate' Dizzee Rascal, whereby he and similarly inclined cultural exponents are advanced a platform regardless of context, but to trouble the very fixing of black with such narrow performative roles.

Similarly, it is worth stressing that such a critical mandate for a multicultural politics is not simply a matter of encouraging a greater culture of civility and politeness in our everyday interactions – as is seemingly the argument of Vertovec (2007, pp. 30–3). Though important, the critical stance to representation advocated here extends, when instantiated, into the very reaches of any noteworthy governmental practice, including the brutality of war itself. For instance, one of the most widely discussed actions under the remit of the War on Terror has been the Guantanamo detention policy. I would contend that the popular support, or at least popular indifference, to such extrajudicial abuses – recall that Tony Blair candidly dubbed it 'a [necessary] anomaly' (*The Guardian* 2006) – is precisely the same symbolic regime which makes automatic, makes intuitive, a default association of Muslims as being constituted of their own volition outside the theatre of liberal democracy (or in stronger terms, with medievalism). The medieval portrayal of a Muslim (as violent, as misogynist, as sectarian) authorises in the court of public opinion a medieval justice. A similar symbolic scenario applies to black over-representation in stop-and-search figures. Namely, the black male is textually apprehended as constitutionally predisposed to 'lifestyle', amoral violence (see here Goodhart's (2011) post-riot causal attribution: 'a nihilistic grievance culture of the black inner city, fanned by parts of the hip-hop/rap scene and copied by many white people'). Targeted policing is as a result deemed a legitimate response. In light of such fraught policies, the critique of representational fields, of entrenched cultural stereotypes, as the primary aim of multiculturalism is one that is not incapable of confronting modern day programmes of state *violence*, which is, of course, only the extreme end in a broad spectrum of exclusion.

VI: Conclusion

Consequently, it is not so much *essentialised* difference requiring tolerance (e.g. the violent or sectarian Muslim) as the asymmetrical control over 'adjudication' concerning *any form* of ethnic difference which needs to be reviewed. Barnor Hesse's summation of the dialectical nature of recognition and misrecognition respectively is particularly apt here:

> Constitutive of the desire for recognition is the objective of questioning the conditions in which certain hegemonic institutions or dominant practices arrogate to themselves a culturally exclusive right to adjudication. [...] I call the response [...] a 'politics of interrogation'. (2000, p. 30)

This *interrogation* of the *conditions* under which identities are inscribed and actualised – in terms of interpreting our own situation and actions as well as the situation and actions of others – would seem consistent with ordinary multiculture, consistent with those urban interactional fields where ethnic difference is habitually breached without it being posited as undesirable. This discussion has attempted to demonstrate the centrality of representational politics to any such multicultural undertaking. Conversely, a wilful erasure of any such critique of representational inequalities allows multiculturalism to be framed in a manner antithetical to salient ethnic diversity. Such absences licence the narration of minority groups – with their excessive cultural attachments – as both constitutionally illiberal and disruptive. In turn, it even renders the basic appeal to tolerance difficult and instead, can be seen to feed an assimilationist purpose. The difference seemingly displayed by certain minority subjects remains a problem when representational privileges go unaddressed; a problem in need of a tolerance which is increasingly presented as something reasonable persons simply cannot consent to. Such inattentiveness to the symbolic violence which outsider, minority subjects encounter can result only in the selective inclusion of vetted individuals (e.g. individuals who are able to successfully de-link themselves from the ethnic associations that they are otherwise attributed) as opposed to the ethnically marked 'communities' at large gaining credibility in the public sphere. Put differently, the chapter has argued that a multiculturalism which is unable to mount a critical *representational* politics *cannot* be considered as possessing the requisite allotment of values and sensibilities appropriate to the furthering of those routines of relatively fluent cross-ethnic interaction not uncommon to many of 'our' Western cities.

In this spirit, it is hoped that this chapter has made apparent how a robust multiculturalism (a desire for recognition/interrogating misrecognition) is entirely different from the unqualified instruction to 'tolerate the other' and the cultural essentialisms such an instruction presupposes. I have argued that a thin multiculturalism which only promises tolerance struggles to even deliver tolerance itself. To tolerate in any viable sense necessarily presumes that 'my' understanding of that other figure is at risk of being unravelled. Consequently, it is a hostility to the prevailing standards of intelligibility which is I contend consistent with the multiculture of open-ended interactional possibilities. This is a multiculturalism informed by the ordinary articulations of urban multiculture, a multiculture described by Gilroy (2006, p. 34) as '"open-sourced" co-production'. It is not one which is about deferring to difference as already intelligible, but arises from the entangled *experience* of difference, of diversity, in 'real time' (2006, p. 28). Multiculturalism is ultimately best realised if it simply reflects the enviable ability of ordinary inhabitants of urban multiculture, in the course of discovering each other through and across difference, to dismiss without much ado the myriad markers of cultural incompatibility and/or deficiency fixed to bearers of difference.

Notes

1. Though the *extent* of such 'convivial' interaction is of course contested, my argument presupposes that such regularised multiethnic lives are, at the very least, both possible and apparent. Such instances of urban multiculture made ordinary which will serve as an implicit assumption informing the broader discussion. In the words of Gilroy, '[We] must necessarily be more alive to the ludic, cosmopolitan energy and the democratic possibilities so evident in the postcolonial metropolis' (2004, p. 178).
2. Sara Ahmed was responding to a Žižek plenary talk, titled 'Walls', given at Birkbeck College in 2007.
3. This extended response to Ahmed, 'Appendix: "Multiculturalism, the Reality of an Illusion" ', appeared originally in 2008 on http://www.lacan.com/essays/?page_id=454. The text is reproduced, nearly verbatim, in *Living in End Times*. There are, however, occasional alterations. Tellingly, concerning the quote above, the book version drops the concluding phrase: 'from the Roma'. I believe the original phrasing to be in the spirit of the broader argument being made and thus, chose to retain it. It is only right, however, to make this minor revision from the earlier manuscript known to the reader.
4. The original quote is '[Light art] is the social bad conscience of serious art' (Adorno and Horkeimer [1947] 2002), p. 107.
5. Leaving his role as founding editor of *Prospect*, the left-of-centre periodical, Goodhart became in 2011 the director the influential think tank Demos. His time as editor was marked by the concerted effort to enumerate the many ills of multiculturalism.
6. This book, though authored by Giovanna Borradori, is a relaying of conversations with Derrida and Habermas about philosophy and politics in the post-9/11 era.
7. The lowest and highest rate respectively for the five countries observed: France, Germany, the Netherlands, Switzerland, and the United Kingdom.

Bibliography

Adorno, T. and Horkheimer, M. (2002 [1947]) *Dialectic of Enlightenment: Philosophical Fragments* (Palo Alto, CA: Stanford University Press).

Ahmed, S. (2005) 'Declarations of Whiteness: The Non-Performativity of Anti-Racism', *Borderlands*, 3(2), http://www.borderlands.net.au/vol3no2_2004/ahmed_declarations.htm

Ahmed, S. (2004) *The Cultural Politics of Emotion* (New York: Routledge).

Ahmed, S. (2008) '"Liberal Multiculturalism Is the Hegemony–It's an Empirical Fact": A Response to Slavoj Žižek', *Darkmatter*, Journal 19 February 2008. http://www.darkmatter101.org/site/2008/02/19/%E2%80%98liberal-multiculturalism-is-the-hegemony-%E2%80%93-its-an-empirical-fact%E2%80%99-a-response-to-slavoj-zizek/#comment-60901

Back, L., Keith, M., Khan, A. Shukra, K. and Solomos, J. (2002) 'New Labour's White Heart: Politics, Multiculturalism and the Return of Assimilation', *Political Quarterly*, 73(4), 445–54.

Barry, B. (2001) *Culture and Equality* (Cambridge: Polity Press).

Barry, B. (2002) 'Second Thoughts: And Some First Thoughts Revived' in P. Kelly (ed.), *Multiculturalism Reconsidered* (Cambridge: Polity Press), pp. 204–37.

Bawer, B. (2010) *Surrender: Appeasing Islam, Sacrificing Freedom* (New York: Anchor Books).

Bernstein, R. (2010) 'The Spectre Haunting Multiculturalism', *Philosophy and Social Criticism*, 36(3–4), 381–94.

Bloomberg (2010) 'Expulsions of Illegal Roma Win Approval from Public in Sarkozy's France', 13 August 2010. http://www.bloomberg.com/news/2010–08–12/expulsions-of-illegal-roma-win-approval-from-public-in-sarkozy-s-france.html

Borradori, G. (2003) *Philosophy in a Time of Terror: Dialogues with Jürgen Habermas and Jacques Derrida* (Chicago: University of Chicago Press).

Brown, W. (2006) *Regulating Aversion: Tolerance in the Age of Identity and Empire* (Princeton, NJ: Princeton University Press).

Bruckner, P. (2007) 'Enlightenment Fundamentalism or Racism of the Anti-Racists', *Sign and Sight*, 24 January 2007, http://www.signandsight.com/features/1146.html

Financial Times (2012) 'Sarkozy Makes Populist Push for Re-election', 11 March, p. 6

Fortier, A.M. (2008*) Multicultural Horizons: Diversity and the Limits of the Civil Nation* (Abingdon: Routledge).

Gaita, R. (2011) 'Introduction' in R. Gaita (ed.), *Essays on Muslims and Multiculturalism* (Melbourne: Text Publishing Company), pp. 1–23.

Gilroy, P. (2004) *After Empire: Melancholia or Convivial Culture?* (Abingdon: Routledge).

Gilroy, P. (2006) 'Multiculture in Times of War', LSE Public Lecture, 10 May 2006. http://www2.lse.ac.uk/publicEvents/pdf/20060510-PaulGilroy.pdf

Goodhart, D. (2005) 'Liberals Should Beware of Giving Rights to People Who Hate Us', *The Sunday Times*, 28 August 2005, p. 8.

Goodhart, D. (2004) 'Too Diverse?' *Prospect*, 95 (February), pp. 30–7.

Goodhart, David (2011) 'The Riots at the End of History', *Prospect*, 9 August 2011. http://www.prospectmagazine.co.uk/blog/the-riots-at-the-end-of-history/

Gooding-Williams, R. (1998) 'Race, Multiculturalism and Democracy', *Constellations*, 5, pp. 18–41.

Guardian, The (2006) 'Blair Admits Guantanamo Bay Is 'Anomaly' but Sidesteps Closure Calls', 18 February 2006, p. 5.

Guardian, The (2010) 'Roma Expulsions by France Overshadow EU Summit Opening', 16 September 2010. http://www.guardian.co.uk/world/2010/sep/16/france-roma-expulsions-eu-summit

Hall, S. (2000) 'Conclusion: The Multi-cultural Question', in B, Hesse (ed.), *Un/settled Multiculturalisms* (London: Zed Books), pp. 209–41.

Hall, S. (ed.) (1997) *Representation: Cultural Representations and Signifying Practices* (London: Sage).

Hesse, B. (1999) 'It's Your World: Discrepant M/multiculturalisms' in P. Cohen (ed.), *New Ethnicities, Old Racisms* (London: Zed Books), pp. 205–25.

Hesse, B. (2000) 'Introduction: Un/Settled Multiculturalisms' in B. Hesse (ed.) *Un/settled Multiculturalisms* (London: Zed Books), pp. 1–30.

Hollinger, D. (2000 [1995]) *Postethnic America: Beyond Multiculturalism* (New York: Basic Books).

Hooker, J. (2009) *Race and the Politics of Solidarity* (New York: Oxford University Press).

Independent, The (2011) 'Leading Article: Cameron's Cynical and Disappointing Approach to Immigration', 15 April 2011. http://www.independent.co.uk/opinion/leading-articles/leading-article-camerons-cynical-and-disappointing-approach-to-immigration-2267901.html

Koopmans, R., Statham, P., Giugni, M. and Passy, F. (2005) *Contested Citizenship: Immigration and Cultural Diversity in Europe* (Minneapolis: University of Minnesota Press).

Kukathas, C. (2003) *The Liberal Archipelago: A Theory of Diversity and Freedom* (Oxford: Oxford University Press).

Kukathas, C. (2002) 'The Life of Brian, or Now for Something Completely Difference-Blind' in P. Kelly (ed.) *Multiculturalism Reconsidered* (Cambridge: Polity Press), pp.184–203

Kymlicka, W. (1995) *Multicultural Citizenship* (Oxford: Oxford University Press).

Lentin, A. and Titley, G. (2011) *The Crises of Multiculturalism: Racism in a Neoliberal Age* (London: Zed Books).

McGhee, D. (2009) 'The Paths to Citizenship: A Critical Examination of Immigration Policy in Britain since 2001', *Patterns of Prejudice*, 43(1), 41–64.

Miller, D. (1995) *On Nationality* (Oxford: Oxford University Press).

New Statesman (2011a) 'Transcript, David Cameron: Speech on radicalisation and Islamic extremism', 05 February 2011. http://www.newstatesman.com/blogs/the-staggers/2011/02/terrorism-islam-ideology

New Statesman (2011b) 'Transcript, David Cameron: Speech on Immigration to Party Members', 14 April 2011. http://www.newstatesman.com/2011/04/immigration-british-visas-work

Pathak, P. (2007) 'The Trouble with David Goodhart's Britain', *Political Quarterly*, 78(2), 261–71.

Parekh, B. (2000) *Rethinking Multiculturalism: Cultural Diversity and Political Theory* (Cambridge, MA: Harvard University Press).

Phillips, A. (2007) *Multiculturalism without Culture* (Princeton NJ: Princeton University Press).

Puar, J. (2007) *Terrorist Assemblages: Homonationalism in Queer Times* (Durham, NC: Duke University Press).

Putnam, R. (2007) '*E Pluribus Unum*: Diversity and Community in the Twenty-First Century,' *Scandinavian Political Studies*, 30(2), 137–74.

Sarrazin, T. (2010) *Deutschland Schafft Sich Ab* (Munich: Deutsche Verlags-Anstalt).

Spivak, G. (1988) 'Can the Subaltern Speak?' in C. Nelson and L. Grossberg (eds), *Marxism and Interpretation of Culture* (Chicago, IL: University of Illinois Press), pp. 271–316.

St Louis, B. (2000) 'Readings within a Diasporic Boundary: Transatlantic Black Performance and the Poetic Imperative of Sport' in B. Hesse (ed.), *Un/settled Multiculturalisms* (London: Zed Books), pp. 51–72.

Taylor, C. (1994) 'The Politics of Recognition' in A. Gutman (ed.), *Multiculturalism* (Princeton, NJ: Princeton University Press), pp. 25–74.

Vertovec, S. (2007) *New Complexities of Cohesion in Britain: A Thinkpiece for the Commission on Integration and Cohesion* (London: Communities and Local Government Publications).

Younge, G. (2010) *Who Are We: And Should It Matter in the 21st Century?* (London: Viking).

Žižek, S. (1997) 'Multiculturalism, or, the Cultural Logic of Multinational Capitalism', *New Left Review*, 1(225), pp. 28–51.

Žižek, S. (2010) 'Liberal multiculturalism masks an old barbarism with a human face', *The Guardian*, 4 October 2010, p. 27.

Žižek, S. (2011) *Living in End Times* (London: Verso).

5
Muslim Women and Gender Stereotypes in 'New Times': From Multiculturalism to Islamophobia

Heidi Safia Mirza

The Arab Spring uprisings in Tunisia, Egypt, Libya, Syria, Bahrain and Yemen have exploded the Western stereotypical image of the oppressed Muslim Arab woman. Daily there are images on the news of Muslim women in designer clothes or their long black *abayas* (Muslim female dress) facing tear gas and baton-wielding troops, or risking sexual assault and even death in their struggles for democracy. From Tahrir Square in Cairo to Pearl Square in Manama, women have leafleted, blogged and led crowds in seemingly 'genderless' mass demonstrations (Moussaoui 2011). In Yemen, Tawakkol Karman, a rights activist, became in 2011 the first Arab woman to win the Nobel Peace Prize. However, as I will argue in this chapter, Muslim women in Britain are still constructed as either the romantic heroine, struggling for the benefits of the 'West' against her 'cruel and inhuman father and family', or as a victim, succumbing to her backward and traditional 'Eastern' culture. There are real physical consequences to such constructions in the highly contested multicultural space occupied by the postcolonial Muslim Diaspora in Britain. The rights and freedoms of Muslim women appear to be 'slipping through the cracks' of everyday policy and politics in a climate where our political leaders in Britain and Europe are heralding the 'death of multiculturalism'.

Rising unemployment and declining social welfare provision in Britain and across Europe has been matched by a strong undercurrent of anti-Islamic feeling, even from the most liberal of quarters. The new and open climate of intolerance against the foreign visible 'other' in our midst is characterised by a belief that things would be better if minorities, and in particular Muslims, assimilated more. In October 2010, the German chancellor, Angela Merkel, proclaimed that the 'multikulti' concept: 'that we are now living side by side and are happy about it...has failed utterly' (cited in Hall 2010). In hot pursuit, British Prime Minister David Cameron announced in Munich, 'The doctrine of state of multiculturalism has failed....it has encouraged different cultures to live separate lives, sometimes behaving in ways that run counter to our values' (cited by BBC 2011).

Two things become clear from these 'new times' of anti-multicultural pronouncements and actions. First, they have been fueled by popularist, Islamophobic political agendas. As history tells us, it is common for frustrations to be vented on convenient scapegoats in times of austerity. Angela Merkel's speech was made in the wake of the publication of Thilo Sarrazin's (2010) popular book *Germany Is Destroying Itself* in which he argued that Islam, practiced by the country's four million Muslims, is a threat to the national Christian identity of Germans (Connolly 2010). A poll showed that one-fifth of all Germans would vote for a party headed by Mr Sarrazin if he chose to form one (Hall 2010). Similarly, in France, where former President Nicolas Sarkozy criminalised the wearing of the *burqa* (total body covering), including the *niqab* (full face veil), and had previously banned the *hijab* (headscarf), the resurgent popular far-right National Front party gained 18 per cent of voters in the 2012 elections (Samuel 2012). In Holland, Geert Wilders's Party for Freedom, whose manifesto includes a ban on the Qu'ran and an end to all immigration from Muslim countries, became the third-largest party in the general election (Marquand 2010).

Secondly, and importantly, is the hidden, unremarked but insidious gendered Islamophobic nature of these anti-multicultural sentiments and actions. Cameron (BBC 2011) in his Munich speech blamed multiculturalism for British 'home-grown' Islamic extremism. He explicitly stated, 'Some young Muslim men find it hard to identify with Britain. ...because state multiculturalism has prevented a vision of society to which these young men can feel attached.' Merkel, addressing fears of 'German-ness' being lost amid new mosques and the rise of Turkish ghettos in Berlin, pointed specifically to headscarves in classrooms as a manifestation of the problem (Hall 2010). While Muslim men are seen as active agents, in the discourses of fear and anxiety which have circulated since 11 September 2001, it is the female Muslim body which has come to represent that which is fearsome and dangerous (Ahmed 2003). It would seem that even though the War Against Terror has been waged by men on both sides, it is the highly visible 'Muslim woman' who has come to symbolise the 'barbaric Muslim other' in our midst. The veil in particular, in all its forms, is the terrain on which the battle is being fought.

Embodying the Veil: Muslim women and gendered Islamophobia

Since 11 September 2001, there has been an overwhelming preoccupation with the 'embodied' Muslim women in our public spaces. Bans of the *hijab* and *niqab* are sweeping across Europe. They now exist in France, Germany, Belgium, and Italy and are under consideration in Spain, Netherlands, Sweden and the UK. This heightened attention raises the question, What is behind this growing concern for the hitherto invisible and marginalised 'Muslim woman?' To answer this question we need to begin by looking at the consequence of the spotlight on Muslim women wearing the veil and the increased focus on 'honour-based' crimes within the current climate of Islamophobia not only in Britain but across Europe.

The heated public debate in Britain triggered by Labour Minister Jack Straw on the matter of Muslim women wearing the face veil demonstrates that in the current discourse the gaze, as ever, is on the woman. In 2006, Jack Straw announced to the press that, after 25 years in office, he felt uncomfortable with Muslim women wearing the *niqab* in his constituency surgery in Blackburn (Bunting 2006). As media hysteria grew over several weeks, stories of the ubiquitous 'Muslim woman' appeared regularly on newspaper front pages. They still do. In 2011, Sayeeda Warsi, co-chair of the Conservative Party and the first Muslim woman to serve in the British Cabinet, caused media outcry with her lecture on Islamophobia and anti-Muslim sentiment in Britain. In her address to Leicester University, she noted that Islamophobia had 'passed the dinner-table test', pointing out that it had become socially acceptable in the UK to be Islamophobic. This, she argued, was exemplified by the racialised representation of the veiled Muslim woman in the national unconscious. As reported (disparagingly) in the *Daily Telegraph*, she noted, 'in the road, as a woman walks past wearing a Burkha, the passers-by think, "that woman's either oppressed or making a political statement"' (Gardiner 2011).

Muslim women wearing the *hijab* or *niqab* in European countries face hostile reactions in a climate of state-sanctioned, gendered, Islamophobic discrimination. In France, the heightened political sentiment against Muslim women has legitimated a public free-for-all 'witch-hunt' against women wearing the veil. Muslim women wearing headscarves have been refused access to voting booths, driving lessons, and have been barred from their own wedding ceremonies at town halls, ejected from university classes and in one case, *The Guardian* reported that a woman in a bank was not allowed to withdraw cash from her own account at the counter (Groskop 2011). Simultaneously, at times there has been a lack of support from within French Muslim communities with *niqab*-wearing women being accused of 'shaming' the entire community, and 'dirtying the religion' (Bouteldja 2011).

Though it is estimated that as few as 2000 women out of five million Muslims in France may wear the *niqab*, *Unveiling the Truth*, a study by Open Society Foundations (2011) documents the impact of the hysterical national discourse on Muslim women wearing the *niqab*. The testimonies of 32 women, 30 of whom are French citizens, reveal the effect of the legislation on their feelings of national identity and belonging. The report challenges many myths, showing how they have been left alienated and abandoned by the republic that they would otherwise call home. Contrary to the usual stereotype of Muslim women forced to wear the face veil, the adoption of the *niqab* was in most cases about 'transforming the self', the result of a personal and extremely individualistic spiritual journey. Most of the women were the first members of their family to adopt the veil, the majority had no *niqab*-wearing peers, their attendance at their mosque was minimal, and their affiliation to any Islamic bodies almost nonexistent.

In Germany, four out of 16 of the country's federal states have put in place legislation to ban teachers and Government employees from wearing Muslim headscarves in the workplace (Human Rights Watch 2009). The laws were introduced following a 2003 Constitutional Court ruling that restrictions on religious dress are only permissible if explicitly laid down in law. While the laws do not explicitly target the headscarf, parliamentary debates and official explanatory documents make it clear that it is the issue. Every court case about the restriction has concerned the headscarf. The report, *Discrimination in the Name of Neutrality: Headscarf Bans for Teachers and Civil Servants in Germany* (Human Rights Watch 2009), analyses the human rights implications of these bans and their effect on the lives of Muslim women teachers and those who have been employed in public service. Tragically, many women have had to give up their careers or leave Germany, where they have lived all their lives.

It is ironic that such 'secular' banning of the headscarf in the name of equality and non-discrimination in democratic societies runs parallel to the actions of Islamic fundamentalist countries, such as Afghanistan,

Saudi Arabia, and Iran, which force women to wear religious clothing. Human Rights Watch (2009) argues that both regimes undercut International Human Rights standards by denying Muslim women their fundamental right to autonomy, privacy, self-expression and religious freedom. As the Islamic feminist Haleh Afshar (2008) points out, a woman's right to wear the veil should be a matter of choice, whether it be a personal, religious, or political one.

While these are contemporary examples of gendered Islamophobia, parallels can be drawn to colonial times, when women's bodies were part of the debate over the West's civilising mission. Frantz Fanon argues the unveiling of the *Muslim woman* is a metaphor for the colonial subjugation of the colonised 'other'. In his treatise on Algeria he writes, 'unveiling equals revealing, baring, breaking her resistance, making her available' (cited in Kanneh 1995, p. 347). Muslim feminist Leila Ahmed (1992) argues that Europeans pointed to the inferiority and barbarism of pre-colonial Islamic societies as a rationale for colonial rule, in particular pointing to the treatment of women. For example, the British abolition of Sati, the practice of widow burning in India, was presented as heroic white male colonists 'saving brown women from brown men' (Spivak 1988). Similarly, in the virulent discourses of Islamophobia and multiculturalism in contemporary Europe, the banning of the face veil does not represent a concern with the Muslim women's human rights and social conditions, as is often invoked. Instead, it constitutes a postmodern reworking of the heroic colonial stance, only now, 'White men and women *are seen to be* saving Muslim women from Muslim men!'

In contemporary Islamophobic discourse, the Muslim female body has become a battlefield in the symbolic war against Islam, the barbaric 'other', and the Muslim enemy 'within'. Muslim women's dress has become interchangeable with essentialist notions of ethnicity, traditionalism and religion. In these constructions the veil is given symbolic meaning far greater than its religious and social status. The Muslim woman's private, faith-based reasons for wearing the *niqab* have become public property, 'weapons' used by many different competing interests, from male politicians in France to white feminists in Belgium, who argue their cases for and against assimilation, multiculturalism, secularism and human rights (Killian 2003; Scott 2007; Coene and Longman 2008). Indeed, it was the weapon drawn by George W. Bush, the then president of the United States, as central justification for war in Iraq (Al-Ali and Pratt 2009), echoing the 'white men saving brown women from brown men sentiment'. In what Chandra Talpade Mohanty (2003) has called the 'latent ethnocentrism' of the West, Muslim women caught up in the *niqab* debate are racialised as voiceless, pre-modern, submissive victims rather than active agents working to determine and engage their rights as individuals.

Violence, Honour and Islamophobic discourses of risk

The visibility of patriarchal and communal cultural practices among some Muslim communities conveniently contributes to the Western 'Orientalist' construction of the racialised 'other's' barbaric customs and cultures (Afshar 2008). This is never more so than in the case of honour crimes committed against women in Muslim communities. Between January 1996 and July 2005, 55 honour killings were reported to the police in Germany, with at least 13 cases in Berlin (BBC 2006). In Britain, following a police review of 22 domestic homicides in 2005, 18 cases were reclassified as 'murder in the name of so-called honour' (Meetoo and Mirza 2007).

Honour crimes are acts of violence against women, where 'honour' is invoked to justify male violence. However, the use of the term 'honour' in such a context is misleading, as the crimes themselves are dishonourable and are merely justified by the perpetrator and wider community in the name of honour. Committing acts of violence against women for breaking an honour code constitutes an abuse of human rights and must be named as such. However, honour crimes are often sensationalised in the press, which engages in a 'pornography of violence' focusing on the individual family and their barbarity and senselessness. This results in cultural stereotyping, and often, following a media frenzy, in a backlash at a national level.

Reading sensationalised press reports of fathers and other close relatives, including women, who inflict violence and brutality on their own children in the name of honour, or *izzat*, we are incredulous. How could they harm their own? On the front pages of our newspapers is the outcome of the case of Banaz Mahmod, a 20-year-old Kurdish woman, who was sexually brutalised and murdered by her father and uncles and cousins because her boyfriend was not a strict Muslim from their community. She was strangled with a shoelace and her body stuffed in a suitcase buried under a patio (BBC 2010). Hannana Siddiqui, of Southall Black Sisters, argues that the use of the term 'honour' in such a context is a misnomer. She states, 'The crimes themselves are dishonourable: they are merely justified by the perpetrator, and wider community, in the name of honour' (Refugee Women's Association 2003, p. 6).

However, it is only in relation to religious communities that the concept of honour is misappropriated by the courts as a mitigating factor when men commit acts of violence against women (Phillips 2003). Honour also prevents women from escaping domestic violence or seeking justice as victims of domestic violence, as they fear punishment for having brought shame on the family or community honour. Focusing on culturally specific forms of violence against women is often seen as very controversial ground. It is generally disputed that culture can explain how and why particular practices happen. By highlighting violence against women in specific cultural and religious ethnic communities are we at risk of stereotyping these communities as backward and barbaric? Does this place a disproportionate emphasis on the Muslim woman – racialising her by separating out these forms of domestic and familial violence as a special cultural phenomena needing special cultural sensitivity? These questions lie at the heart of understanding the tensions between recognising gender oppression and preserving multicultural difference.

Phillips (2007) makes the point that culture is widely employed in the discourse on multiculturalism to deny the human agency of minority or non-Western groups, who (unlike their Western counterparts) are seen to be 'driven' by cultural traditions and practices that compel them to behave in particular ways. Thus, while Muslim women are seen to suffer 'death by culture', that is, are subject to honour crimes, white European or North American women (with their societies characterised by freedom, democracy and mobility) are deemed to be immune from culture, even when they become victims of culturally specific forms of Western patriarchal violence such as gun crime, date rape, or domestic violence.

However, the killing of women must never be seen as a cultural matter, but always as a human rights issue. We must take a global perspective on violence against women and see honour killing and forced marriage as part of a wider global patriarchal phenomenon of violence (Gupta 2003). Women are beaten and murdered across the globe for similar reasons, and it is not particular to one culture or religious group or community. Violence against women cuts across race, class, religion and age. Patriarchal structures use violence extensively to subjugate women in different forms in relation to class, race and ethnicity. Violence against women is not an issue of racial or ethnic differences; it is a question of the economic, political and social development of a society and the levels of democracy and devolution of power within communities (Gill 2006).

While the focus on honour-based crimes has opened up the issue of individual human rights for ethnicised Muslim women, it has also exacerbated Islamophobia and fear of the 'other'. Honour-based crimes are constructed as ethnicised, often Islamic phenomena within the racialised multicultural discourses in Europe. As such they also contribute to the anti-Islamic discourse. Risks, such as honour crimes, are selected at particular times and constructed and legitimated for public attention. Describing the global threat to security from Islamic extremism, Liz Fekete (2004) argues that we are living in a time of fear not only of 'outsiders', but of Muslims 'within' our European societies. The heightened sensationalised focus on honour-based crimes must be seen within this climate of Islamophobia.

Multiculturalism and the marginalisation of Muslim women

While liberal multiculturalism is popularly and politically conceived as celebrating diversity and 'tolerating' different cultural and religious values among groups, the notion of mutual tolerance is fragile. It could be argued that one way in which multiculturalism negotiates this fragility is by maintaining a laissez-faire approach to gendered cultural difference (Okin 1999; Phillips 2007). Multiculturalism in this sense is 'skin deep', and it works only if the demands of visible and distinct ethnic groups are not too 'different' and not too rejecting of the welcoming embrace or 'gift' of the 'host' society (Ahmed 2004). The figure of the veiled Muslim woman challenges the values that are crucial to the nation, such as values of freedom and culture. As Sara Ahmed explains, 'She becomes a symbol of what the nation must give up to be itself, a discourse that would require her unveiling in order to fulfil its promise of freedom' (2004, p.132).

Clearly liberal multiculturalism in Britain in its many shifting manifestations, including Community Cohesion, has consistently functioned to privilege race and ethnicity, and now religion, over gender (Samantrai 2002; Phillips 2007). It fails to recognise the gendered power divisions within ethnic groups dealing with problems *between* communities, but turning a blind eye to problems *within* communities. A gender-blind multiculturalism has consequences for Muslim women, who remain largely invisible, locked in the private sphere of the home, where despite state recognition of the human rights abuses of forced marriage and honour violence, gender-oppressive cultural and religious practices are still played (Patel and Siddiqui 2010). Beckett and Macey (2001, p. 311)

highlight the contradictions of gendered multiculturalism which invisi-
bilises women. They write,

> Multiculturalism does not cause domestic violence, but it does facili-
> tate its continuation through its creed of respect for cultural differ-
> ences, its emphasis on non-interference in minority lifestyles and
> its insistence on community consultation (with male, self-defined
> community leaders). This has resulted in women being invisibilised,
> their needs ignored and their voices silenced.

To understand the social construction of gender and violence within
multiculturalism, we need to look at the way ethnicity has been reified
and fixed among minority ethnic groups. This process of reification,
whereby ethnic group identity becomes defensive and cultural and
religious practices are constructed within imagined but rigid boundaries, leads to a form of 'ethnic fundamentalism' (Yuval-Davis 1997).
Migration, whether forced or planned, often leads to the breakdown of
traditional certainties and structures, thereby heightening anxieties of
loss and belonging. Patriarchal practices can be amplified for migrant
Muslim women, who are seen as upholding traditional values when
they are estranged from their homelands (Abbas 2010). Under threat,
certain aspects of culture may be preserved, ossified or romanticised –
what I call 'pickled in aspic'. When this happens, as in the context of the
discourse on Islamophobia, we witness a resurgence and persistence of
fixed and regressive notions of ethnicity and nationalism underpinning
traditional beliefs (Elliot 2002).

Halima Begum (2008) demonstrates how this plays out in the secular
yet religious and ethnically inscribed multicultural space of Banglatown
in the East End of London. She argues the streets of Banglatown have
become nationalistic, male-dominated Bengali public spaces, from which
Bangladeshi women feel excluded and often unsafe. Second-generation
young Bengali women, whose bodies are still inscribed with conservative cultural values, in turn prefer to express their 'Muslimness' as an
private inner belief and transcendental identity. Thus, it would seem
in the secular British multicultural national context, where, according
to Werbner (2007), religious practice, though valorised, is still located
in the unregulated private sphere of civil society, Islam can been mobilised as a power resource in the construction of an unfettered hegemonic masculine Muslim identity (Balzani 2010). Hasmita Ramji (2007)
discusses the way in which young working-class Asian Muslim men in
Britain exercise patriarchal power by invoking common-sense and often

contradictory readings of the Qur'an which they use to legitimate the regulation and surveillance of women through policing their 'modesty'. To be a 'proper' Muslim man means being the provider and protector of women, whose freedom of movement, including the right to work, must ultimately be curtailed.

However, Islamic feminist scholars argue that patriarchy and gendered oppressive practices are not foundational to Islam (Wadud 1999). Leila Ahmed's (1992, p. 55) detailed scholarly history of women in Islam finds egalitarianism to be a constant element of the ethical utterances of the Qur'an and states, 'Nowhere is veiling explicitly prescribed.' The Qur'an provides women with explicit rights to inheritance, independent property, divorce and the right to testify in a court of law. It also prohibits violence towards women and duress in marriage and community affairs (Wadud 2002). Fatima Mernissi (1996) suggests that, despite the progressive role of women in Islam, including the Prophet's third wife, A'ishah, who led troops into battle, the lowly image attributed to women in Islamic societies is not due to the absence of traditional memory or historical evidence, but rather to conservative forces shaping the image making in the Muslim world which discriminate against women. The rise of Islamic fundamentalism has had much to do with this negative gendered representation. Haidah Moghissi argues, as with the rise of Western capitalism, the control of women and the authority of the patriarchal family are central to the Islamic fundamentalist utopia. To this end, she explains, 'Islamic fundamentalists dig up medieval Islamic texts, prescribe moral codes or invent rules of conduct when the need arises' (1999, p. 73). For Asma Barlas (2002), the solution to the disputes on gender equality in Islam lies in what she sees as understanding the libratory hermeneutics, of the Qur'an. Writing in *The Guardian,* she contends that 'As long as Muslims continue to read gender inequalities into the Qur'an, we will not be able to ensure gender equality in Muslim societies' (Barlas 2008). Saba Mahmood (2005), however, takes the argument of Muslim women's religious disposition a stage further. For Mahmood, acts of piety, or *taqwa,* such as obedience to God, brings spiritual rewards. The Egyptian women she studied in the mosque movement produced 'virtuous selves' through conscious acts of 'shyness' in which the female body is used as an instrument to attain state of embodied piety. Mahmood suggests that to understand Islamic female forms of moral subjectivity and embodied spiritual interiority, we must move beyond Western imperialist notions of libratory emancipation and the deterministic binaries of resistance/subordination by which Muslim female subjectivity and agency are judged.

It could be argued that it is controversial to focus on religious and culturally specific forms of gender oppression and violence against women (Dustin and Phillips 2008; Gill and Mitra-Khan 2010). By highlighting issues of communal and familial violence in Muslim communities, are we perpetuating the stereotype of these communities as backward and barbaric? Similarly, it could be argued that by distinguishing these forms of gendered violence as special cultural phenomena, we are placing an undue emphasis on the 'Muslim woman' and, in effect, racialising her. The debate centres on highlighting gendered sexualised practices in particular Islamic cultures, such as female genital mutilation, forced marriages and honour killings, where the sanctity of (male) community rights is privileged over the bodily rights of individual (female) victims. To develop a truly multicultural, multi-agency policy framework in our education, health, criminal justice and social services that uncompromisingly responds to cultural forms of domestic violence, we need a 'mature multiculturalism' (Patel and Siddiqui 2010). Such an approach would address the tensions between recognising gender oppression and valuing multicultural difference by challenging cultural and social attitudes through public education and informed anti-racist professional practice (Mirza 2010).

Spaces of recognition: Muslim women, activism and the 'third space'

In the face of growing racist political rhetoric, Islamophobia, and anti-asylum and immigration policies in Britain, we are witnessing a retreat from multiculturalism and a move towards civic integration. The now longstanding policy of Community Cohesion through civic integration has been the official state discourse on multiculturalism in Britain since New Labour's rule. In the multicultural 'post-nation', integration and active citizenship are seen as the solution to economic inequality, political under-representation and structural segregation in housing and education in the ethnic enclaves that serve our cities (Wetherell et al. 2007). Community Cohesion emphasises building bridges between faith-based communities, in particular targeting what are seen as segregated Muslim communities which are deemed to live 'parallel lives' (Cantle 2001). The focus on interfaith and cultural understanding in the context of civic integration legitimates the link between citizenship and nationhood as essential for multicultural coexistence. However, the shift to a faith-based approach within the multicultural discourse has many implications for equality and the human rights of Muslim women in their communities. Pragna Patel and Hannana Sidiqqui (2010) argue that since the Rushdie affair in 1980s, the overarching aim of the British multicultural state has been to isolate religious extremists by creating a space for religious moderates to take up key leadership positions in their communities.

This move to multi-faithism has resulted in what in what Patel and Siddiqui (2010) call 'the shrinking of secular spaces' for black and minority ethnic women to autonomously struggle for their human rights. The rise in power of unelected and unaccountable Muslim (male) community leaders means that those who are able 'to shout the loudest' establish a platform and the authority to impose conservative patriarchal religious interpretations which traditionally discriminate against women. An example of this is the establishment of Muslim Arbitration Tribunals (MATs) and Sharia Councils affiliated to mosques (Bano 2010). Both act as an alternative to dispute resolution in Muslim communities, using Islamic law in family matters including domestic violence and forced marriage. These unofficial quasi legal bodies which are sanctioned within the multicultural state draw on the knowledge of unelected male elders in their conservative interpretation of Islamic law (Patel and Siddiqui 2010).

While there are successful Muslim women's organisations campaigning against human rights abuses, such as Iranian and Kurdish Women's Rights Organisation (IKWRO) and Women Living Under Muslim Laws (WLUML), it has been secular, activist coalitions of black and minority ethnic women such as Southall Black Sisters, Woman Against Fundamentalism (WAF), Newham Asian Women's Project (NAWP) and Foundation for Women's Health Research and Development (FORWARD) among many others, which since the 1970s have been central in placing Muslim women's issues on the public policy agenda in Britain. They have made many gains in the law and services as well as tackled the thorny issue of cultural and religious conservatism within minority ethnic and Muslim communities (Dustin and Phillips 2008; Patel and Siddiqui 2010; Wilson 2010).

The power struggle between male Muslim community leaders and women's groups within a British multicultural policy framework needs to be openly addressed. As the Muslim Women's Network (WNC) report *She Who Disputes* records, 'We can't pussy foot around community leaders and not address issues for fear of getting their backs up. By not addressing controversial issues our communities are destroying themselves' (2006, p. 9). British Muslim women's activism across all communities has been local, grassroots and in response to immediate concerns such as their own and their children's education and health, as well as public and communal violence against women. Building basic capacity among Muslim women and finding a safe space for them to express their concerns has been a priority for Muslim women activists, but one achieved largely without much access to 'hard to get' Government funding or support from male community leaders (WNC 2006). Projects such as the Ashiana, Karma Nirvana, and the Muslim Women's Help Line, refuges and care centres that cater to the specific needs of Muslim women, have struggled to survive under the new blunt, racist Community Cohesion funding regimes, which, in response to fears about Muslim segregation and national security have withdrawn specialist funding for specific ethnic communities (Wilson 2010).

With the setting up of the Home Office Working Group on Forced Marriage, the Southall Black Sisters with others, including Muslim women activists, secured a major watershed victory in 1999, when they secured state recognition of gender based violence in minority ethnic communities. This led to the Forced Marriage Civil Protection Act (2007) which gave statutory footing to the work of the Forced Marriage Unit in the Foreign and Commonwealth Office. Other gains have been made in relation to marriage related immigration rules, such as amendments to the discriminatory Primary Purpose Rule and the One, now Two-Year Rule, which states that immigrant women must stay with their husbands for minimum period or face deportation (Shama and Gill 2010). This rule effectively works to trap women who are experiencing domestic violence, ruling that a break-up of marriage before the end of this period means that women will lose their right to stay in the UK. Another recent cruel and devastating rule is the 'No Recourse to Public Funds' rule which leaves women with insecure immigration status, unable to claim welfare and thus destitute or forced to stay in abusive relationships. Patel and Siddiqui (2010) document the contradictory actions of the state with regard to black and minority ethnic women. On the one hand, the state pays lip service to progressive human-rights-based legislation, with its action on forced marriage, while it also regulates minority ethnic communities through using cultural issues to tighten immigration controls. In this regard, a critical eye must be cast on the true motives behind the passing of forced marriage legislation to begin with.

Such human rights victories by women's groups can irrevocability shift the image and identity of the state as it is forced to make adjustments that embrace broader concepts of gendered rights which challenge hegemonic notions of British citizenship, British justice and the underpinning principle of British 'fair play'. Muslim and black and minority ethnic women activists have had a significant impact on the multicultural state by slowly instigating state behavioural change with regard to gendered human rights issues for women. Ranu Samantrai (2002) argues that black and minority ethnic feminist activism has been more than just about accessing rights and services. They are a contingent and politically destabilising force, in a constant state of flux, where neither allies nor enemies are readily identifiable and where even their own campaigns and activists may become obsolete when gains are made. But more importantly, she argues, they play a central role in challenging the fundamental core of British identity. It could be argued by challenging the racial subtext of British majority and minority identities, black and minority ethnic feminists, including Muslim women activists, are engaged in the very radical project of refining the 'We' of the nation – in effect 'who are the British'. Muslim, black and minority ethnic women are writing themselves into the British multicultural national story.

Muslim and black and minority ethnic women's grassroots and human rights activism sheds new light on traditional conceptualisations of citizenship. In the classical political and social discourse on citizenship and belonging that underpins the current debates on multiculturalism and Community Cohesion, little space is given to 'gendered acts of citizenship' which require 'other ways of knowing'. In their gendered/racialised version of citizenship Muslim and black and minority ethnic women activists use international and domestic law to challenge the patriarchal alliance between white and minority ethnic male leaders – an alliance that, despite state racism, remains secure and at the heart of the liberal democratic state in Britain. Muslim and black and minority ethnic women collectively combine their social and emotional capital skills of resourcefulness and networking which enables them to carve out new spaces of contestation as radical collective transformative agents (Mirza 2009). It could be argued their activism offers up a form of 'experiential socio-analysis', which opens up a 'third space' of strategic engagement. Such a discursive 'third space' has largely remained invisible in the traditional public (male) and private (female) dichotomy in current citizenship theorising, which, as in the Government's current vision of the 'Big Society', obscures other ways of knowing and thus other ways of being a British citizen.

For Muslim and black and minority ethnic women's activists, raising difficult issues of sexism and domestic violence brings to the fore issues of power and patriarchy in their own communities (Crenshaw 1994).

In vulnerable and racialised Muslim communities there are tensions between protecting men from the racism of state agencies and negative media representation on the one hand, and the need to raise the issue of gendered violence and protect women's rights in these communities on the other. As Sawsan Salim (2003) explains, in the Kurdish community there is a fear amongst some that putting honour crimes on the public agenda might cause a dangerous backlash in the immigration debate and heighten xenophobic sentiments against asylum seekers. However, Muslim women scholars and Islamic feminists must and do raise difficult issues of sexism and violence against women within their communities. The call to 'a return to *Shari'ah'* by Islamist political ideologues in Iran in 1970s had devastating consequences for Muslim women globally with the return to outdated models of feudal social relations, gendered segregation, compulsory dress codes and the revival of cruel medieval punishments. The Islamic feminist Ziba Mir-Hosseini (2011) argues that the setting up of the United Nations General Assembly for the Convention on the Elimination of All Forms of Discrimination against Women (CEDAW) in 1979 was the watershed that gave Muslim women the language and tools to resist Islamist patriarchy by giving gender equality a clear international human rights mandate. Women's NGOs in Muslim countries together with the transnational women's movement made visible various forms of fundamentalist gender based discrimination and violence rooted in patriarchal cultural traditions and religious practices.

However, as Amina Wadud (2002) explains, the relationship between feminist activism and Islam has not been easy:

> Today Muslim women are striving for greater inclusiveness in many diverse ways, not all of them in agreement with each other. At the Beijing Global Women's Conference in 1995, nightly attempts to form a Muslim women's caucus at the NGO forum became screaming sessions. The many different strategies and perspectives just could not be brought to a consensus.

Wadud suggests there are three main stands of thinking within Islamic feminism. Firstly, on the left are the Marxist informed secular feminists and activists who, though Muslim themselves, see Islam in terms of its oppressive cultural manifestations in the Western national postcolonial context. On the far right are the Muslim male authorities and their female representatives, known as Islamists who identify an ideal Islam as the one lived by the Prophet. They take a reactionary, neoconservative approach adopting an unquestioned *Shari'ah* state imposed onto modern complexity. Between the secular Muslim feminists and the Islamists is Islamic feminism, which gained currency in the 1990s. These Muslim women scholars keep their allegiance to Islam as an essential part of their identity but strongly and empathically critique patriarchal control over the male Islamic world view, including the feminist theological interpretation of *Shari'ah* compared to 'man-made' *fiqh*, or 'Islamic jurisprudence' (Mir-Hosseini 1999).

Muslim women scholars, Islamic feminists and black and postcolonial feminists have been in the front line of opposing the postcolonial racist assertion that black, Asian and Muslim men are more barbaric. If we take a global perspective, honour killings and forced marriage are part of a wider patriarchal phenomenon of violence against women (Gupta 2003; Balzani 2010). Women are beaten and murdered across the globe for similar reasons. Violence against women cuts across race, ethnicity, class, religion and age. Violence is not particular to one culture, religion or community. Patriarchal structures use violence extensively to subjugate women in relation to all these dimensions. While the intersectionality of race, religion, class, patriarchy and gender power dynamics produce culturally specific manifestations of violence against women which are important to acknowledge and address in local service delivery, the responses and funding should be mainstreamed into informing domestic violence interventions more generally (Dustin and Phillips 2008). In evidence to the Working Party on Forced Marriage, Southall Black Sisters highlighted the failure of service providers to address the cultural needs of women and girls at risk of forced marriages and honour killings (Siddiqui 2003). Service providers cited cultural grounds for this failure, the assumption being that minority communities are self-policing and that services do not need to intervene on behalf of women (Burman et al. 2004; Sangehera 2006). However, policies such as not putting non-English-speaking women into white-run refuges because of a perceived lack of 'cultural fit' can also leave desperate women without care or shelter (Wilson 2010). At the same time, it is important for Muslim and minority ethnic women's sense of empowerment to be in a refuge that enables their equal participation and values their decision-making (Gill and Rehman 2004).

Conclusion: Muslim women and spaces of gendered visibility/invisibility

The issues raised in this chapter lead us to ask: How do Muslim women escape the racialised and gendered stereotypes that mainstream Western society have of them? Stereotypes are powerful forms of knowledge which construct a repertoire of possible identities and hence subjectivities which, through powerful systems of representation, shape the lived experience of the ethnicised and racially constructed Muslim women in Britain and Europe. Despite the radical images of Muslim women's self-determination in the Arab Spring uprisings, in Britain and Europe Muslim women are still highly *visible* through their dress and as such have become symbolic in the discourse of Islamophobia. The pathological pattern of visibility which characterises the popular representation of the 'Muslim woman' is underpinned, on the one hand, by a Eurocentric universalism, which reduces the complexity and individuality of these women's lives to a single objectified category – in this case, the ubiquitous, stereotypical oppressed 'Muslim woman'. On the other hand, Muslim women are also characterised by a particular form of cultural relativism that highlights specific barbaric cultural practices. In these media narratives the young women are constructed as either romantic heroine, struggling for the benefits of the 'West' against her cruel and inhuman father and family, or victim, succumbing to her backward and traditional 'Eastern' culture. My concern in this chapter has been to understand the tensions between recognising patriarchy and gender oppression within Muslim communities, on one hand, and preserving the important but contested space of multicultural difference, democratic freedom, and the right to religious expression, on the other.

Islamic feminists have taken issue with the cultural superiority of simplistic, sensationalised cultural constructions of Muslim women in the Western media, constructions that negate Muslim female identity and agency, and depoliticise their (embodied) struggles for self-determination (Abu-Loughod 2002; Mahmood 2005). However, this tendency is not just preserved for Muslim women. In postwar Europe there has been a continuous postcolonial preoccupation with the ethnicised woman's victimhood and sexuality (Mama 1989). For example, black and postcolonial feminists have shown how African and Asian migrant women have been represented in Britain (Mirza 1997; Mirza and Joseph 2010). If they have agency they are often depicted as manipulative, scrounging refugees and asylum seekers or overbearing black female matriarchs who marginalise and emasculate their men folk. They are often constructed as the 'jezebel' or exotic other – a sexual temptress who invites rape, violation and prostitution. If they are victims, they are portrayed as disempowered, sexually exploited mail-order brides or sold into sexual trafficking.

While we need to be vigilant about the post-9/11 Islamophobic media discourse and its preoccupation with the veil and highlighting Muslim barbarism against women, we must accept that violence against women is a reality for Muslim communities, as it is in all communities. It is easy not to see cultural forms of domestic violence as part of the bigger picture of endemic universal violence against women which must be challenged in no uncertain terms. Muslim women are largely absent and *invisible* in the mainstream normative (white) discourse on domestic violence, and as such are at risk of not being protected as equal citizens. Professionals working in health, educational and welfare who are tasked with delivering multicultural services to ethnically diverse populations often find themselves 'walking on eggshells' – that is, accommodating gendered cultural practices for fear of offending Muslim communities and inviting accusations of racism (Mirza 2010).

If we are to develop a more equitable and culturally neutral perspective where Muslim women's human rights are ensured and privileged over Islamic patriarchal cultural practices we need a pragmatic and contingent dual approach to progressing the debate on violence against women in Britain. Such a dual approach includes both religious Islamic feminist perspectives and secular Muslim and black and minority ethnic women's human rights activism in a multi-pronged 'transversal' (Yuval-Davis 1999) coalition in the campaign for state action to combat violence against women.

We need to urgently address the human rights violations of young Muslim women's bodily rights both within Muslim communities and in our mainstream British and European societies. There is a fine line to walk between recognising patriarchy and gender oppression within Muslim communities and preserving a woman's right to freedom of religious expression. To keep our balance, we need to be prepared to move beyond stereotypical views of Muslim women and see the complexity of the issues that lie behind our narrow political agendas and limited public policy perspectives in Britain and across Europe.

References

Abbas, T. (2010) 'Honour-related Violence towards South Asian Muslim Women in the UK', in M. Idriss and T. Abbas (eds), *Honour, Violence, Women and Islam* (London: Routledge), pp. 16–28.

Abu-Loughod, L. (2002) 'Do Muslim Women Really Need Saving? Anthropological Reflections on Cultural Relativism and Its Others,' *American Anthropologist*, 104(3), 783–90.

Ahmed, L. (1992), *Women and Gender in Islam: Historical Roots of a Modern Debate* (New Haven: Yale University Press).

Ahmed, S. (2003) The Politics of Fear in the Making of Worlds. *International Journal of Qualitative Studies in Education*, 16(3), 377–98.

Ahmed, S. (2004) *The Cultural Politics of Emotions* (Edinburgh: Edinburgh University Press).

Afshar, H. (2008) 'Can I See Your Hair? Choice, Agency and Attitudes: The Dilemma of Faith and Feminism for Muslim Women Who Cover', *Ethnic and Racial Studies*, 31(2), 411–27.

Al-Ali, N. and Pratt, N. (2009) *What Kind of Liberation? Women and the Occupation in Iraq* (Berkeley: University of California Press).

Bano, S. (2010) 'Shariah Councils and the Resolution of Matrimonial Disputes: Gender Justice and the Shadow of the Law,' in R. Thiara and A. Gill (eds), *Violence against Women in South Asian Communities: Issues for Policy and Practice* (London: Jessica Kingsley Publishers), pp.182–210.

Balzani, M. (2010) 'Masculinities and Violence against Women in South Asian Communities: Transnational Perspective', in R. Thiara and A. Gill (eds). *Violence against Women in South Asian Communities: Issues for Policy and Practice* (London: Jessica Kingsley Publishers), pp. 80–101.

Barlas, A. (2002) *'Believing Women' in Islam: Unreading Patriarchal Interpretations of the Qur'an* (Austin: University of Texas Press).

Barlas, A. (2008) 'Toward a Feminist View of Islam', *The Guardian*, 31 October 2008, http://www.guardian.co.uk/commentisfree/2008/oct/31/religion-islam

BBC (2006) 'Honour Killing Brother Jailed', *BBC News London*, 13 April 2006, http://news.bbc.co.uk/1/hi/world/europe/4905758.stm

BBC (2010) 'Banaz Mahmood 'Honour' Killing Cousins Jailed for Life', *BBC News London*, 10 November 2010, http://www.bbc.co.uk/news/uk-england-london-11716272

BBC (2011) 'State Multiculturalism Has Failed, Says David Cameron', *BBC News London*, 5 February 2011, http://www.bbc.co.uk/news/uk-politics-12371994.

Beckett, C. and Macey, M. (2001) 'Race, Gender and Sexuality: The Oppression of Multiculturalism', *Women's Studies International Forum*, 24(3/4), 309–19.

Begum, Halima (2008) 'Geographies of Inclusion/Exclusion: British Muslim Women in the East End of London' *Sociological Research* [online], 13(5), http://www.socresonline.org.uk

Bouteldja, N. (2011) 'France's False Battle of the Veil', *The Guardian*, 18 April 2011, http://www.guardian.co.uk/commentisfree/2011/apr/18/france-false-battle-of-the-veil

Bunting, M. (2006) 'Straw's Storm of Prejudice', *The Guardian Unlimited Weekly*, 13 October 2006. http://www.guardian.co.uk/guardianweekly/story/0,,1896807,00.html

Burman, E., Smailes, S. L. and Chantler, K. (2004)). 'Culture as a Barrier to Service Provision and Delivery: Domestic Violence Services for Minoritized Women', *Critical Social Policy*, 24(3), 332–57.

Cantle, T. (2001), *Community Cohesion: A Report of the Independent Review Team* (London: Home Office).

Crenshaw, K. (1994), 'Mapping the Margins: Intersectionality, Identity Politics, and Violence against Women of Color', in M. Albertson Fineman and R. Mykitiuk (eds), *The Public Nature of Private Violence* (New York: Routledge), pp. 93–118.

Coene, G. and Longman, C. (2008) 'Gendering the Diversification of Diversity: The Belgium *hijab* (in) Question', *Ethnicities*, 8(3), 302–21.

Connolly, K. (2010) 'Germany's Central Bank Decides to Sack Board Member', *The Guardian*, 2 September 2010, http://www.guardian.co.uk/world/2010/sep/02/germany-central-bank-decide-sack-thilo-sarrazin

Dustin, M. and Phillips, A. (2008) "Whose Agenda Is It? Abuses of Women and Abuses of Culture in Britain', *Ethnicities*, 8(3), 405–24.

Elliot, A. (2002), 'Beck's Sociology of Risk: A Critical Assessment', *Sociology*, 36(2), 293–315.

Fawcett Society (2006) 'The Veil, Feminism and Muslim Women: A Debate', 14 December 2006, www.fawcettsociety.org.uk/index.asp?PageID=378

Fekete, L. (2004) 'Anti-Muslim racism and the European security state', *Race and Class*, 46(1), 3–29.

Gardiner, N. (2011) 'Britain Is No Nation of Bigots Baroness Warsi', *Daily Telegraph*, 20 January 2011, http://blogs.telegraph.co.uk/news/nilegardiner/100072880/britain-is-no-nation-of-bigots-baroness-warsi/

Gill, A. (2003) 'A Question of Honour', *Community Care*, 27 March 2003.

Gill, A. (2006) 'Patriarchal Violence in the Name of "Honour"', *International Journal of Criminal Justice Sciences*, 1(1), 1–12.

Gill, A. and Mitra - Khan, T. (2010) 'Moving toward a "Multiculturalism without Culture": Constructing a Victim-Friendly Human Rights Approach to Forced Marriage in the UK', in R. Thiara and A. Gill (eds), *Violence against Women in South Asian Communities: Issues for Policy and Practice* (London: Jessica Kingsley Publishers), pp.128–55.

Gill, A. and Rehman, G. (2004) 'Empowerment through Activism: Responding to Domestic Violence in the South Asian Community in London', *Gender and Development*, 12(1), 75–82.

Groskop, V. (2011), 'Liberté, égalité, fraternité – Unless, of Course, You Would Like to Wear a Burqa', *The Observer*, 10 April 2011, http://www.guardian.co.uk/commentisfree/2011/apr/10/france-burqa-niqab-ban

Gupta, R. (2003) 'Some Recurring Themes: Southall Black Sisters 1979–2003, and Still Going Strong', in R. Gupta (ed.), *From Homemakers to Jailbreakers: Southall Black Sisters* (London: Zed Books), pp.1–27.

Hall, A. (2010) 'Multiculturalism in Germany Has "Utterly Failed"' Claims Chancellor Angela Merkel', *Mail Online*, 18 October 2010, http://www.dailymail.co.uk/news/article-1321277/Angela-Merkel-Multiculturalism-Germany-utterly-failed.html

Human Rights Watch (2009) *Discrimination in the Name of Neutrality. Headscarf Bans for Teachers and Civil Servants in Germany*, http://www.hrw.org/en/news/2009/02/26/germany-headscarf-bans-violate-rights

Kanneh, K. (1995) 'Feminism and the Colonial Body' in B. Ashcroft, G. Griffiths and H. Tiffin (eds), *The Post Colonial Studies Reader* (London: Routledge), pp.346–8.

Killian C. (2003) 'The Other Side of the Veil: North African Women in France Respond to the Headscarf Affair', *Gender and Society*, 17(4), 567–90.

Mahmood, S. (2005) *The Politics of Piety: The Islamic Revival and the Feminist Subject* (Princeton, NJ: Princeton University Press).

Mama, A. (1989) 'Violence against Black Women: Gender, Race, and State Responses', *Feminist Review*, 32, summer, pp. 30–48.

Marquand, R . (2010) 'Why "Islamophobia" Is Less Thinly Veiled in Europe', in H. Bruinius and R. Marquand, *Islam and the West*, 102(41), 10 September 2010, http://freethoughtmanifesto.blogspot.co.uk/2010/09/why-islamophobia-is-less-thinly-veiled.html

Mir-Hosseini, Z. (1999) *Islam and Gender: The Religious Debate in Contemporary Iran* (Princeton, NJ: Princeton University Press).

Mir-Hosseini, Z. (2011) 'Beyond "Islam" vs. "Feminism"', *IDS (Institute of Development Studies) Bulletin*, 42(1), 67–77.

Meetoo, V. and Mirza, H.S. (2007) 'There is Nothing Honourable about Honour Killings: Gender, Violence and the Limits of Multiculturalism', *Women's Studies International Forum*, 30(3), 187–200.

Mernissi, F. (1996) *Women's Rebellion and Islamic Memory* (London: Zed Books).

Mirza, H. S. (1997) *Black British Feminism: A Reader* (London: Routledge).

Mirza, H. S. (2009) *Race, Gender and Educational Desire: Why Black Women Succeed and Fail* (London: Routledge).

Mirza H. S. (2010) 'Walking on Egg Shells: Multiculturalism, Gender and Domestic Violence', in M. Robb and R. Thomson (eds), *Critical Practice with Children and Young People* (Bristol: Policy Press), pp.43–57.

Mirza, H. and Joseph, C. (eds) (2010) *Black and Postcolonial Feminisms in New Times: Researching Educational Inequalities* (London: Routledge).

Moghissi, H (1999) *Feminism and Islamic Fundamentalism: The Limits of Postmodern Analysis* (London: Zed Books).

Mohanty, C. T. (2003) *Feminism without Borders: Decolonising Theory, Practicing Solidarity* (Durham, NC, and London: Duke University Press).

Moussaoui, R. (2011) 'A Woman's Touch in the Arab Spring', 25 December 2011, *The Daily News Egypt /Agence France-Presse*, http://www.thedailynewsegypt.com/people/a-womans-touch-in-the-arab-spring.html

Okin, S.M. (1999) 'Is Multiculturalism Bad for Women?', in J. Cohen, M. Howard and M. C. Nussbaum (eds), *Is Multiculturalism Bad for Women? Susan Moller Okin with Respondents* (Princeton, NJ: Princeton University Press), pp.7–26.

Open Society Foundations (2011) *Unveiling the Truth. Why 32 Women Wear the Full-Face Veil in France*, http://www.soros.org/initiatives/home/articles_publications/publications/unveiling-the-truth-20110411

Patel, P. and Siddiqui, H. (2010) 'Shrinking Secular Spaces: Asian Women at the Intersect of Race, Religion and Gender', in R. Thiara and A. Gill (eds), *Violence against Women in South Asian Communities: Issues for Policy and Practice* (London, Jessica Kingsley Press), pp.102–27.

Phillips, A. (2003) 'When Culture Means Gender: Issues of Cultural Defence in English Courts', *The Modern Law Review*, 66(4), 510–1.

Phillips, A. (2007) *Multiculturalism without Culture*, (Princeton, NJ: Princeton University Press).

Ramji, H. (2007) 'Dynamics of Religion and Gender amongst British Muslims', *Sociology*, 41(6) 1171–89.

Refugee Women's Association (2003) *Refugee Women's News*, June and July 2003, issue 23.

Samantrai, R. (2002) *AlterNatives: Black Feminism in the Post Imperial Nation* (Palo Alto, CA: Stanford University Press).

Samuel, H. (2012) 'France Election 2012: Nicolas Sarkozy Says Far-Right Vote Cannot Be Ignored', 23 April 2012, http://www.telegraph.co.uk/news/worldnews/europe/france/9219926/France-election-2012-Nicolas-Sarkozy-says-far-Right-vote-cannot-be-ignored.html

Salim, S. (2003) 'It's About Women's Rights and Women's Rights Are Human Rights', interview with Sawsan Salim, Coordinator of Kurdistan Refugee Women's Organisation (KRWO), Stop Violence against Women Honour Killing Conference, 28 October 2005, London.

Sanghera, J. (2006) 'Honour Abuse: The Victims' Story', Karma Nirvana, IKWRO/ Amnesty International 'Honour Killings' Conference, London, 1 December 2006, http://www.karmanirvana.org.uk/component/content/article/30-what-is/75-honour-killing.html

Sarrazin, T. (2010) *Deutschland schafft sich ab: Wie wir unser Land aufs Spiel setzen* (Munich: Deutsche Verlags-Anstalt).

Scott, J. W. (2007) *The Politics of the Veil* (Princeton, NJ: Princeton University Press).

Shama K. and Gill A. (2010) 'Protection for All? The Failures of the Domestic Violence Rule for (Im)migrant Women', in R. Thiara and A. Gill (eds), *Violence against Women in South Asian Communities : Issues for Policy and Practice* (London: Jessica Kingsley Press), pp. 211–36.

Siddiqui, H. (2003) 'It Was Written in Her Kismet: Forced Marriage', in R. Gupta (ed.), *From Homebreakers to Jailbreakers* (London: Zed Books), pp. 67–108.

Spivak, G. C. (1988) 'Can the Subaltern Speak?', in C. Nelson and L. Grossberg (eds), *Marxism and the Interpretation of Culture* (London: Macmillan), pp. 271–313.

Yuval-Davis, N. (1997) *Gender and Nation* (London: Sage).

Yuval-Davis N. (1999) 'What Is Transversal Politics?' *Soundings,* 12(Summer 1999), pp. 94–8.

Wadud, A. (1999) *Qur'an and Woman: Rereading the Sacred Text from a Woman's Perspective* (Oxford: Oxford University Press).

Wadud, A. (2002) 'Aishah's Legacy', *New Internationalist,* 345 (5 May 2002), http://www.newint.org/features/2002/05/01/aishahs-legacy/

Werbner, P. (2007) 'Veiled Interventions in Pure Space: Honour, Shame and Embodied Struggles among Muslims in Britain and France', *Theory Culture and Society,* 24(2), 161–86.

Wetherell, M., Lafleche, M. and Berkeley, R. (eds) (2007) *Identity, Ethnic Diversity and Community Cohesion* (London: Sage).

Women's National Commission (2006) 'She Who Disputes: Muslim Women Shape the Debate', *Muslim Women's Network, Women's National Commission,* November, http://www.thewnc.org.uk/publications/doc_details/356-she-who-disputes-.html

Wilson, A. (2010), 'Charting South Asian Women's Struggles against Gender-based Violence' in R. Thiara and A. Gill (eds) *Violence against Women in South Asian Communities: Issues for Policy and Practice* (London: Jessica Kingsley Press), pp. 55–79.

Part II

6

Can You Have Muslim Soldiers? Diversity as a Martial Value

Vron Ware

> When people raise the subject of racism with me and ask whether it is a matter of political correctness, I remind them that the most glorious hours of the British armed forces were spent when they stood alone against the most poisonous regime ever to emanate from the European continent. The poison at the heart of that regime was racism. There is no place for racism in the ethos of the British armed forces.[1]
>
> > (John Reid, Minister for the Armed Forces 1997)

> Nationalism and Patriotism are values that are totally compatible with Islam and Islamic teachings. Actually they not only compatible but are actually encouraged and seen as commendable traits. Therefore there a famous Islamic saying in Arabic "Hubbul watan minal eeman" – the love of your nation is part of your faith.
>
> > (Imam Asim Hafiz, Muslim chaplain to HM Armed Forces 2010)

> Diversity increases operational effectiveness.
>
> > (Slogan on RAF diary 2012)

The British Army website is a movable feast. Like many corporate employers, the organisation constantly updates the online information and images so as to entice young men and women with the prospect of an exciting, fulfilling career. In February 2012, a page could be found in the section on joining the army, providing answers to frequently asked questions. 'Army life has a lot of similarities to civilian life,' it stated, 'but there are times when it makes very different demands of the people who live it.'[2] A list of 12 questions could be found below, formatted in 'accordion' style so that the answers only appeared when the viewer clicked on the corresponding arrow. Thus it was possible to read them not just as a list but also an index of public ignorance surrounding the nature of military work.

The questions ranged from what soldiers ate and where they lived to whether they could go home or were allowed to leave the army. They also included inquiries about different types of food, pensions, injuries, wages and contact with friends and family. In the middle of the list, however, a more incongruous example leapt out: can you have Muslim soldiers? This prompted the compact reply:

> The Army has soldiers from all faiths and communities. There are Muslim soldiers as well as Jewish soldiers, Hindu soldiers and others from Britain and Commonwealth countries. The only thing that matters is that soldiers are prepared to work for each other and towards a common goal.

This brief response is notable for the fluency with which it conveys the wide diversity of the workforce while simultaneously stressing the particular demands of soldiering. The only thing that matters is that people are prepared to work for each other, it declared.

There are good reasons to doubt that this was a routine question faced by recruiters talking to young British Muslims eager to sign up, and it is clear that its presence in this more humdrum list requires an alternative explanation. For one thing, it provided an opportunity to articulate the army's embrace of diversity, speaking directly to young Asian applicants from Muslim or Hindu backgrounds. Not only could you have Muslim soldiers, we are told, but they also worked happily alongside soldiers of other faiths. This assertion, along with the supporting information that halal food was provided where possible, indicated that the army had embraced modern forms of diversity management in line with the rest of Britain's public institutions. The extent of this integrated, cohesive work environment even hinted that military institutions might provide a space for minorities, including Muslims, to negotiate their identities as fully qualified national subjects, premised on their readiness to fight and die for their country.

The mention of soldiers from Commonwealth countries reflected the fact that non-British applicants were eligible to apply, although this was not addressed to them. But more troubling was the question itself: can you have Muslim soldiers? Asking why 'Muslim soldiers' might not be possible, permissible, feasible even, is a good place to start to reflect on the ways that war and racism are connected in twenty-first-century Britain. The uncertainty about whether British Muslim citizens are either entitled or prepared to perform military service articulates a 'common-sense' viewpoint that multiculturalism has become inseparable from national security. When the nation's security is perceived to be under threat, either from inside or from outside the country, the appeal to national character, patriotism, and ethno-racial familiarity are asserted more forcefully (Goldberg 2009, p.55). Soldiers are commonly associated with patriotism, service to Queen and Country, and a heroic readiness to sacrifice their lives. The category of 'Muslims' is identified with the very causes of global insurgency, not least the dubious loyalties that lie beyond the borders of the national state (Qureshi and Zeitlyn 2013).

Against this background, the grounds for doubting the existence of the British Muslim soldier appear more solid. Yet the UK armed forces are seldom factored into political debates about citizenship, multiculturalism and immigration. They are regarded as operating on a different terrain, separate from the rest of the public sector to which they nominally belong, and their employment policies obscured behind the carefully managed screen of military public relations. It has long been accepted that national military institutions play a significant role in representing countries in the global arena, including the combat zone, but their role in shaping social structures and values in domestic spheres is rarely acknowledged outside the confines of specialist military sociology (Krebs 2004, p.89). In some periods the question of who joins the army is relatively dormant as a public concern. But studied over time, military recruitment strategies can be seen to play an important role in shaping the definition of the political community. Approaching military service through the framework of the state-funded public sector offers insights into concepts of citizenship and national belonging because it raises in acute form the question of what the country owes those who volunteer to join the armed forces (Ware 2010a). This is because, at certain moments, the act of volunteering to be a soldier is thought to reach into the heart of what it means to be a citizen and to 'serve' the country. And when greater attention is paid to the conditions of military service and the personal costs borne by the 'ordinary' women and men involved, the presence (or absence) of ethnic, cultural, sexual and religious minorities comes into view as an index of inclusion (or exclusion) in the wider society.

Reviewing the 'diversification' of the UK armed forces over the last decade, this chapter will argue that the policies and practices introduced to manage a multicultural workforce have themselves been militarised. That is, the various strategies associated with equality and diversity have not only been absorbed into a military setting, they have also been associated with the core values adopted by the military as their organisational ethos. As it turns out, not only can you have Muslim soldiers who are exemplary patriotic citizens, but, along with other minorities, they can also provide tools for the emerging defence, development and diplomacy nexus that shapes US-led foreign policy (Finney 2010). Accepting the potent meanings of soldiering as particularly symbolic work demands a much more rigorous analysis of the roles that the military institutions play, not just in defining the bounds of the nation, but also in arbitrating the terms of belonging as well (Cowen 2008).

Political communities

Military organisations, including veterans' charities, provide substance to the national apparatus of Britishness, whether through the pomp and pageantry of royal occasions or the annual ceremonies of remembrance which give voice to the full expression of national identity reiterated in a timeless language of war and sacrifice. Assumptions about how the military relates to civilian society are formed by a range of factors: historical events, traditional practices, political settlements, legal agreements, media representation and personal experience. They also depend to a large extent on what citizens think about the wars that national armies are sent off to fight. As a consequence, recruitment into the armed forces is a supremely social issue as well as an intensely political one, and the line between military and civilian spheres exists as an unpredictable and unstable fissure. For those researching the politics of citizenship, belonging, and national identity, scrutinizing military employment policies and strategies when the country is at war becomes an important way of investigating the limits of the nation – both as an idea and in policy terms as well.

Recent events have demonstrated how military service in the cause of defending Britain's interests in the past remains an important qualification for enacting modern claims to citizenship and defining the bounds of the political, national and postcolonial community (Paul 1998). This issue was exemplified by the media furore over the plight of elderly Nepalese ex-servicemen, many of whom had fought alongside the British Army in South East Asia in the 1960s. In 2008–9, the Campaign for Gurkha Justice, led by actor Joanna Lumley, pressurised the government to permit those who had served for a minimum of four years to live in the UK with full access to public funds. The Gurkha soldiers' record of fierce loyalty to the British Crown, demonstrated by countless deaths in both 1914–18 and in 1939–45, provided the basis of public support for their right to social welfare in the UK. It was an important campaign, not least because the strength of public support signalled the resilience of a powerful idea about what it meant to be a soldier in the service of the nation, regardless of nationality or ethnic origin (Ware 2010, p. 321).

While the continuing policy of employing Gurkha soldiers drew attention to Britain's historic recruiting practices, these was little comment at the time that the armed forces contained hundreds of other migrant personnel, particularly in the army. In 1998 the New Labour government relaxed the residency rules for Commonwealth citizens in response to severe manpower shortages. Individual regiments were recruited directly from countries such as Fiji and Jamaica to deploy in Northern Ireland, Kosovo and Sierra Leone, but by 2002 the army had begun to send 'overseas pre-selection teams' (OPTs) to process applicants so that they could travel directly to the UK and begin training immediately. These expeditions were carried out at intervals until the summer of 2008 when the financial crash began to alter patterns of retention and recruitment in the UK (Taylor 2009).

The annual report on UK Defence Statistics issued in April 2011 showed that 92.2 per cent of personnel in the army recorded British nationality, leaving 7.8 per cent (7600 soldiers) who were not UK citizens.[3] Of these, 7.3 per cent were from either the Republic of Ireland or from Commonwealth countries, while 0.5 per cent (460 soldiers) were Nepali citizens who had transferred from the Brigade of Gurkhas. Breaking down these figures even further reveals that there were soldiers from 33 Commonwealth countries who were serving in the British Army.[4] Over 2000 were from Fiji, 800 from Ghana, 790 from South Africa and 440 from Jamaica. Although Zimbabwe and Fiji had been suspended from the Commonwealth, their citizens were still eligible under the British Nationality Act 1981.

The employment of migrant-soldiers with strong postcolonial ties to Britain challenges the 'common-sense' racism and nationalism that delineates the boundaries of our political community by colour and concepts of indigeneity. Although the majority of these soldiers, some of whom are also designated as white, might otherwise be cast as ineligible skilled and unskilled migrants from outside the EU, they are not automatically rewarded with citizenship as a condition of employment in the armed forces. Nor is their path to citizenship, should they wish to apply, significantly expedited by their readiness to 'serve'.

The inclusion of so many Commonwealth citizens has been fortuitous because it has allowed military institutions – particularly the British Army – to prove their commitment to successive diversity and equality policies, despite initial resistance on the grounds that HR policies devised for the civilian world did not apply (Dandeker 1994, p. 649). Anthony Forster has argued convincingly that military leaders fought a losing battle to control a professional space that remained outside legal interventions and impervious to societal pressure (Forster 2006). Collating the interventions and initiatives that took place in the late 1990s brings into view the convergence of legal, administrative, political and constitutional motors of reform that challenged the Ministry of Defence's (MoD's) claim to be an exceptional form of employer.

Corporate diversity

In 2011, the MoD issued a revised policy statement on diversity that was notable for the manner in which it moved away from the legalistic discourse of racial discrimination that had previously characterised its approach. 'Equality and diversity is not a policy we pursue just because the legislation requires us to,' it announced. 'We pursue the policy simply because it is morally right and because it makes excellent business sense.' Referring to the importance of recruiting civil and military employees across the breadth of society, it continued, 'We encourage people throughout society to join us, and remain with us, to make their distinctive contributions and achieve their full potential.' To do this effectively, the policy made clear that the ministry would not tolerate 'any form of intimidation, humiliation, harassment, bullying or abuse'.[5]

Over a decade earlier, the British Army issued a set of recruitment posters based on Alfred Leese's well-known 'Your Country Needs You' image of Lord Kitchener from the First World War. In one of these, Kitchener's face had been replaced by that of Ghanaian-born Captain Fedelix Datson of the Royal Artillery.[6] 'Britain is a multi-racial country,' the poster declared in small print at the bottom of the picture. 'It needs a multi-racial Army.' The word 'need' in this context illustrated the somewhat crude agenda set by a corporate version of multiculturalism, defined by Stuart Hall as an attempt 'to "manage" minority cultural differences in the interests of the centre' (Hesse 2000, p. 210). This process was driven in part by the climate of reform ushered in by the Macpherson Report, published in early 1999, and the Race Relations (Amendment) Act which followed in 2000, extending the definition of 'public authorities' to cover the police, and also, for the first time, the prison service and the armed forces. The new bill also gave the Commission for Racial Equality (CRE) further powers to promote 'race equality', whether by issuing tighter codes of practice or by imposing specific duties on public bodies.

The evident disparity between this vocabulary of equal opportunities and 'racial groups' and the confident assertion of the moral economy of corporate diversity ten years later is not unique to the defence sector, but it requires a separate analysis. While it is possible to look back and assemble all the different measures of reform in a chronological pattern, we should also note that it has been a more chaotic, uneven and contested development, characterised by Stuart Hall in the Parekh Report on the future of multi-ethnic Britain as 'multicultural drift' (2000, p. 14). Although in hindsight this process has often been represented as a coherent programme driven by ideology, the reality has been far more complex.

The drive towards increasing the proportion of ethnic minorities in the military stemmed from three interconnected factors. The first was that New Labour was elected into office in 1997 with a mandate that promised a substantial reorganisation of the country's defence policy (Cornish and Dorman 2009, p. 248). In his introduction to the Strategic Defence Review (SDR), published in 1998, Secretary of State for Defence, George Robertson, wrote the chillingly memorable words: 'The British are, by instinct, an internationalist people. We believe that as well as defending our rights, we should discharge our responsibilities in the world. We do not want to stand idly by and watch humanitarian disasters or the aggression of dictators go unchecked. We want to give a lead, we want to be a force for good' (Robertson 1998). The proposals laid out in the Review ranged from matters of global security to the minutiae of equipment to be used by each of the three services, and from the future shape of the armed forces to the conditions of service for both civilian and military personnel working within the defence sector.

The second factor was the chronic shortage of men that had plagued the armed forces since the end of conscription in 1960. In the early 1990s the military was facing an uncertain role in the post-Cold War environment; and, at the same time, the armed forces were struggling to maintain employment levels. By 1998 there was a deficit of at least 5000 personnel. 'The matter is not open to simple solutions', Minister for the Armed Forces John Reid told the House of Commons in a debate about the SDR. 'It involves a range of problems not only of numbers but of culture, retention, the nature of the modern armed forces and the nature of the community from which they draw their raw material.'[7]

Among the solutions to these problems was the widening of the recruitment pool to include ethnic minorities and homosexuals and a review of military occupations open to women. Seen in this light, the opportunities provided by the obligation to increase diversity offered a pragmatic approach to shortfalls in recruiting.

The third and related explanation for targeting minority recruits was the documented issue of racism inside the armed forces. In the same debate, Reid stated that 'We face a greater challenge in recruitment from the ethnic minorities. The armed forces have until relatively recently remained distanced from the progress in racial awareness made in other areas of society.'[8] He also made it clear that this was not merely the view of the new government. The Chief of the General Staff had earlier issued a press release confirming that 'The Army's view that there was a perception of racism inside the Army. The Chief of the General Staff – not politicians – made it plain that he would not tolerate it.'[9]

The SDR contained the statement that the government was 'determined that the Armed Forces should better reflect the ethnic composition of the British population'.[10] The rationale for increasing the percentage of ethnic minority recruits was presented in the context of employing 'our fair share of the best people this country has to offer'. This was partly connected to the theory that public bodies should reflect the socio-demographic mix of the country, an idea that had gained credibility as an instrument for dealing with institutional racism. It was also a recognition of the 'business case' since ethnic minorities provided a potential pool of young, fit recruits (Dandeker and Mason 2003). A paper outlining the policy shifts referred, somewhat obliquely, to the reasons the current figure was so low: 'We are also committed to making real progress on improving our record on equal opportunities through tackling the complex web of underlying factors which have inhibited people from various backgrounds choosing to join us in the past.'[11]

The history of under-recruitment reflected patterns of outright discrimination and exclusion which identified the armed forces as a particularly negligent employer. In 1997, for instance, the Office of Public Management released a damning report that found evidence of widespread racism in the armed forces.[12] The CRE had intervened in the army's grievance procedures in 1991 in order to give complainants an opportunity to sidestep internal procedures which were not seen to be impartial. In 1994 the CRE initiated a more formal inquiry into the Household Cavalry after two serious incidents of discrimination and bullying (Bellamy 1994) A year later, Mark Campbell, the first black trooper to join the Household Cavalry, was discharged from the Queen's

Life Guards on medical grounds. In his evidence he claimed that he had faced taunts of 'nigger', been handed a note saying 'there is no black in the Union Jack' and had his bed soaked with urine (BBC 2006). The regiment had come under scrutiny before for its suspected policy of hiring an all-white workforce, and it was no surprise that the resulting investigation found it to have contravened the law on several counts: direct and indirect discrimination in recruitment and selection; abuse and harassment of ethnic minority soldiers; inducement and instructions to discriminate (CRE 2000).

One of the results of the inquiry was that the MoD was threatened with a non-discrimination notice, but in 1997 this was deferred after the MoD agreed to work with the CRE to implement a campaign for equality across the armed forces. In March 1998 the MoD and the CRE signed a five-year Partnership Agreement which included an 'action plan' with a series of fresh initiatives intended to eliminate discrimination and harassment from the three services. Among these was the collection of data on minority recruitment to be presented and analysed in quarterly reports. Other forms of monitoring were to be introduced, along with new models of equality training and outreach schemes targeted at ethnic minority communities in the UK. An exhibition, entitled 'We Were There', was prepared by the MoD 'to honour the invaluable contribution made by the ethnic minorities to the Armed Forces for more than 200 years'.[13] The recruitment posters mentioned in the introduction were also part of this drive to target minorities as prospective recruits. The language of 'need' evidently expressed the legal pressures to take racism seriously as much as the ideological components of a state programme.

Britishness

In terms of numbers, the lengthy process of reform that began in the 1990s can be deemed a success story. In 2011 the figure for ethnic minorities in all three services and in all ranks was 6.7 per cent (DASA 2011). Among officers the figure was 2.4 per cent and other ranks, 7.6 per cent. In the British Army the percentages start to vary more widely: the overall figure rose to 9.6 per cent (2.8% among officers and 10.7% in other ranks). However, if we investigate how these figures were achieved, a more complicated picture emerges. From 1999 the figure for ethnic minorities started to rise exponentially, exceeding planned recruitment targets set by the SDR, but the increase had little to do with these measures. The ethno-racial diversity of the British Army today derives largely from migrants whose eligibility for military service began, as we have seen, as a strategy to cope with this crisis in recruitment and retention.[14] By the end of the decade the requisite targets for ethnic minorities had been reached and their numbers had risen from 360 to more than 6600.

So successful was the sustained recruitment drive in the eastern Caribbean and Fiji, that, concern began to be expressed that there might be too many minorities accumulating in particular sections of the army. In 2009 the government announced that a cap would be placed in certain sections of the army where the number of Commonwealth citizens was already approaching or had exceeded the 15 per cent mark (Norton-Taylor 2009). This was being done in the 'interests of operational effectiveness', Defence Secretary John Hutton explained, since the aim was to restrict the number of personnel whose foreign citizenship could leave them 'potentially subject to legislation contrary to our own decisions – on, for example, operational deployments' (ibid). The decision to apply the cap to certain trades was an outcome of extensive calculations aimed at steering a path between breaking the law of the land and damaging the army's attempts to be seen an enthusiastic equality and diversity employer. Introducing the decision to restrict foreign nationals in certain parts of the army, Hutton told the Commons that they had also borne in mind 'the importance of ensuring that the armed forces continue to be identified with and representative of the UK' (ibid).

Two years previously the *Daily Mail* had reported that 'Defence chiefs want to limit the number of Commonwealth troops in the Army to retain its "Britishness"' (Leake 2007). Under the headline: 'Race uproar over Army troop quota,' it reported that 'confidential papers prepared by the Army General Staff, headed by General Sir Richard Dannatt, suggest Commonwealth troops – mostly non-white – should be limited to 10 per cent of the 99,000 total.' One of the main reasons for restricting the number of Commonwealth troops was 'cultural'. The article only hinted at what this actually meant.

> One source said: 'The main reason is this view of Britishness, ensuring that the norms and values of society are reflected in its armed forces.' For example, gender equality in Britain means that the dominant view is that women should have a role in the armed forces. It's different in other countries (Leake 2007).

The implications of this statement were that some nationalities had issues serving alongside women, and that this was causing problems within the organisation. There was also a suggestion that foreign nationals produced more administrative work for the army due to logistical factors; but combined with the earlier point about 'norms and values', there was clearly a more substantial charge being made: that dealing with the different cultures of some of the Commonwealth soldiers was proving an additional burden that had not been anticipated. It was fortuitous that the rhetoric of Britishness promoted by Brown's government at the time allowed the legitimacy of a cap on migrant soldiers to pass as an imperative of social cohesion in the nation as a whole as well as a requirement for 'operational effectiveness'.

However, the same decade saw a number of other reforms that forced the armed forces to fall in line with the public sector. In 2005 the appointment of Buddhist, Muslim, Sikh and Hindu chaplains replaced a system whereby religious leaders were engaged as advisers on issues specific to each faith group. These non-uniformed civilians joined 300 commissioned Christian chaplains who, until then, bore responsibility for providing spiritual care for all members of the armed forces. This was a direct consequence of the Employment Equality Regulations which came into force in December 2003, incorporating the religion and belief elements of the European Employment Framework Directive into UK legislation. As the *Guide on Religion and Belief* published by the MoD made clear, this new legal obligation made it unlawful to discriminate against personnel on the grounds of religion or belief (MoD 2004–5):

> The Armed Forces and MOD Civil Service have been practising policies that respect individuals' religion or belief for some time. However, it is important to understand that, where in the past MOD as a matter of policy aimed not to discriminate, the new Regulations make discrimination on the grounds of religion or belief unlawful and give individuals a right to bring Employment Tribunal claims for breaches of the Regulations. (p. 5)

The transition to an officially multi-faith employer was thus mandated by law, reflecting the extent to which, as a national institution, the armed forces were obliged to conform to a corporate multiculturalist script.[15] Within a relatively short period, Muslim servicemen and women, in common with sexual minorities and other faith groups, saw the recognition of their position within the institution as an opportunity to organise their own forms of mutual support. In doing so they were able to articulate incontrovertible claims to citizenship as well as perform a strategic role within the defence–diplomacy nexus.

Bridging the gap

When the Imam took up the post of Muslim Chaplain to the Armed Forces in 2005, it was unclear how many Muslims were serving in the three services, although the majority were in the army and a significant proportion were migrants from Gambia and Nigeria. When comprehensive statistics began to be collected in 2007, a more accurate picture emerged (UKDS 2011). By 2009, when there were 500 Muslims in the regular armed forces, 410 of whom were in the army, the Armed Forces Muslim Association (AFMA) was set up as a support network for individual Muslims scattered across the institution. Writing in the first AFMA newsletter, the secretary of AFMA, Cpl Mohsin Al Mughal, spelled out the reasons it was so important for Muslims to be recognised within the armed forces: 'The make-up of the armed forces is increasingly becoming a mirror of modern-day Britain.' The AFMA was an important step in supporting 'this diverse community to maintain and foster their individual and respective cultural and religious beliefs, practices and identity' (Al Mughal 2010).

In the same publication Imam Hafiz explained how the organisation also hoped to persuade Muslim civilians about the significance of their work:

> Unfortunately there is a huge…ignorance in some parts of the Muslim community and I hope that AFMA will be able to bridge the gap between the Armed and the Muslim community and be a reminder that HM Forces are as integral to British society as are other British institutions such as the Police Force, the fire service and the NHS that are here to serve this nation as whole including the Muslim community. (Hafiz 2010)

By the end of 2010, the importance of acknowledging Muslims within the British armed forces was demonstrated in Helmand Province itself. On 16 November that year the Muslim chaplain gave a sermon to a multinational congregation in the festival of Eid ul Adha in conjunction with the Imam of the local 205 Corps of the Afghan National Army (ANA). A lengthy report on the MoD's Defence News site revealed that there were 600 Muslims present, including representatives from across International Security Assistance Force (ISAF) military forces, defence contractors and civilian workers as well as 'local Afghans'. The occasion was hailed as a reflection of 'the united relationship' between ISAF and the Afghan National Army (MoD 2012).

The report stated that, 'The sight of ISAF troops and the local community joining together to celebrate their faith offered some respite for the whole camp from the difficulties being faced in Afghanistan.' Linking the timing of the occasion to the services of remembrance held to mark Armistice Day, the Imam also played his part in emphasising that Muslims were integral to the mission in Afghanistan (MoD 2012). 'This mission', he continued, 'need not be a combat one but could be a partnership of development and progress for ordinary Afghans. ISAF has again demonstrated that Islam and the West are compatible, and that Muslims are proud citizens of their countries – they fly their flags with pride and willingly serve their nations.'

Proof that some military leaders had grasped the importance of diversity within the armed forces was provided when the Chief of the General Staff, General Sir David Richards, accepted the offer to become patron of the AFMA. Endorsing the launch of the organisation he observed that Britain 'had a commitment to Afghanistan and the region and all those Muslims with whom we have a natural identity, given our own core values reflect very strongly to those of Muslim faith (Versi 2009).[16] Meanwhile a decade of disastrous military expeditions had taught NATO forces that a better knowledge of 'culture' and specifically of 'cultural difference' was an essential tool in modern warcraft (Kilcullen 2006; Gusterson 2010, p. 280).

On the frontline

The representation of Muslim soldiers in Afghanistan as ambassadors for a multicultural Britain reinforces the centrality of culture in the War on Terror as well as the importance of propaganda, providing a link between the management of information about the aims and objectives of the global counter-insurgency and the representation of the war aims to sceptical publics at home. The BBC, a global institution which plays a strategic role in airing UK defence and security issues, demonstrated the salience of these calculations in a report in 2011 entitled 'UK's Muslim soldiers "fighting extremists not Muslims"', published the same day as a radio documentary, broadcast through its Asian network, called *Muslims on the Frontline* (Taneja 2011). In both items, journalist Poonam Taneja interviewed a number of British Muslim servicemen and women in Afghanistan as well as British Muslim opponents of the war. Cpl Raziya Aslam, for example, a citizen of the UK whose parents migrated from Pakistan before she was born, talked enthusiastically about her work as a linguist, acting as interpreter in negotiations with villagers. 'I don't see it as a war against Islam,' she said. Pte Shehab El-Din Ahmed El-Miniawi was reportedly even more emphatic: 'My home is the UK,' he said. 'As a Muslim, that's the place I'd happily die for and kill for. That's the same way it's going to remain until my dying day' (ibid).

Another informant was Zeeshan Hashmi, one of the first British Muslim servicemen to be deployed to Afghanistan in 2002 and a member of the Intelligence Corps for five years. In 2006, his brother Jabron Hashmi became the first British Muslim soldier to die in Afghanistan. Zeeshan spoke of the pride his family felt when they were asked to lay the foundation stone for the National Memorial Arboretum which was opened in 2007. Since his brother's death they had received over 100 letters from well-wishers of all faith and backgrounds, which, he said, were a great source of comfort. However, he also described how 'There were certain remarks put on the Internet, on a given website, certain people see my brother as a traitor because of his role as a soldier, because of his role in the armed forces, in Afghanistan' (ibid).

The importance of employing Muslims 'on the front line' was emphasised by the MoD as well. In 2010, the website hosting the 'We Were There' exhibition was revised and updated, placing the original project within a revised historical perspective. The first incarnation, launched a decade earlier, was intended as 'a significant statement about the contribution of Britain's ethnic minority communities to UK defence over the last 250 years', explained the new introduction. The initiative was seen at the time as an educational resource describing the benefits of cultural diversity as well as helping to promote 'better understanding between communities by showing how men and women from Africa, Asia, the West Indies and other Commonwealth countries fought and served alongside British forces during many major conflicts'.[17]

In the more recent version, a new dimension was added which provided evidence that the role of military history in asserting the rights of minorities had become more important in the meantime, particularly in the context of debates about Britishness and national identity. 'For students of history and citizenship,' the new website suggested, 'the exhibition offers a wider and more inclusive perspective of our military past. It demonstrates how people from different religions, races, and cultures came together at times of great social, political, military and geographical change to help create and then defend the British Empire and democratic freedom. What has surprised many people is that most of those who served from the colonies were volunteers, including the whole of the Indian Army.'

The final page of the current exhibition was the most relevant because it illustrated the convergence of diversity management with national security, foreign policy and the proliferation of roles that national militaries were expected to play. 'The MOD and the Armed Forces now operate on a global scale,' read the text, 'in a wide variety of roles such as war fighting, counter-terrorism, defence diplomacy, peacekeeping and the delivery of humanitarian aid.'[18] The expanded list of military roles from war fighting to peacekeeping reflected the transformations in global warcraft that had taken place in the intervening years. The constellation of geopolitical, technological, economic and moral factors that sanction the deployment of NATO forces was neatly compressed under the much-laundered banner heralding international peace and stability, thus concealing the true costs of the global counter-insurgency, aggressive nuclear proliferation and the rapid fragmentation and privatisation of military work.

The same panel reiterated the importance of representing and including minorities: 'Men and women from ethnic minorities make up 5.6% of the Armed Forces and 2.9% of the MOD and Civil Service. They all contribute to the common aim of defending their country through strengthening international peace and stability and being a force for good in the world.' But it was the image that captured the fused political imperatives of a securitised multiculturalism. It showed the back view of a uniformed man giving the thumbs up to a Chinook helicopter delivering aid, with a caption that read: 'Flight Lieutenant Sohail Khan in Pakistan where he helped with the earthquake relief effort.'[19] The choice of this image demonstrated that military service was not about fighting Muslim antagonists, it was about helping them, bringing aid to the vulnerable in the interests of global security.

Enemies within

The question Can you have Muslim soldiers? dramatises the connection between what happens inside the armed forces and the purpose of the operations they are required to carry out. In other words, it accepts that the institution's approach to racism and diversity among its workforce is intrinsically related to foreign policy, national security and the global counter-insurgency. While statutory obligations have ensured that military institutions take equality and diversity seriously, the uneven pace of reform must be analysed against a background of intense deployment in unpopular wars as well as increased securitisation at home.

During this period war has become normalised in the political life of the UK. One consequence is that the figure of the soldier is ubiquitous throughout the media, constantly visible in news, military bulletins, films, digital games, forums, art and photography. The image of the flag-draped coffin, however, remains a site of intense struggle, over not just the meanings of military sacrifice but also the perceived value of the war in which the individual soldier 'gave' their life. Until the repatriation of bodies was re-routed in 2011, the homecoming parades at Wootton Bassett demonstrated the volatile mix of political opportunism, public alarm and private grief that resulted from the deaths of soldiers in Helmand Province. Paying close attention to the figure of the soldier as a particular kind of worker-citizen can expose the hidden material and financial resources that are required to commit the country to war. It can also provide a focus for tracking the ideological energy involved in securing public acquiescence, and in marginalising opposition as a form of disloyalty to the national state. (Ware 2010a).

Following the mass demonstrations against the proposed invasion of Iraq in 2003, oppositional spaces for protesting against war have steadily diminished. In 2005, activist Maya Evans became the first person to be convicted under Section 132 of the Serious Organised Crime and Police Act, the controversial new law that banned unauthorised protests from taking place within half a mile of Westminster. At the time she was reading out the names of soldiers killed in Iraq in solidarity with Military Families Against the War, a group formed in opposition to what they saw as Blair's cavalier attitude to the safety of UK soldiers. But as anti-war protestors attempted to hold a line between ambivalent support for ordinary soldiers and criticism of the politicians that deployed them, interventions such as the Military Covenant Campaign and the charity Help for Heroes effectively rendered the concept of military service as an exceptional form of employment undertaken for the benefit of the nation as a whole, regardless of the rights and wrongs of the war in question. One effect was to narrow the ground on which protestors have been able to express dissent against military operations in Afghanistan, Libya and Somalia.

Meanwhile, those Islamist groups and individuals who opposed the War on Terror on the basis that fellow Muslims were being slaughtered by British soldiers have come under particularly intense surveillance. Militant groups such as Islam4UK and Muslims Against Crusades, which articulated vocal opposition at soldiers' homecoming marches and commemorative ceremonies, were systematically banned under the Terrorism Act 2000 on the grounds that they were glorifying terrorism. Muslims who were prepared to enlist were not only threatened by members of these groups, but their participation in the armed forces was cast as a form of apostasy. In 2008, for example, Parvis Khan, pleaded guilty to plotting the kidnap and execution of a British Muslim soldier, which he planned to film and release for propaganda purposes (Gardham 2008). During this period, the mobilisation of the fascist English Defence League under the banner of fighting the spectre of Islamic extremism infused racism and Islamaphobia with militaristic expressions of patriotism, masculinity and whiteness.

More recently, increased surveillance of social media sites has led to the criminalisation of those who criticise soldiers on Facebook. In March 2012, teenager Azhar Ahmed was charged with racially aggravated public order after posting angry comments about the publicity given to the deaths of six UK soldiers in Afghanistan.[20] This charge was subsequently amended to one of sending a message that was grossly offensive under the Communications Act 2003. At his hearing, protestors from the group Combined Ex Forces carried banners that read: 'Jail those who insult our troops' (Champion 2012). This case can be linked to an earlier incident in Coventry when a group of five Muslim boys and a non-Muslim girl calling themselves the 'Muslim Defence League' were investigated by police after posting threats of violence on a classmate's wall. The 13-year-old boy had written a supportive comment about British troops with two photos of Armistice Day, and in response the group had announced their intention to kill him (Ellicott 2010).

These incidents have contributed to a further identification of Muslim citizens who are critics of UK foreign policy as a homogenous and unpatriotic section of the population. There has been minimal attention paid to the impact that Blair's wars have had on younger generations, many of whom were barely in primary school in 2001. Research among young Pakistani Muslims in Birmingham, for example, has indicated that many have responded to the questioning of their citizenship in the media 'with reflexivity, introspection and explicit political engagement' (Qureshi and Zeitlyn 2013, p. 16).

The young Pakistanis had joined in enthusiastically in public protests against the wars in Iraq and Afghanistan. Whilst echoing the wider patriotic terming of the armed forces as 'our boys', they understood them as victims of the conflicts and the new imperialism. Their analysis stressed the role of power and imperialism in the war and the deaths of civilians and combatants on both sides. (ibid)

War crimes

This chapter has attempted to describe the importance of military work for delineating the grounds for inclusion in and exclusion from national citizenship in the UK. In doing so, it has argued for a rethinking of what is meant by multiculturalism and a radical re-evaluation of its effects on British public life. While comparison with other national institutions such as the police and prison service can be useful, the armed forces play a unique role in mediating between domestic and international politics (Krebs 2004, p. 123). A critical examination of the ways in which military organisations have weathered the external pressures to diversify their workforces is therefore important but not sufficient. It is a task that is inseparable from the work of monitoring and resisting the ways in which the national community becomes defined by and inured to militarism as a defining aspect of British national identity.

In this final section I suggest that the equality and diversity laws that protect soldiers' individual and collective rights must be studied in relation to the enforcement of military regulations governing the treatment of civilians and detainees by occupying armies. In the British Army, for instance, the overlap between these two policy areas has resulted in a renewed commitment to inculcate 'the military ethos' through teaching a set of core values, one of which is 'respect for others' (Aitken 2008).[21]

It was these same values to which former Chief of the General Staff General Dannatt referred when, in 2011, he told a theological think-tank that society was no longer providing new recruits with 'an understanding of the core values and standards of behaviour' that the military looked for in young people. 'Given that much of our society is pretty unstructured these days,' he wrote, 'and given that the military has the unique opportunity to educate its own into the importance of a proper moral understanding, then perhaps the military community may have a wider contribution that it can make to the nation' (Dannatt 2011). His thrust was that the concept of values was a defining characteristic of military culture, differentiating it from civilian society, which was perceived as individualistic and amoral. The mental and moral preparation of our soldiers was as important as their physical training, he declared. 'They must be able to kill and show compassion at the same time; they must be loyal to their country, their regiment and their friends without compromising their own integrity.' One implication of his speech was that the army could not be blamed if individual soldiers failed to live up to these values. Much more controversial was his claim that civil society could benefit from adopting the values espoused by the military.

His intervention took place shortly after the inquiry into the unlawful killing of Iraqi citizen Baha Mousa reported that had been 'an appalling episode of serious gratuitous violence' (Cecil and Cheston 2011). The Gage report, published in 2011, revealed that the chain of command right up to the MoD was implicated both in the atrocities and in subsequent attempts to investigate. Baha Mousa was one of seven suspected insurgents arrested by British soldiers while working as a hotel receptionist in Basra, southern Iraq, in September 2003. The men, who were innocent of any crime, were systematically abused and tortured while they were held in detention, resulting in Mousa's death 36 hours later. An extract from a press report of the inquiry detailed their treatment at the hands of the soldiers.

> The seven hotel workers, together with three other men arrested later the same day, were hooded with hessian sandbags by Cpl Donald Payne as soon as they arrived at the TDF. Soon afterwards, one detainee described 'being beaten and having his feet kicked into a stress position'. For most of the next 36 hours Baha Mousa would be hooded and kept in a 'ski' position, with legs apart and bent at 45 degrees and hands raised, whilst being subjected to repeated beatings. Soldiers would also kick and punch him if his arms began to drop or he relaxed in any way.
>
> The men described having fingers pressed in their eye sockets, water being squeezed into their mouths and being kicked in the genitals and kidneys while they were kneeling. One man said he had petrol rubbed in his face before a cigarette lighter was lit close to him...One of the prisoners, referred to in the report as D001, described how the detainees would be 'arranged in a circle on their knees, and soldiers going around the circle hitting and kicking' them, which made them 'emit groans and other noises and thereby playing them like musical instruments.' (Rayner 2011)

Mousa was found to have sustained 93 injuries while he was bound and hooded in conditions of 'intense heat and extreme squalor'.(Bingham and Hough 2011) After an internal inquiry headed by Brigadier Aitken, seven members of the 1st Battalion, the Queen's Lancashire Regiment, were court-martialed in 2007, including the battalion's former commanding officer Jorge Mendonca. Only one was found guilty. The MoD agreed to pay £2.83m compensation to the ten Iraqis who were tortured (BBC 2008), and the subsequent report made recommendations to change internal procedures. However, there was lingering evidence of complicity among more senior personnel, and doubts about the reliability of the Royal Military Police who carried out the internal investigation.

In 2008 a public inquiry was ordered by then Defence Secretary Des Browne, and it was to become a ground-breaking examination of military conduct in the aftermath of the Iraq invasion. In a devastating indictment of military culture, retired appeal court judge Sir William Gage's 1400-page report, released in September 2011, ruled there was widespread ignorance of the correct way to deal with prisoners of war, and that senior officers bore a 'heavy responsibility' for troops using banned interrogation techniques. The impact of this investigation, and of the earlier army-led Aitken Inquiry in 2008, would be profound, leading to a revision of the procedures involved in the detention of prisoners: 'Managing the process of detention properly is now a mainstream military skill which requires mandatory education, specific permissions, and well-practised procedures' (Wall 2011).

Just as the Macpherson report acknowledged the extent of 'institutional racism' within the Metropolitan Police in 1999, so this inquiry in 2011 laid bare the extent of the army's culpability in failing to prepare soldiers to handle civilian detainees in a war situation and then protecting those soldiers who were guilty. Dannatt's successor, CGS General Sir Peter Wall, admitted that Baha Mousa's death in 2004 cast a 'dark shadow' over the Army's reputation. He articulated the conventional pact between the national armed forces and civilian society in his acceptance that 'The nation places its trust in us and we expect our soldiers' conduct to reflect that trust.'

Despite this summoning of the nation as an entity that could be betrayed by the actions of a few, the responsibility was seen to fall squarely within the institution rather than reflect attitudes and behaviours emanating from UK culture more generally. In an interview with *Guardian* journalists, Lt Col Nicholas Mercer, the army's former chief legal adviser in Iraq, accused the MoD of 'moral ambivalence' and a 'cultural resistance to human rights' that allowed British troops to abuse detainees (Norton-Taylor 2011).

While Dannatt had fully condemned what had happened in Iraq, he would also have known that further revelations would continue to emerge as other families who suffered abuse at the hands of British soldiers sought compensation. Although the Baha Mousa inquiry formally ended in late 2011, campaigning lawyers continue to pursue two further inquiries with wide-ranging remits to investigate allegations that UK forces abused and unlawfully killed Iraqi civilians while they controlled parts of southern Iraq (Marsden 2012). After more than a decade of military operations in Afghanistan, it is likely that the UK armed forces will continue to face legal challenges of abuse and unlawful killing for many years to come (Cobain 2012).

Britain's more recent military exploits, particularly under Blair's leadership from 1997 to 2007, have clearly had momentous effects on public perceptions of the place of the military in society. Military institutions constitute a valuable field of postcolonial study because it is here, at the intersection of defence, security and foreign policy, that the country's adjustment to the loss of empire is registered on multiple levels. The modern history of the British Army, which includes the reform of the ways soldiers are treated as employees as well as how they handle their detainees, can only be understood against the backdrop of Britain's transition from a once imperial power to its current status as a junior partner of the USA within NATO. In this protracted scenario, racism continues to bind the politics of postcolonial citizenship to the bloody context of military occupation and the conduct of war itself.

Acknowledgements

I am grateful to James Rhodes, Nisha Kapoor and Benjamin Zeitlyn for commenting on earlier versions of this piece.

Notes

1. House of Commons. HC Deb 28 October 1997 vol 299 cc724–808. 724 http://hansard.millbanksystems.com/commons/1997/oct/28/defence-policy#S6CV0299P0_19971028_HOC_201, accessed 15 February 2012.
2. http://www.army.mod.uk/join/25629.aspx, accessed 12 February 2012.
3. http://www.dasa.mod.uk/modintranet/UKDS/UKDS2011/c2/table214.php.
4. Trained UK Regular Forces by Service and nationality at 1 April 2011. Obtained under FOI.
5. Ministry of Defence. What We Do. Personnel. Equality and Diversity. Foreword by PUS and CDS. http://goo.gl/Lo6Zv, accessed 10 January 2012.
6. Online. Available at http://www.nam.ac.uk/exhibitions/permanent-galleries/conflicts-interest-1969-present/gallery-highlights/equality, accessed 15 March 2011.

7. House of Commons HC Deb 28 October 1997, vol. 299 cc728–29, http://goo.gl/PntWc, accessed 15 February 2012.
8. House of Commons HC Deb 28 October 1997, vol. 299 cc728–730, http://goo.gl/jJGFk, accessed 15 February 2012.
9. Ibid.
10. Modern Forces for the Modern World, Strategic Defence Review, July 1998, Supporting Essay Nine, 'A Policy for People', section 41, p. 214.
11. Ibid., Introduction, p. 205.
12. National Army Museum, NAM 1998-10-244, Equality. http://goo.gl/YA9XS accessed 20 October 2011.
13. The exhibition was launched by the Minister of State for the Armed Forces, Mr John Spellar and the Chair of the Commission for Racial Equality, Mr Gurbux Singh. The We Were There exhibition. Ministry of Defence, launched 28 November 2000. http://goo.gl/tNuWb, accessed 30 October 2011.
14. In 2004–5, for example, the shortfall of trained soldiers rose by 300 per cent, and although recruitment improved the following year, with an increase of 9.2 per cent, poor retention of existing personnel led to an overall shortfall of 1,500. http://goo.gl/bNI3x, accessed 13 April 2012.
15. By 2010, the list of other faiths recorded in the annual survey of religious backgrounds for 2010 included Buddhist (0.3%), Sikh and Christian tradition, meaning Seventh Day Adventists, Jehovah's Witnesses, Mormons and others (0.1%), Hindu (0.6%), Muslim and other religions (0.5%). Minority religions included Druid, Pagan, Rastafarian, Spiritualist, Zoroastrian (Parsee), Wicca and Baha'i.
16. In the same interview Richards also said, 'It is very important for the Muslim community to be exposed to an alternative view as it is for the rest of the nation. The Taliban kill many more Muslims than we do.'
17. Introduction, 'We Were There', MoD, http://goo.gl/6iLtl, accessed 30 October 2011.
18. 'We Were There' home page.http://goo.gl/OJoN0, accessed 31 October 2011.
19. The exhibition was subsequently updated to provide short biographical accounts of individuals, including Sohail Khan. However, underneath his personal entry, the same image of Khan working in Pakistan was featured, with the caption: a Chinook helicopter. http://goo.gl/ll2LU, accessed 28 February 2012.
20. In 2012 a Yorkshire teenager was charged with a racially aggravated public order offence after posting on Facebook allegedly offensive comments about six UK soldiers killed in Afghanistan. 'Teen Charged Over Dead Soldiers Facebook Post', *Sky News*, Monday 12 March 2012, http://goo.gl/TeMwb, accessed 16 March 2012.Noting that there was nothing in the incriminating post that mentioned race or religion, one commentator remarked that: '"Soldier" is not a race but, if you're Muslim in Britain, you can pretty much forget any freedom of speech niceties that we bandy around when we compare ourselves to despotic foreign regimes that crush peoples' human rights.' 'SHUT YOUR FACEBOOK. Anti-occupation rant leaves one Facebook user facing serious charges', *Weekly Schnews, Brighton,* 16 March 2012, http://goo.gl/F1vn3, accessed 17 March 2012.

21. See also 'Values and Standards of the British Army', 2008. AC 64813. http://www.army.mod.uk/documents/general/v_s_of_the_british_army.pdf, accessed 10 February 2011.

References

Aitken Report (2008) *An Investigation into Cases of Deliberate Abuse and Unlawful Killing in Iraq in 2003 and 2004*, Ministry of Defence, 25 January 2008, http://www.mod.uk/NR/rdonlyres/7AC894D3–1430–4AD1–911F-8210C3342CC5/0/aitken_rep.pdf

Al Mughal, Cpl M. (2010). Secretary AFMA, 'Journey of AFMA', Armed Forces Muslim Newsletter, July 2010, pp. 4–5.

BBC (2006) 'Oldest Regiment Serves Dual Role', *BBC News*, 25 January 2006, http://goo.gl/1Ui1n

Bellamy, C. (1996) 'Army Pledges to Stamp Out Racism in Ranks', *The Independent*, 28 March 1996. http://goo.gl/DAVtt

BBC (2008) 'Timeline: Iraqi Abuse Trial', *BBC News UK*, 10 July 2008, http://goo.gl/a8MkS

Bingham, J. & Hough, A. (2011) 'Baha Mousa Inquiry: Soldiers Suspended in "Dark" Day for Army', *Daily Telegraph*, 8 September 2011, http://www.telegraph.co.uk/news/uknews/defence/8749760/Baha-Mousa-inquiry-soldiers-suspended-in-dark-day-for-Army.html

Cecil, N. & Cheston, P. (2011) 'Day of Shame for British Army as 14 Soldiers Suspended over Horrific Killing', *London Evening Standard*, 8 September 2011, http://goo.gl/AOnUr.

Champion, M. (2012) 'Azhar Ahmed to Stand Trial over Facebook Post About Dead Soldiers', *Metro*, 20 March 2012, http://goo.gl/g3dXj

Cobain, I. (2012) 'RAF Helicopter Death Revelation Leads to Secret Iraq Detention Camp', *Guardian*, 7 February 2012, http://goo.gl/xFuYk

Cornish, P. and Dorman, A. (2009) 'Blair's Wars and Brown's Budgets: from Strategic Defence Review to Strategic Decay in Less Than a Decade', *International Affairs*, 85(2), 247–61.

Cowen D. (2008) *Military Workfare: The Soldier and Social Citizenship in Canada* (Toronto: University of Toronto Press).

Commission for Racial Equality (CRE) (2000) Memorandum from the Commission for Racial Equality, Select Committee on Defence, Parliamentary Business, 2 October 2000, http://goo.gl/xdutb

Dandeker, C. (1994) 'New Times for the Military: Some Sociological Remarks on the Changing Role and Structure of the Armed Forces of the Advanced Societies', *The British Journal of Sociology*, 45(4), 637–54.

Dandeker, C. & Mason, D. (2003) 'Diversifying the Uniform? The Participation of Minority Ethnic Personnel in the British Armed Services', *Armed Forces & Society* 29(4), 481–507.

Dannatt, CGS, Gen. Sir R. (2011) 'Military Must Teach Morals', Defence Management, 8 November 2011, http://goo.gl/nRAX4

DASA (2011) 2.10. Strength of UK Regular Forces by Service, Ethnic Origin and Rank. Defence Analytical Service and Advice, UK Defence Statistics.

Ellicott, C. (2010) 'Five Muslim Boys and White Girl, All 12, Excluded over Facebook Death Threats to Classmate Who Supported British Troops', *Daily Mail*, 18 November 2010. http://goo.gl/ucpMk

Finney, N. Capt. (2010) 'A Culture of Inclusion: Defense, Diplomacy, and Development as a Modern American Foreign Policy', *Small Wars Journal*, September 2010. http://smallwarsjournal.com/jrnl/art/a-culture-of-inclusion

Forster, Anthony. (2006) 'Breaking the Covenant: Governance of the British Army in the Twenty-first Century', *International Affairs*, 82(6), 1043–57.

Forster, A. (2012) 'The Military Covenant and British Civil-Military Relations: Letting the Genie out of the Bottle', *Armed Forces & Society*, 38(2), 273–90.

Gardham, D. (2008) Man Guilty over Muslim Soldier Beheading Plot', *Daily Telegraph*, 15 February 2008, http://goo.gl/VhfXJ

Goldberg D.T. (2009) *The Threat of Race: Reflections on Racial Neoliberalism* (Oxford: Wiley Blackwell).

Gusterson, H. (2010) 'The Cultural Turn in the War on Terror', in J. D. Kelly, B. Jauregui, S. T. Mitchell, and J. Walton (eds), *Anthropology and Global Counterinsurgency* (Chicago: University of Chicago Press), pp. 279–96.

Hafiz, A. Imam (2010) 'The Love of Your Country Is Part of Your Faith', Armed Forces Muslim Newsletter, July 2010, pp. 6–8.

Hesse, B. (ed.) (2000) *Un/settled Multiculturalisms: Diasporas, Entanglements, Transruptions* (London: Zed Books).

Kilcullen, D. (2006) 'Twenty-Eight Articles: Fundamentals of Company-level Counterinsurgency', edition 1, March 2006, http://goo.gl/VsIoY

Krebs, R. (2009) 'The Citizen-Soldier Tradition in the United States: Has Its Demise Been Greatly Exaggerated?' *Armed Forces & Society*, 36(1), 153–74.

Leake, C. (2007) 'Race Uproar over Army Troop Quota', *Mail Online*, 1 April 2007, http://goo.gl/k9C59

Marsden, S. (2012) 'New Iraq War Inquiry Set to Open', *The Independent*, 2 January 2012. http://goo.gl/vb5BY

Mason, D. & Dandeker, C. (2009) 'Evolving UK Policy on Diversity in the Armed Services: Multiculturalism and its Discontents', *Commonwealth & Comparative Politics*, 47(4), 393–410.

Ministry of Defence (2004–5) 'Guide on Religion and Belief in the MoD and Armed Forces'. Designed and produced by TES-TI Media. Bath, http://goo.gl/FZ6Is

MoD (2010) 'British Imam Leads Eid celebrations in Kandahar', Ministry of Defence, *Defence News*. 19 November 2010, http://goo.gl/Eg4l1

Norton-Taylor, R. (2009) 'Army Puts Cap on Number of Foreign Recruits', *The Guardian*, 3 February 2009, http://goo.gl/LozNQ

Norton-Taylor, R. (2011) 'MoD's Resistance to Human Rights in Iraq Blamed for Death of Baha Mousa', *The Guardian*, 24 November 2011, http://goo.gl/shcPq

Parekh, B. (2000) *The Future of Multi-Ethnic Britain: The Parekh Report* (London: Profile Books).

Paul, K. (1998) 'From Subjects to Immigrants', in R. Weight, R. and A. Beach, A. (eds), *The Right to Belong: Citizenship and National Identity, 1930–1969* (London: LB Taurus), pp. 223–43.

Qureshi, K. & Zeitlyn, B. (2013) 'British Muslims, British Soldiers: Cultural Citizenship in the New Imperialism', *Ethnicities*, (13)1, 110–26.

Rayner, G. (2011) 'Baha Mousa: How a Young Father Met His Violent Death at the Hands of British Soldiers', *Daily Telegraph*, 8 September 2011, http://goo.gl/xaXLC

Roberston, G. (1998) Introduction, 19. Strategic Defence Review. July. Ministry of Defence.

Somers, M. R. (2008) *Genealogies of Citizenship* (Cambridge: Cambridge University Press).

Taneja, P. (2011) 'UK's Muslim Soldiers "Fighting Extremists not Muslims"' *BBC News*, 21 February, 2011, http://goo.gl/uWiYv

Taneja, P. (2011a) 'Muslims on the Frontline', Asian Network Reports Special, *BBC Asian Network*, 21 February 2011.

Taylor, M. (2009) 'Army Recruitment Surge due to Patriotism and Recession', *The Guardian*, 27 September 2009, http://goo.gl/RwrKE

UK Defence Statistics (2011) *Chapter 2.13: Strength of UK Regular Forces by Service and Religion, at 1 April each year*, http://goo.gl/VgA86

Versi, A. J. (2009) 'Army Chief Admits Failure to Convince Muslims over Afghan Policy', *The Muslim News*, issue 247, 27 November – 10 Dhu al-Hijjah 1430, http://goo.gl/OZ1Vs

Wall, CGS Gen. Sir P, (2011) 'Chief of the General Staff Responds to Baha Mousa Inquiry Report', MoD Defence Policy and Business, 8 September 2011, http://goo.gl/4zf3T

Ware, V. (2010a) 'Lives on the Line', *Soundings*, issue 45, summer 2010, pp.147–58.

Ware, V. (2010b) 'Whiteness in the Glare of War: Soldiers, Migrants and Citizenship' *Ethnicities*, 10(3), 313–30.

Ware, V. (2012) *Military Migrants: Fighting for YOUR Country* (Basingstoke: Palgrave Macmillan).

7

'Prevent'ing Education: Anti-Muslim Racism and the War on Terror in Schools

Shamim Miah

Introduction

Since the events of the 2001 riots, 9/11 and the terrorist attacks in London in 2005, we have witnessed in Western Europe an 'end of [state] multiculturalism' (McGhee 2008), replaced by a policy debate on the integration of Muslim communities within a heightened security context. These policy debates on racialised minority groups have coincided with the emergence and popular appeal of a 'new British fascism' (Goodwin 2011) in the form of British National Party (BNP), English Defence League (EDL) and the Infidels of Britain. This chapter will focus on the dichotomy between the rhetorical discourse of 'postrace', and the securitised governance of racialised minority groups within the context of education and schooling. It will discuss how the national meta-discourse of Muslims as a 'pariah group', as informed through the 'Bush years' (Imtiaz 2009), shapes the experiences of anti-Muslim racism within schooling. In the first section I explore the intense educational policy imperative which has emerged during the last decade and has attempted to address the 'Muslim question' through ethnic integration, segregation and securitised de-radicalisation policies. Major socio-political and security events at an international and domestic level have given way to policy approaches attempting to address the 'Muslim question' by problematising and pathologising Muslims. The second section will draw on empirical data and highlight how the framing of Muslims at a national level informs the experiences of anti-Muslim racism within the context of schooling. I conclude by suggesting that, since the publication of the MacDonald Inquiry into 'Murder in the Playground' over

20 years ago (MacDonald et al. 1989), racism continues to shape the experiences of Muslims in British schools.

'Postrace' and Schooling

The postracial has been theorised as representative of the disconnect between dominant racial rhetoric, which claims we are 'postrace', implying race is no longer the salient excluding marker that it once was, and the continuing racist practices of the state and institutions which impact on the racial experiences of many racialised minorities (Goldberg 2009). This postracial sentiment has featured strongly in the policy framing of the Stephen Lawrence Inquiry, which resurfaced in January 2012 following the sentencing of two of Lawrence's killers, David Norris and Gary Dobson. Despite initial claims signalling a landmark shift in British race history, where even the *Daily Mail* reported the Inquiry as a 'damming report on race murder [that] will change Britain' (cited in Gillborn 2008, p. 125), little has been done subsequently to implement the report's recommendations. Drawing upon the Critical Race Theory (CRT) tradition (Delgado and Stefancic 2001), Gillborn (2008) sees the Lawrence Inquiry as a *contradiction-closing case*, whereby 'occasional symbolic victories' are used to indicate that meaningful change has occurred, when in reality very little change has taken shape. So, despite the optimism and the focusing of public attention on institutional racism, racism within the police, and the public duty to promote racial equality, the experiences for many minority communities remain less informed by these more progressive acknowledgements and more informed by the new forms of exclusion and targeting based upon the legacies of the War on Terror. For example, following the London bombings of 2005 there has been conscious racial profiling of young Muslim men, which was publicly defended by the Chief Constable of the British Transport Police and supported by the then minister at the Home Office, Hazel Blears MP (Gillborn 2008).

Within the context of education, entrenched racisms remain evident, despite the changes promised by the Lawrence Inquiry. Firstly, we have witnessed an increase in racist incidents within schools in the UK. In response to a Freedom of Information request, it was disclosed that 88,000 incidents of racist bullying were recorded in British schools between 2007 and 2011. Some areas, such as Oldham, Luton, Croydon and Middlesbrough, saw an increase of 40 per cent or more over the period 2007/08 to 2009/10 (Talwar 2012). Secondly, despite occasional success stories of ethnic minority achievement in educational league tables, racial inequality is so profoundly embedded in the educational system that some educational sociologists are talking about *'locked-in inequality'*, that is, a situation where the levels of inequality are so deep that the removal of existing barriers will not create a level playing field (Gillborn 2008). Finally, we have seen the implementation of integration and counter-terrorism discourses and practices, whereby certain groups are pathologised and put under greater scrutiny within a security context.

Framing Muslims: Politics of Anti-Muslim Prejudice

Islam is often presented as being diametrically opposite to the West. The former is often projected as obscurantist, undemocratic and misogynistic, whilst the latter is seen as secular, advanced and grounded upon the principles of liberalism. Whilst this type of reasoning has gained particular momentum following the events of 9/11 and 7/7, the ideological antecedents have a long intellectual and historical tradition and can be traced back to the eighth century and the rise of Islam as a dominant political force (Said 1978, 1997; Daniel 1991; Sardar 1999; Macfie 2000). A strong critical response to this form of Manichean framing of the 'other' has been developed by a number of academics and policy analysts. The framing of the 'other' or the non-European is, for Said (1978, 1997) and Tibawi (1964), largely associated with the colonial positioning of the non-European as an inferior, antiquated and alien subject of the West. The 'other' is formed through Western ideological biases articulated through scholarship and systems of thought. The current treatment of Muslims, as discussed by Back et al. (2002), Fekete (2008, 2009) and Kalra and Kapoor (2009), is seen as part of a continuation of the colonial legacy and the racialised political treatment of minority communities in Britain. And, of course, this is deeply intertwined with the centrality of race in the development and emergence of the modern nation state, as Goldberg (2002) has demonstrated in his discussions of the writings of those such as John Locke, Friedrich Hegel and John Stuart Mill. The central themes that emerge from this literature are, firstly, the importance of locating anti-Muslim prejudice within a wider historical setting; secondly, the recognition of power dynamics in understanding racialised minority groups; and, thirdly, the influence of the state or the racial state in 'producing and reproducing racist ends and outcomes' for racialised groups (Goldberg 2002, p. 113).

The increasing Muslim presence in Europe, together with the growing security concerns about Muslim communities, has given rise to this discursive framing of the Muslim problematic, often labelled as anti-Muslim racism (Kundnani 2007) and Islamophobia (Runnymede Trust 2004; Marranci 2004; Allen 2010). Both notions reflect dominant approaches which have attempted to make sense of the current discourse on integration within a wider context of 'new racism' (Barker 1981). Islamophobia came to public attention following the publication of *Islamophobia: A Challenge for Us All* by the Runnymede Trust (1997). The report defined Islamophobia as 'referring to dread or hatred of Islam and, therefore, to fear or dislike of all or most Muslims'. Thus it is not surprising to note that the Runnymede Trust places anti-Muslim prejudice within its subtext.[1] The report articulates the 'hatred of Islam' by exploring the *Closed and Open View of Islam*[2] and a detailed assessment of anti-Muslim prejudice in British society, including the criminal justice system, the media and religiously motivated attacks, thus combining the macro framing of Islam with the micro experiences of Muslims in Britain. This is further articulated by the following:

> The term Islamophobia refers to the unfounded hostility towards Islam. It refers also to the practical consequences of hostility in unfair discrimination against Muslim individuals and communities, and to the exclusion of Muslims from mainstream political and social affairs (Runnymede Trust 1997, p. 1).

The Runnymede Trust's follow-up report *Islamophobia: Issues, Challenges and Action* (2004) highlighted how hostility towards Islam and Muslims has taken various forms over 'different times and different contexts' (Runnymede Trust 2004, p.7). The report acknowledges how, within the context of 9/11 and 7/7, Islamophobia has become pervasive and has developed a global reach, with an increasing characterisation of a humanised West and a de-humanised 'other'. Marranci (2004), also drawing upon a contextualised reading of Islamophobia, suggests that it is not an unfounded prejudice against Islam, but rather one whose roots lie in European perceptions of Islam acting as a 'transruptive force' with regard to Judeo-Christian values. Marranci (2004, p.2) goes on to argue that some of the contemporary concerns about multiculturalism lie in 'Europe's fear that, in a real multicultural environment, Islam might transform what Europe is today'. This is further supported by Fekete (2009) who has demonstrated how the political discourse on Muslims in Europe often accuses Muslim cultural practices of representing a 'threat' to Europe from within. She also notes how 'the adherence to Islamic norms and values threatens the notion of Europeaness itself' (Fekete 2009, p.44). Similarly, Allen (2010) sees Islamophobia as akin to a *new racism* which essentialises and demonises Muslims as the 'other'; as a result, Muslims are likely to be on the receiving end of discriminatory practices. This is further clarified by Allen's definition of Islamophobia:

> Islamophobia is an ideology, similar in theory, function and purpose to racism and other similar phenomena, that sustains and perpetrates negatively evaluated meaning about Muslims and Islam in contemporary setting in similar ways in which it has historically ... As a consequence of this, exclusionary practices – practices that disadvantage, prejudice or discriminate against Muslims and Islam in the social, economic and political sphere ensue, including the subjection to violence – are in evidence. (Allen 2010, p. 190)

Allen brings together the discursive ideological function of Islamaphobia with the practical discrimination faced by Muslims (and others who look like them). In that sense, where the focus is on the institutional and practical forms, then the concept of anti-Muslim racism, which builds upon colonial and orientalist schemata, is best used to explain the phenomenon of 'new racism' in this current context, as a term that focuses less on the hostility against Islam and more on the aggression and prejudice against Muslims – that is to say, anti-Muslim prejudice focuses on the 'lives of Muslims' in the West (Malik 2009). Anti-Muslim racism in its present form sees the current portrayal of the Muslim problematic arising from a transition from anti-Asian racism, revolving around the essentialised *'Paki'*, to anti-Muslim racism – with the objective of the hate being transferred from race to culture (Poynting and Mason 2007). Contemporary discourses on 'integrationism' are grounded upon an anti-Muslim political culture manifested through the War on Terror, forced assimilation and accusations of self-segregation and alien values (Kundnani 2007). In fact a range of terminology has developed to describe the phenomenon. For example Kundnani (2007) and Poynting and Mason (2007) prefer to use 'anti-Muslim racism', Malik (2009) uses 'anti-Muslim prejudice' whilst Halliday (2002) chooses to use 'anti-Muslimism'. I have preferred to use the term 'anti-Muslim racism' throughout this chapter. The reason for this is based upon the observation that most young people we interviewed chose to use 'racism' as a way of understanding and explaining their experiences. Most were unfamiliar with the terms Islamophobia and anti-Muslim prejudice.[3]

New Labour, Schooling and the De-radicalisation Imperative

> By analysing the role of 'race' and ethnicity in policy discourse, we are able to trace a dynamic and often complex link between issues of racism and key policy pronouncements. We are able to critically deconstruct policies that claim (often explicitly) to be unconnected with 'race' whilst simultaneously granting legitimacy to a particular racist definition of 'us' (the "real" British, the heart of the nation) as opposed to 'them' (outsiders- such as 'alien' ethnic minorities – and the enemies within). (Gillborn 1995, p. 20)

The above observation by Gillborn provides an insight into a growing body of evidence that has articulated the intricate relationship between race, racism and educational policy and practice. Whilst the quote is taken from Gillborn's early books on racism and schools, it nevertheless captures the current sentiments surrounding Muslims and educational policy by highlighting the way in which racism is produced and reproduced over a period of time by the state. Given what we know about the nature of the racial state (Goldberg 2002), it thus was not surprising to note that, following the 7 July, 2005, London bombings, British Muslims increasingly became racially governed through *soft* and *hard* approaches. For McGhee (2008), hard approaches include anti-terrorism legislation, such as the Crime and Security Act 2001 (linked to internment of foreign national terror suspects), the Prevention of Terrorism Act 2005 (connected with placing terror suspects under control orders) and the Terrorism Act 2006 (clamping down on extremist influences with the introduction of acceptable and unacceptable behaviours). Soft approaches to de-radicalisation include a 'community-relations' approach to fighting terrorism which, 'examines the central problematic associated with presenting Muslim communities as suspect communities in the "war on terror"' (McGhee 2008, p. 8). Part of this 'community-relations' approach, which includes Cantle's (2005) thesis of ethnic segregation leading to racial conflict, was extended to argue that ethnic segregation could lead to radicalisation and extremism (Davies 2008). The extension of community cohesion to national security is a theme that can be identified in the Department for Children, Schools and Families' prevention of violent extremism toolkit, entitled *Learning Together to Be Safe* (2008), which was launched after the conviction of Hammad Munshi – the youngest Muslim to be sentenced under the UK Terrorism Act. Munshi, aged 15 at the time, was arrested in West

Yorkshire on his way home from school in 2006, and sentenced to two years' imprisonment for 'downloading information about bomb-making material from the internet and hidden notes about martyrdom under his bed' (Gammell 2008). This toolkit provides 'advice' and 'guidance' to schools, with a three-tiered approach to countering the extremist narrative carried out in the name of Islam. The first tier is defined as *universal actions,* which include the school 'promoting community cohesion and promoting equality and wellbeing'. The second tier strengthens *targeted* work, which includes schools using the 'curriculum to challenge extremist narratives'. Finally, and perhaps most controversially, is the *specialist tier* which encourages schools to 'form good links with police and other partners to share information'.

The CONTEST strategy (HM Government 2006), which is the government's over-arching counter-terrorism policy, provides compelling evidence of anti-Muslim prejudice, especially given the discursive framing of Muslims as an essentialised problematic group. The CONTEST strategy has four central themes: Prevent, Pursue, Protect, and Prepare. *Prevent* focuses on stopping people becoming terrorists or supporting violent terrorism, and is considered the spearhead of counter-terrorism work (HM Government 2006). *Pursue* responds by stopping terrorist attacks through prosecution, intelligence and increased international cooperation. *Prepare* places emphasis on vulnerability and risk assessment by the emergency services. *Protect* strengthens the civic infrastructures such as border control and public transport systems. Whilst these strands appear to function independently, some would regard them as interconnected. For example, many have argued that the Prevent and Pursue strands of the strategy are interconnected, or, simply put, 'Prevent is Pursue in sheep's clothing, implying that Prevent provides a cover for the active pursuit of suspected terrorists' (see House of Commons 2010, p. 8). The revised CONTEST strategy (HM Government 2009), otherwise known as CONTEST II, further intensified the grip on Muslim communities by extending surveillance and disciplinary measures to target any verbal expression of dissent, in practice targeting any Muslim seen to be articulating illiberal views or sentiments. This curtailment of any space for open debate was legitimated through an integrationist agenda, leading to a synthesis of the counter-terrorism and integrationist strategies:

> We will also continue to challenge views which fall short of supporting violence and are within the law, but which reject and undermine our shared values and jeopardise community cohesion – the strong and positive relationships between people of different ethnic, faith and

cultural backgrounds in this country. Some of these views can create a climate in which people may be drawn into violent activity. (HM Government 2009, p. 88)

The degree of scrutiny and the micromanaged nature of public policy vis-à-vis the Muslim community is historically unprecedented. Indeed, such a view has even been expressed from the unlikely quarter of the National Association of Muslim Police, who reported to the House of Commons Select Committee that:

Never before has a community been mapped in a manner and nor it will be ... The hatred towards Muslims has grown to a level that defies all logic and is an affront to British values. The climate is such that Muslims are subject to daily abuse in a manner that would be ridiculed by Britain, were this to occur anywhere else. (Davies 2010, cited in Husband and Alam 2011, p. 102)

The Government's *'Learning together to be safe'* specialist tier guidance changes the role of teachers, making them potential agents of the state whose function is not to educate but rather to provide security surveillance, monitoring and feeding back problematic behaviours to the security agencies. Kundnani (2009, p.7) has shown how the emphasis on tackling violent extremism puts the integrity of the teaching profession at risk as teachers are increasingly expected to 'become the eyes and ears of counter-terrorism policing'. As Dodd (2009) explains, 'The government programme aimed at preventing Muslims from being lured into violent extremism is being used to gather intelligence about innocent people who are not yet suspected of involvement in terrorism.' In his discussion, Dodd reports how a 'nine-year-old schoolboy in east London was referred to the authorities after allegedly showing "signs of extremism" – the youngest case known in Britain. He was [then] "de-programmed" according to a "source with knowledge of the case"' (ibid.).

The coalition-led government's revised Prevent Strategy (HM Government 2011) also reinforced the partnership work between the Department of Education (DoE) and the Office for Security and Counter-Terrorism (OSCT), which further reinforced links between racialised anti-Muslim discourse and security, with the support of £4.7 million to work with local authorities and schools. A further £950,000 of regional funds was also allocated to embed the aforementioned *Learning Together to be Safe* toolkit within schools. Furthermore, the revised Prevent Strategy

(HM Government 2011) gave the Channel Project a strategic and central role in the fight against terror. The Channel Project is the government's multi-agency risk-management initiative; it has been strongly criticised by Kundnani (2009) and others, who submitted their objections to the Preventing Violent Extremism Select Committee on the grounds of its possible human rights infringements, given that young students are referred to the police simply for expressing controversial opinions (see House of Commons 2010). This is succinctly summarised by Kundnani (2009, p.6):

> There is strong evidence that a significant part of the Prevent programme involves the embedding of counter-terrorism police officers within the delivery of local services, the purpose of which seems to be to gather intelligence on Muslim communities, to identify areas, groups and individuals that are 'at risk' and to then facilitate interventions, such as the Channel programme.

Despite the serious criticism of the Channel programme, the revised 2011 Prevent Strategy further integrated the Channel Project within the government's child protection and safeguarding policies.

Schooling and the War on Terror

There are clear links to be made between the national and international positioning of Muslims and Islam in the ongoing War on Terror, articulated through media and political discourses on Muslim communities, and the experiences of anti-Muslim racism within the school environment. In our research in schools, it was evident that international events and the rhetoric of the War on Terror have nurtured a sense of hostility displayed by non-Muslim pupils and teaching staff towards Muslim pupils. The empirical findings I discuss draw upon focus-group interviews with Muslim young men, aged 15 and 16, in youth clubs and community centres in Greater Manchester and Lancashire. In total, seven focus-group interviews were conducted, and each focus group had five to six respondents.

Imagining the 'other': It's you Muslims killing our soldiers

The national debate on the Muslim problematic is deeply intertwined with the ongoing military campaign led by the USA, the United Kingdom and their allies. The intense effects of these campaigns on 'Muslim conditions in the West' have been succinctly elucidated by Imtiaz (2010) in his collections of highly thought-provoking short essays and stories. In his commentary on the impact of the George Bush II's presidential reign, he rightly notes, 'It's difficult to remember the Bush years except as one long, enduring, painful moment that will not go away. At various moments, different aspects of it rise to the surface to heighten the pain and these may then go away but the pain nevertheless remains' (Imtiaz 2010, p.138). The implications of the Bush years for racial experiences are evident within the experience of schooling for Muslim pupils, where the rhetoric used to extend the War on Terror is often used as a repertoire of abuse in the classroom.

In the focus-group interviews with 15-year-old Muslim boys, their responses exemplified how international events shape the way in which Muslims are 'excluded' from particular activities in schools. It is important to note how micro narratives or stories that are told informally through various school activities play a crucial role in essentialising the 'other'. Muslim pupils are able to pick up these narratives to inform their understanding of hostile spaces within the school environment. Certain spaces or extra-curricular activities are avoided by Muslim pupils because of the implicit messages conveyed by members of staff. In one of the focus-group discussions, the discussed how teachers running a School Cadets Team (SCT) reinforced a particular reading of the War on Terror by portraying 'all Muslims' as being responsible for 'killing our British soldiers'. The Muslim school pupils demonstrated how 'stories' informed by the War on Terror are used in schools to reinforce the idea of the enlightened insider and demonised outsider. It is also interesting to note how by extension 'all Muslims', regardless of nationality or ethnic group, are seen as one monolithic problematic group.

Recently with all that's been happening in Afghanistan, with the bodies of soldiers coming to the England for burial, things have been very bad. You ask anyone they will tell you the grief we get....We are not from Afghanistan, we were born here, and yet they think we are all the same. This obviously affects what happens in school... We joined the SCT; we thought it would be fun, but we had to leave really quickly. With what's happening in Afghanistan and the British soldiers and stuff, people that go there [SCT] they get told stories about all these [Muslim] Talibans killing "all our" British soldiers; that's having an impact. People turn against us, things become very bad – you don't know. We had to leave very quickly, there was racism and I mean TOO MUCH RACISM, that's why we left.'

This quote exemplifies how stories about 'us and them' drawn principally from the War on Terror have created a hostile cultural environment within the confines of the school. It demonstrates how Muslim pupils can often feel vulnerable and insecure as a consequence of international events because those events have an impact upon what happens in schools. Some students were even reluctant to attend school the next morning if a national or international story had been discussed in the national media. They feared the backlash or the subtle racist remarks that they would experience in the classroom or walking along the corridors. The fears that the students articulated were not 'imaginary' but were rather informed by previous experience. The pupils provided countless examples of anti-Muslim racism by teachers and fellow pupils. These experiences of racism were not just confined to the school premises but continued during the journey to and from school. In the following account, a Yemeni Muslim student from Manchester shares an experience inflicted by a member of staff:

> The other day I was messing about in class, we can't understand the teacher so we all mess about. So the teacher told me to leave the room, so I did, and the teacher followed me out. He then got hold of my tie, and in a very angry voice called me a "**scruffy Arab**"...I didn't think nothing of it, this is not the only time something like this has happened.'

This example raises two important points. Firstly, Muslim pupils can experience complete powerlessness in the face of racism, and secondly, and more importantly, racism is a normalising presence, especially given the fact that incidents of racism on school premises are not addressed. Pupils described feeling that there was no point in taking matters any further, particularly in view of the similar treatment they endured from other, more senior members of staff. Emerging from the focus-group interviews was a clear picture that anti-Muslim racism is not a series of isolated incidents but rather reflects how the logic of the pathological 'other' has permeated the institutional fabric of the schools. Pupil testimonies revealed how teacher-pupil relationships had been transformed in light of the counter-terrorism policies, and pupils experienced subtle changes in the way in which some members of staff interacted with them. Muslim pupils were often wary of talking to teachers in case they were 'spies' or informants for other agencies.

It was clear that issues of religious and political extremism were widely discussed in schools, often through direct intervention, such as in the form of classroom discussions and theatre performances, or in a more covert form through outreach work with young people. An example of intervention, included within the Department for Communities and Local Government's (DCLG's) (2010) examples of best practice, is *The Muslimah: Make a Difference* performance. This drama, delivered to secondary school pupils, uses the medium of theatre as a way of exploring terrorist activities and emphasising Muslim women's duty to prevent violent extremism. It acts as an extension of *Watch over Me*, an interactive DVD accompanied by teacher resources aimed at secondary schools, which was supplied to every secondary school in England as part of the DoE's school Prevent strategy (HM Government 2011). Perhaps the most worrying feature of this counter-terrorist work is the covert operations carried out by public-sector workers, such as youth workers outside formal school hours, who historically have played a 'supportive role' for young people. This aspect of Prevent is alarming not only because it breaches notions of trust but also because it uses trust and loyalty as devices to support counter-terrorism. Such practices have infiltrated the most mundane of activities, such as football games played among groups of school friends. By the DCLG's (2010) own admission, 'work with young people is the most important focus ... since it is this group that are felt most susceptible to becoming attracted to extremism' (DCLG 2010, p. 24). One of the features of successful work with young people, according to DCLG (2010, p. 25), is the high levels of trust that can be gained through long-term engagement, which can be developed through a 'respectful listening mode of interaction'. The impact of Prevent on schools is clearly evident in the DoE's own assessment in March 2010, which noted that 61 per cent of local authorities' children's services were actively engaged with Prevent work (HM Government 2011, p. 69). A poll by MORI confirmed this finding, highlighting how over 84% of schools 'knew at least something about their role in preventing violent extremism' (DCLG 2010, p. 25).

The suicide repertoire: You're gonna blow me up?

One of the major motifs of racial hostility following the War on Terror was the angry Muslim male. In recent years the caricature of Muslims as intolerant, violent, misogynistic suicide bombers has become a dominant iconography in the media representation of Muslim communities. The image of the Muslim suicide bomber has come to dominate the public image of young Muslim men, often either based upon a political reading, through the lens of the Palestinian struggle, or through the theological lens of the concept of *jihad*. The image of the suicide bomber in the UK came to dominate the popular imagination following the London bombings of 7/7, through the names of Muhammad Siddique Khan, Shahzaad Tanweer, Germain Lindsay and Hasib Hussain. The implications for Muslim students in Leeds and the neighbouring areas, from where these men came, were intense. This particular image of the angry irrational Muslim, with the default position of a person prepared to cause mass casualties, is a caricature often found in the experiences of young Muslim students in school. An impression often articulated by the students we interviewed, and most often condoned by teachers, has come to be a defining experience of schooling. In a discussion with students from a secondary school in one of the towns near Leeds, they explicitly articulated the routine nature of this experience, highlighting how the image of a suicide bomber is used to mock the Muslim 'other'. Simple matters of disagreement, or just mere presence, provide opportunities for insult:

> The big stereotypical view of us Muslims in school [to] put it plain and simple is that we're terrorist. The white students think we're terrorist, but I also think the teachers also think the same. We know that the white teachers and the kids don't like us. It doesn't take a genius to figure that you know... For example we'll be in class, like the other day we were talking about something in history and this white guy said something which I did not agree with him so I told him I think you wrong. And suddenly he jumped up and said OK you're right otherwise **'YOUR GONNA BLOW ME UP'**. Or, I'll give you another example, it will be like, you'll be walking down the corridor in school, you know, minding your own business, and a group of white students would say 'tick tick tick tick' – like a bomb going off.

It is important to note how the above account focused particularly on gendered experiences of anti-Muslim prejudice. It was principally Muslim young men who complained of being caricatured as suicide bombers. The racial imagery of the suicide bomber is seen to be closely associated with notions of masculinity, which are often considered to be senseless, hyperactive and, above all, prone to the use of violence to convey a point of view. This particular construct is central to racial mythology, which has evolved from the problematic young black male of the 1980s (Hall et al. 1978; Gilroy 1987) to contemporary notions of 'dangerous brown men' (Bhattacharyya 2008). The recent racist carica-ture of Muslim masculinity is based upon a development of much older myths, which have been central to orientalist literature (Said 1978). For Bhattacharyya (2008), contemporary racial mythology has evolved from the 'demonised figure of 'dangerous black man' [to] become the 'dangerous brown man', an adaption of early racial mythologies that may refer to the same groups of men but that enables the inclusion of more recent racialised anxieties' (Bhattacharyya 2008, p. 96). This point is further supported by Alexander, who has demonstrated how 'Muslims have then ironically become the new "black" with all the associations of cultural alienation, deprivation and danger that came with this problem' (Alexander 2000, p.15).

Conclusion

For Muslim pupils, racist experiences, in the climate of 9/11 and 7/7, were increasingly seen as a fact of life, a normalising presence or even a rite of passage that Muslim pupils inevitably had to undergo. The War on Terror not only manifests itself in foreign policy but also permeates the educational system via the militarisation and securitisation of schooling. School experiences came to reflect the political mood of the wider society; they were a casual reflection of what was articulated by politicians whilst *talking* about domestic counter-terrorism or the War on Terror, or *failing to talk* about other international events, such as the Palestinian oppression. National and international events would often inform or dictate the type of racist abuse or physical attacks experienced by Muslim pupils, whether in relation to the 'angry suicide bomber' following 7/7 or the 'Muslim Taliban' following the deaths of servicemen or women in Afghanistan.

Racism in this context was not a product of a few disruptive children, but rather a product of a much wider and more deeply ingrained social and institutional phenomenon. Certainly, the interconnected nature of wider political events at national and international levels and the increasing levels of anti-Muslim racism at a grass-roots level have been emphasised in numerous other empirical studies. Noret and colleagues (2007), for example, has shown how levels of antagonism towards Muslims increased following the events of 9/11 and the invasion of Iraq, and Crozier and Davies' (2008) study on Muslims' experiences of schooling highlighted that the question of safety was paramount for Muslim parents and pupils. Their study also made it 'clear that racist abuse is a lived experience for some on a daily basis, but for all as a feature of their schooling' (Crozier and Davies 2008, p. 295). The impact and the legacy of 'Prevent' continues to have a deep and profound effect on the experience of schooling for Muslims in Britain.

Notes

1. In fact, the title of chapter 2 of the report is 'Islamophobia: The Nature of Anti-Muslim Prejudice'. Despite this, Allen (2010) is highly critical of the way in which Islamophobia is used to refer to Muslims of Asian heritage, thus associating religion with ethnic identity. According to Allen (2010, p.62), the report substitutes 'Muslim' with markers of South Asian heritage 127 times, which is 'equivalent to 70.5 per cent of all references in the text'.
2. Closed and Open views of Islam are tabulated based upon eight distinctions of Islam. These distinctions are then compared with an open and a closed view of Islam. For example, is Islam monolithic or diverse? A closed view will consider it to be monolithic whilst an open view of Islam will consider it to diverse with internal differences. Other distinctions include whether Islam is separate/interacting, inferior/different, enemy/partner, manipulative/sincere, criticisms of the West rejected/considered, discrimination defended/criticised and Islamophobia being seen as natural/problematic.
3. Recently there has been an attempt to undermine, delegitimise and marginalise the experiences of Muslim communities by dismissing their genuine fears of Islamophobia in Europe as 'hysterical to the point of delusion' (Malik 2009). It has often been argued that, far from experiencing discrimination, Muslims have in fact been privileged, benefiting from special treatment brought about through multicultural civic policy. This rather optimistic view of the workings of multiculturalism is also combined with a view of racism which is poorly theorised. If one assumes that racial identity is based on fixity, whereas religious identity is about choice, there is an underlining assumption being that it is the Muslims who are responsible for their own marginalisation.

References

Alexander, C. (2000) *The Asian Gang: Ethnicity, Identity and Masculinity* (Oxford: Berg).

Allen, C. (2010) *Islamophobia* (London: Ashgate).

Back L., Keith, M. Khan, A., Shukra, K., and Solomas, J. (2002) *The Return of Assimilation: Race and Multiculturalism and New Labour.* Sociological Research Online, 7(2), http://www.socresonline.org.uk/7/2/back.html, date accessed 17 July 2007.

Barker, M. (1981) *New Racism: Conservatives and the Ideology of the Tribes* (London: Junction Books).

Bhattacharyya, G. (2008) *Dangerous Brown Men: Exploiting Sex, Violence and Feminism in the War on Terror* (London: Zed Books).

Cantle, T. (2005) *Community Cohesion: A New Framework for Race and Diversity,* (Basingstoke: Palgrave).

Crozier, G. and Davies, J. (2008) '"The Trouble is They Don't Mix": Self Segregation or Enforced Exclusion? Teachers' Constructions of South Asian Students', *Race, Ethnicity and Education,* 11(3), 285–301.

Daniel, N. (1991) *Islam and the West: The Making of an Image* (Oxford: Oneworld).

Davies, L. (2008) *Educating Against Extremism* (Stoke on Trent: Trentham Books).

Delgado, R and Stefancic, J. (2001) *Critical Race Studies: An Introduction* (New York: New York University Press).

Department for Children, Schools and Families (DCSF) (2008) *Learning Together to Be Safe: A Toolkit to Help Schools Contribute to the Prevention of Violent Extremism* (London: The Stationary Office).

Department for Communities and Local Government (DCLG) (2010) *Preventing Support for Violent Extremism through Community Interventions: A Review of the Evidence – Full Final Report* (London: The Stationary Office).

Dodd, V. (2009) 'Government Anti-terrorism Strategy 'Spies' on Innocent', *Guardian*, 16 October 2009, http://goo.gl/aigsJ.

Fekete, L. (2008) *Integration, Islamophobia and Civil Rights in Europe* (London: Institute for Race Relations).

Fekete, L (2009) *A Suitable Enemy: Racism, Migration and Islamophobia* (London: Pluto).

Gammell, C. (2008) 'Britain's Youngest Teenage Terrorist: "A Wake-up Call for Parents"'. *Daily Telegraph*, 19 September 2008, http://goo.gl/j8ciD.

Gilroy, P. (1987) *There Ain't No Black in the Union Jack: The Cultural Politics of Race and Nation* (London: Hutchinson).

Gillborn, D. (1995), *Racism and Anti-Racism in Real Schools* (Buckingham: Open University Press).

Gillborn, D.(2008), *Racism and Education: Coincidence or Conspiracy* (London: Routledge).

Goldberg, D. T. (2002) *The Racial State* (London: Blackwell).

Goldberg, D. T. (2009) *The Threat of Race* (Malden, MA: Blackwell).

Goodwin, M.J. (2011) *New British Fascism: Rise of the British National Party* (London Routledge).

Halliday, F. (2002) *Two Hours that Shook the World: September 11, 2001: Causes and Consequences* (London: Saqi Books).

Hall, S., Critcher, C., Jefferson, T., Clarke, J., and Roberts, B. (1978) *Policing the Crisis* (London: Macmillan).

HM Government (2006) *Countering International Terrorism: The United Kingdom's Strategy*, Cm 6888 (London: The Stationary Office).

HM Government (2009) *Pursue, Prevent, Protect Prepare. The United Kingdom's Strategy*, Cm 7547 (London: The Stationary Office).

HM Government (2011) *Prevent Strategy*, Cm 8092 (London: The Stationary Office).

House of Commons, Home Affairs Select Committee (2005) *Terrorism and Community Relations, Sixth Report of Sessions 2004–2005*, Volume 1, HC 165–1 (London: The Stationary Office).

House of Commons, Communities and Local Government Committee (2010), *Preventing Violent Extremism, Sixth Report of Sessions 2009–10*, HC 65 (London: The Stationary Office).

Husband, C. and Alam, Y. (2011) *Social Cohesion and Counter-Terrorism: A Policy Contradiction* (Bristol: Policy Press).

Imtiaz, A. S. (2010) *Wandering Lonely in a Crowd: Reflections on the Muslim Condition in the West* (Markfield: Kube Press).

Kalra, V. S. and Kapoor, N. (2009) 'Interrogating Segregation, Integration and the Community Cohesion Agenda,' *Journal of Ethnic and Migration Studies*, 35(9), 1397–415.

Kundnani, A. (2007) *The End of Tolerance: Racism in 21st Century Britain* (London: Pluto Press).

Kundnani, A. (2009) *Spooked! How Not to Prevent Violent Extremism* (London: Institute of Race Relations).

Macfie, A. L. (ed.) (2000) *Orientalism: A Reader* (Edinburgh: Edinburgh University Press).

Malik, M. (2009) 'Anti-Muslim Prejudice in the West, Past and Present: An Introduction', *Patterns of Prejudice*, 43(3/4), 207–12.

Marranci, G. (2004) 'Multiculturalism, Islam, and the Clash of Civilization Theory: Rethinking Islamophobia', *Culture and Religion*, 5(1), 107–19.

McGhee, D. (2008) *The End of Multiculturalism: Terrorism, Integration and Human Rights* (Berkshire: Open University Press).

Noret, N., Brockett, A. A., Harenwall, S., Baird, P. D. and Rivers I. (2007) 'Adolescent Attitudes in York towards Muslims and Islam', in S. Kim and P. Kollontai (eds) *Community Identity: Dynamics of Religion in Context* (London, T & T Clark International), pp.253–78.

Poynting, S. and Mason, V. (2007) 'The Resistible Rise of Islamophobia: Anti-Muslim Racism in the UK and Australia before 9/11', *Journal of Sociology*, 43(1), 61–86.

Runnymede Trust (1997) *Islamophobia: A Challenge for Us All* (London: Runnymede Trust).

Runnymede Trust (2004) *Islamophobia: Issues, Challenges and Action* (London: Trentham Books).

Said, E. (1978) *Orientalism* (London: Routledge).

Said, E. (1997) *Covering Islam: How the Media and Experts Determine How We See the Rest of the World* (London: Vintage).

Sardar, Z. (1999) *Orientalism* (Buckingham: Open University Press).

Talwar, D. (2012) 'More than 87,000 racist incidents recorded in schools', BBC Online, 22 May 2012, http://www.bbc.co.uk/news/education-18155255

Tibawi, A.L (1964) 'English-Speaking Orientalists', *Islamic Quarterly*, 8(1–4), 25–45.

8
Resisting Technologies of Surveillance and Suspicion

Virinder S. Kalra and Tariq Mehmood

Following the 7/7 bombings in London, a distinct desire to target Muslims for scrutiny and surveillance pervaded the British security establishment in its national arms (MI5) as well as its local elements (police). The panic that pervaded these institutions and its long-term consequences was exemplified in the fact that the 2012 Leveson Inquiry into phone hacking cited the 7/7 attacks as one reason why the police were not able to fully investigate that particular scandal effectively.[1] The charged atmosphere led to the creation of a large number of policy developments all of which aimed to create mechanisms for the assertion of biopolitical power over the Muslim population of Britain. The Preventing Violent Extremism agenda (Prevent) was developed in this regard by the then Labour government to implement the general ideological notion that a certain population was in need of greater control. Though this was not the first time the British state targeted a population it deemed in need of isolation and domination, there was nonetheless a range of new technological tools at the state's behest as well as a number of hindrances. Most notably, the presence of a more effective European Court of Human Rights and British equalities legislation enabled, at some level, an engagement with the legal process to protect against the states interventions. It was this problem, of a desire to discipline and target but restricted by legal convention, that meant that certain proposals of the state were never formally instigated but nonetheless operated at the informal level, such as special visas to the US for British Pakistanis and, until recently, open extradition to the US.[2] Perhaps the most fundamental shift which was implemented was the removal of British citizenship from those who have been accused of engaging in 'terrorist' activities as part of dealing with the problem of too many rights for European citizens. Much has been written on the creation of non-state persons, particularly in Guantanamo Bay, but the rendering of whole populations as liminal citizens marks a new aspect of securitisation and is particularly well demonstrated in the UK context.

Fekete (2004) outlines the process by which the European security establishment initially created a 'shadow criminal justice' system to deal with foreign nationals, including extraordinary extradition and detention without trial and torture. She also raises the problem for the War on Terror of suspects who are citizens and therefore supposedly protected by the conventions of legal frameworks, constitutions and the European Convention on Human Rights. As Gareth Peirce (2010, p.65) has systematically described in the brilliant and incisive book *Dispatches from the Dark Side*: 'Through a myriad of routes Britain has continued to attempt to evade internationally recognised legal restraints.' One mechanism for this process of evading the legal process is suggested by Brown (2010) in her analysis of the impact of the anti-terror legislation on Muslim communities. Firstly, Muslim communities have become collectively criminalised, then terrorists are reduced to criminals. These dual processes effectively de-racialise and de-politicise.[3] Finally, and perhaps most crucially for this argument, the dichotomy between Islamic radicalism and British values is established. The suspect status of British Muslims is then intimately connected with a suspect citizenship. It is therefore not problematic for the creation of mechanisms which avoid citizenship rights as these are held liminal for the population in question. Indeed, the premise of the police surveillance that this chapter describes was that all Muslims are a suspect population, regardless of their citizenship status. Peirce (2010) also asks the question of whether the situation of the Irish was any different under the Prevention of Terror legislation. The idea of the 'suspect community' was developed by Hillyard (1993) to describe the relationship of the Irish to the state after the passing of the Prevention of Terrorism Act in 1974. It was deemed effective shorthand for discussing the relationship between the state's security apparatus and the Irish population. Pantazis and Pemberton (2009) review the concept in terms of its applicability to Muslims in Britain post-9/11 and 7/7. They conclude: 'The 'terror of prevention' continuum, which ranges from the day-to-day harassment of Muslims through stop and search to high-profile police raids, has had a corrosive effect on the relations between Muslim communities and the police' (2009, p. 662). Even though the rhetorical question that Peirce (2010) asks in this context: 'Was it like this for the Irish?' is answered by Pantazis and Pemberton, the more important question about the mechanisms by which the situation changed for the Irish is much more difficult to address when it comes to Muslims. For the Irish, the support of the USA and the end of the Soviet Union combined to provide the correct climate for a cessation of hostilities. The global geopolitical situations offer no such immediate relief for British Muslims. Indeed, it is much more likely that the notion of 'suspect community' will perhaps be deemed too lightweight to encompass the kinds of new strategies of surveillance and targeting that the state is engaged in with regard to Muslims. One of the central planks of the new securitised racial state is in the utilisation of surveillance technologies. At every juncture in the interaction between aspects of the state apparatus, from mundane delivery of services to implementation of the law, scrutinisation and electronic surveillance is the norm. These were not widely available at the time of the Irish insurrection. However, it is also important to note that neither was the European Court of Justice a presence (it was formed in the early 1990s), which has enabled greater weight to be placed on human rights abuses than was previously the case in the British courts.[4]

Policing this Crisis

Although it is important to understand the continuities with the demonisation of the Irish population, it is also important to recognise that the way Black African/ Caribbean populations were constructed as the source of moral panic in the 1970s (Hall et al. 1978) also resonates with the contemporary. At that time, the police were clearly in a crisis, as illustrated by the following quote by the Metropolitan Police commissioner: 'Policing a multi-racial society is putting the fabric of our policing philosophy under greater stress than at any time since the years immediately after the Metropolitan Police was established in 1829' (*The Guardian*, 25 September 1979, quoted in Gilroy 1982, p. 144). These kinds of comments were not repeated in 2005 by the police, as it was left to then Prime Minister Tony Blair to articulate that the 'rule of the game had changed'.[5] This broad ideological positioning in effect enabled a much greater involvement of intelligent agencies in routine police work. Racist policing and institutional racism have been established as one of the cornerstones of the implementation of law and order in Britain (Sivanandan 1981; Bowling and Phillips 2001; Patel and Tyrer 2011). The brief period of introspection and self-flagellation following the McPherson Inquiry, where race was at least an issue for the police to deal with, only lasted until the public disorder of 2001 and the falling of the twin towers. The legacy of that brief period of police introspection comes in the form of 'community engagement' (Spalek and Imtoual

2007), which is essentially about community self-policing. Racism as an issue has therefore become muted by the necessity of racist policing in the name of national security. The contradiction in the notion of community policing in this context is of course apparent; on the one hand, there is a demand for self-policing by the community, on the other hand, it is the 'self' who is deemed to be the enemy in need of control. It is this problematic that is played out in the Birmingham spy camera saga that will be considered at some length later in the chapter.

The nature of the police response to the presence of Muslims in the metropole has been categorised by the criminology fraternity in terms of 'hard and soft' approaches (see Spalek 2009); hard responses being those that engage in overt and covert surveillance, counter-terrorist operations and the implementation of anti-terror legislation, whilst soft approaches involve forums for dialogue, police–community initiatives, and other forms of community participation in securitisation. This kind of split can be seen in the separation between CONTEST as the overall counter-terrorism strategy controlled and run by the Home Office and the intelligence services and Prevent, which is meant to be a multi-agency program with the police as only one partner. Though clearly the raft of legislation that has come into force since 2001 has all been concerned with creating a space for targeting Muslims as a collective, this chapter demonstrates that it is through increasingly blurring the distinction between policing and military, intelligence and spying, that this targeting has become possible. Indeed, the increased focus on counter-terrorism works on a number of levels: firstly, by making counter-terrorism a pervasive aspect of all policing; secondly, by increasing the resources for this activity; and, thirdly by taking specific powers away from the local police and moving them into a centralised counter-terror unit. The first activity blurs the boundaries between police and community counter-terror efforts. Thus, doctors, university lecturers, hoteliers, security guards, and so on, are all supposed to be vigilant about suspicious activity. In effect, all those engaged in any kind of service delivery (private or public) are part of the security apparatus of the state. This of course is an uneven and contested process, but it nonetheless drives the logic of the securitisation mechanism. Secondly, the funding for counter-terrorism activities and the proportion of this that has been allocated to the mainstream of policing has increased dramatically. In just three years, between 2007 and 2010, counter-terrorism police budgets increased by 30 per cent, leading to a total of 7700 officers, which means that 5 per cent of all officers are working in activities related to increased state securitisation.[6] By 2011 it is estimated that the budget on counter terrorism will be £3.5 bn with money for this activity ring-fenced against austerity (Brown 2010). This alone should indicate that any kind of differentiation between hard and soft arms of police activity are perhaps a little naïve. Rather, there is a blurring of the lines between the activities of intelligence agencies and routine local policing. Of most importance, and what is crucial to this strategy, is to avoid the possibility of any form of accountability of the system which would allow for the assertion that Muslims have any rights as subject of Britain and citizens of Europe. Indeed, the Prevent 2011 agenda addresses the way in which the state wishes to maintain a blurred set of boundaries when it comes to counter-terrorism work (HM Government 2011). This review consistently states that the police are not the main agency involved in Prevent. However, in each and every other point made in the document, the police role is clearly demonstrated to be central in terms of the resources allocated to them through the program, in terms of their role in the local implementation of activities, and ultimately, in terms of being the final destination for any information gleaned. To some extent this rhetoric about partnership working is in place because Prevent was presented as the soft public face of counter-terrorism, though it was clear to those who were engaged with it that it was more a smokescreen for surveillance and spying, and therefore much distrusted and maligned by Muslim commentators and spokespeople (Awan 2011; Brown 2010).

> It is also clear that the state has gone from a responsive mode to an aggressive targeting of Muslim communities and anyone seen as their supporters. An example of the way in which the intelligence services were directly involved in local-level surveillance that might have previously been under the remit of the police was in the creation of a network of mosque infiltrators. These were funded outside the normal mechanisms of Prevent, with direct linkages to the Home Office, MI5 and the organisations concerned. The process of funding itself was not subject to any of the public scrutiny usually associated with public grants and as such reflects the murky nature of the agenda. In Manchester, the organisations that were engaged in this way were asked to directly intervene with those young Muslims identified at risk of 'extremism'.[7] Though the methodology being deployed by MI5 at the time, in collaboration with Queens University in Belfast (no surprise here given their 'experience' with Irish insurgents), meant that over 80 per cent of Muslims would be seen as holding some extremist views. Indeed, the Prevent 2011 strategy presented to Parliament makes fairly clear that the role of the police is to work on the ideological as well as the practical level: Propagandists for terrorism and for ideologies taken up by terrorists should not be

permitted to make use of publicly owned venues. Local authorities and others must be ready to take appropriate action. Where conferences and speaker meetings involving propagandists are taking place in universities and colleges, communities and privately-owned locations, authorities – including the police – should always be ready to brief the owners and ensure they understand what is taking place. (HM Government 2011, p. 53)

The level of scrutiny should not be underestimated. In March 2012, an advert for a Ph.D. studentship looking critically at the role of the police in relation to Prevent was circulated through the usual academic channels. One of the authors of this chapter, who was the principle supervisor for the project, received an email, in May 2012, from the regional prevent coordinator, who responded to the proposal in this way: 'Having read the outline, I would query some key fundamental assertions contained in the text – I won't go into them at this stage.' This was followed by an offer of a meeting along with the regional Channel coordinator. Clearly the police role in terms of asserting the authority of state propaganda and quelling dissent has become fairly explicit. It is not that these contradictions have not surfaced before when considering the way in which the police have come to be a central plank in the monitoring and control of racialised others; rather there is at play a new level of sophistication and intrusion. On the one hand, soft policing has always worked through other agencies, such as social work and mental health institutions. As neoliberal reforms reduce these institutions to hollow shells, the actual work of community control falls on the police. At the other end of the spectrum, the work of the intelligence agencies is becoming routinised in the policing context, and is increasingly being played out through the counter-terrorism unit. This, again, relies on the police for local implementation but runs into the problem of local accountability through police authorities and other mechanisms, though ways of sidestepping these through elected police commissioners is in process (Roth 2010). It is precisely this juncture, of local accountability of police action, of the blurring of lines between intelligence agencies and local policing, and of the relentless demand of the state to target Muslims that was exposed in the Birmingham spy cameras case.

Spy Cameras

In 2007, the West Midlands Police Authority applied to the Home Office for funding from its counter-terrorism unit to install CCTV cameras in two areas of Birmingham, specifically, Alum Rock and Sparkhill. Both areas had been previously identified as having populations with larger numbers of those charged with terrorist related activities, relative to other parts of the city.[8] These areas are also the most economically disadvantaged and have the largest concentration of Muslims – mainly from South Asia.[9] The technologies of Automatic Number Plate Recognition (ANPR) cameras and CCTV were to be deployed to create a 'ring of steel' around these areas so no vehicle leaving or entering would go undetected. The plan was for 106 traffic lanes to be covered by multiple ANPR cameras, some with overview CCTV to record vehicle details. The information would be fed into the national feed of ANPR cameras, which is open to all police forces to view. In addition there were to be a further 38 CCTV cameras covering streets with a feed only going to the Central Terrorism Unit. In total, 193 cameras were planned. When the notion of a 'suspect' community was aimed at the Irish, large-scale surveillance technology of this kind was not available. The placement of these cameras was a clear policy of targeting a predominantly Muslim area for overt and covert surveillance, in effect creating the suspect community.

The seeds of the scheme to place these cameras, called Project Champion, began, according to the police inquiry into the affair in the wake of Operation Gamble (Thornton 2010). This police operation took place in 2007, when nine men were arrested in Birmingham, Alum Rock, for planning to behead a Muslim soldier.[10] Seven hundred police officers were involved in the operation. Of those arrested, five were charged and convicted, and four were released. One of those detained but not charged, Mr Bakr, was quite vociferous in his understanding of the way in which the anti-terror legislation operated: '"It's a police state for Muslims. It's not a police state for everybody else because these terror laws are designed specifically for Muslims and that's quite an open fact," he added.'[11] These statements were subsequently sharply refuted by a swathe of MPs. But given the paucity of creativity in the West Midlands Counter Terrorism Unit (CTU), which had underspent their 2007 budget, Mr Bakr's comments probably presented the germ of an idea. Concurrent with neoliberal practice, the first step was to employ consultants. They put together a bid that focused solely on anti-terror-related surveillance, with the objective of establishing a surveillance scheme that followed suspect targets into the 'community'. A bid was made to the Association of Chief Police Officers (ACPO) which secured the funding from the Home Office. In April 2008 the bid was approved and a further group of consultants employed; this time it was the Olive Group. This was to be the implementing agency for installing and maintaining the cameras. In its own promotional materials, the Olive Group represents itself as on of the main contractors operating surveillance in Iraq and Afghanistan.[12] Their main operations are concerned with handling covert surveillance. Indeed, it is apparent by the use of the Olive Group, that this was an attempt at bringing the kinds of tactics deployed in the wars abroad onto the home turf. Even though the UN has expressed concern that the increasing use of private security firms leaves much greater room for infringements of human rights with no mechanisms of accountability, it seems this has no impact on the implementation of counter-terrorism policy.[13] But then perhaps, someone in the West Midlands police force began to understand the implications of the scheme.

In a number of closed-door meetings with senior members of Birmingham City Council administration, the scheme was sanctioned and funding approved. However, it is not clear why at some point there was a realisation that for the cameras to be implemented there had to be some form of local involvement or consultation. Though this was raised in the subsequent inquiry in terms of the fact that Project Champion would obviously involve violations in terms of Human Rights and Equalities legislation, this does not seem to be the impetus behind the change in strategy (Thornton 2010). In fact, none of the procedures governing the use of CCTV and ANPR in public areas was followed, due to it being part of an anti-terror strategy. The open gamut that was available to the police in the post-7/7 environment seemed to be taken full advantage of. Nonetheless, at a certain point senior officers within the West Midlands police force it was felt necessary to 'sell' the scheme as part of a wider crime-prevention strategy in the area. In a sense the police force were attempting to reverse the usual criticism that black areas were under-policed but over controlled. In this repackaging and reselling (it is surprising more consultants were not bought in at this point), the anti-terror aspects were no longer emphasised. The role of the Safer Birmingham Partnership (SBP), a body that consists of elected council-lors, the police and other agencies, was forwarded to emphasise crime reduction and community safety aspects. Indeed, the CTU insignia were replaced by the SBP logos. A public document on Project Champion was released, in the spirit of a 'too little, too late' public consultation.

Despite this attempt by the police to shift emphasis away from the anti-terror elements of the scheme to one with more general anti-social behaviour and crime-prevention emphasis, this was not clearly felt by representatives from the area. In the Project Champion briefing session which took place on the 29 April 2009 and involved councillors in the effected areas and representatives from the police and the SBP, it was only the ward councillors, who were all Muslims, who raised concerns in the meetings, which are quoted as follows in the minutes of the meeting:

> Cllr Idress advised the group of the need to reassure the wider community that there is nothing to worry about in terms of this project. Cllr Ansar Ali Khan voiced concerns around Islamaphobia and that reassurances must be made that this project is not targeting the Muslim community and how will these issues be tackled to get the balance right. When Cllr Yaqoob 'declared she believed that this meeting was regarding Preventing Violent Extremism and if the funding was for tackling the extremism agenda this would breach the very little trust that has taken so long to build in the community and that it will be viewed as targeting the Muslim community'. (Thornton 2010, p. 20)

The sleight of hand carried out by the police in terms of general public-safety concerns and specific anti-terrorism claims is deeply embedded in the way the scheme was designed. Indeed, the racial profiling is deeply integrated in the way the technology was planned. The ANPR cameras were designed to feed into the general police database of this information and therefore would be able to be used for general crime-prevention matters. All the CCTV cameras, overt and covert, were designed to be fed into the CTU network only. It was these that were to exclusively focus on and concentrate on monitoring of Muslims. Another councillor, Ayoub Khan, himself a lawyer, articulates a sense of being mislead:

> The initial briefing that I had with the Assistant chief constable, which lasted no more than maybe half an hour, was talk about how CCTVs and ANPR system will be utilised in order to cut crime. And the majority of the discussion was around the likes of anti-social behaviour, uninsured vehicles and very little in relation to counter terrorism. The fact that this one element was mentioned towards the latter part of the meeting does not mean that we were given a true reflection of the project.[14]

The presence of Muslim councillors in Birmingham City Council and the fact that Salma Yaqoob, a member of the explicitly anti-war, 'Respect' party were present in these consultation meetings, may have been one of the reasons that the police felt it necessary to increase the level of public consultation. Yet, these attempts at community engagement were obviously just aimed at generating consent, as the scheme itself was implemented without modification. Indeed, Cllr. Ayoub Khan goes on to state that they were aware that the cameras would be used for counter-terrorism activities, but that he still felt misled: The reality is, yes we were informed of the potential of [the cameras being used for counter-terrorism], in relation to a small aspect of these cameras being utilised, but at no stage was there any information in relation to where the funding had come from. For example it was only after the implementation that we realised that this came from a funding pot which was targeting counter terrorism. We were never told of that. In fact my meeting with the Assistant Chief Constable was that this money has been given on behalf of the Home Office.

It is fairly clear that the councillors, rather than representing the public in these areas or even opposing the targeting of Muslims, were being established as the source of legitimacy for the program of implementation.

CCTV has become an established part of increased surveillance of public space in the UK. Arguably one of the most digitally encoded places on earth, CCTV for public surveillance was first used in 1985 at the Conservative Party conference in response to the Irish Republican Army's attack at the previous year's event. Given that there are estimates of over 4 million cameras in the UK (private and public), it is remarkable that systematic research gives mixed results in terms of the impact on crime prevention (Welsh and Farrington 2009). Whereas there has been no research on the role that CCTV can play in the prevention of terrorism, the basis of the Birmingham spy cameras initiative. Indeed, the use to which most CCTV is put is in the post-detection of those who have committed crimes and can be tracked through the technology. More significantly, the one conclusive element of CCTV research is that it results in racial profiling (Norris and Armstrong 1999; Stutzer and Zehnder 2012). The implementation of the cameras was clearly racist in identifying and targeting a particular population for differential treatment, through an apparently generic tool of governmentality. A point made generally by John Fiske (2004) in his review of the use of video surveillance technologies, which he labels as 'non-racist racism' or what some are calling 'post-race'. For Fiske, this technology is apparently neutral and put in place for community security and crime prevention, but it is in fact racism that is recoded into these discourses so that effects appear to be non-racial. In the Birmingham case, the racism was explicit from the outset, but it was the availability of post-racial discourse embedded in the surveillance technology that was utilised as a cover-up. The apparent universality of the desire for security, something repeated throughout the police response to criticism, was used by the police to mask their intention of monitoring Muslims.

Despite the obvious problems with implementation of CCTV in this area, the installation of the cameras began in January 2010. Given that the intention was to track all vehicles coming in and out of the areas, the cameras were located not just in the two wards but also in the other seven surrounding wards. Indeed, by April 2010, in the Mosley area of Birmingham, the presence of cameras on street corners was noted by residents. Mosely is an ethnically mixed Asian/white area close to the University of Birmingham, and houses students but also a quite sizeable liberal/left middle class. It was from here that the first complaints about the cameras arose. One resident in the area and ultimately one of the main campaigners to get the cameras removed described his first interaction with them:

> I found out about the cameras when one of them just appeared, just up the road. I walked up the main road which is just down there, and this is my usual route back to where I live and I came across this post. And I just stopped and stared at it for ages wondering what on earth it was doing there. I got home and read an email from a local councillor who said he had had a number of enquiries from local people, erm, about these camera posts. And people were asking what are they? What are they for? And the local councillor didn't know, so he contacted the local police station. And they didn't know either. (Steve Jolly)

A campaign was launched to put pressure on the police to reveal the purpose of the cameras, the main aims of which were to argue that they should be removed, that those responsible for putting them there should be questioned about the rationale for their placement, and finally, to ask what the justification was for their presence in the first place. In April 2010, the local Birmingham newspaper the *Birmingham Mail* ran an article about the concerns of Moseley residents about the appearance of these CCTV cameras. Its focus was on the lack of consultation within the locality. By June 2010, the national media had begun to take an interest in the case, but by this time the emphasis had changed. For example, a national liberal daily paper, *The Guardian* took up the story, with the headline, 'Surveillance Cameras Pop up in Muslim Areas of Birmingham – the Targets? Terrorists', with the journalist Philip Lewis repeating much of the literature released by the campaign group.[15] Pressure put on local councillors in some sense enabled them to speak out against the cameras. The following interview with Councillor Tanveer Choudhry demonstrates this point:

> There's two things here actually. Unfortunately and for my sins, I was the lead member for the West Midlands Police authority when actual scheme in 2008 was brought forward. And again the guise in which it was sold, and as Steve alluded to, it was sold under the pretext that it was for the whole of the Birmingham area, and it was going to reduce crime and anti-social behaviour within certain part of the communities. And which, which councillor in the right mind would say no.

The fact this interview took place quite a while after the campaign had won the battle against the cameras reflects not just upon the importance of the police in controlling aspects of local politics but also on the role campaigning can play in altering hegemonic positions. On the 16 June, the Birmingham SBP, Birmingham City Council and West Midlands Police Authority issued a press release i which announced that Project Champion was to be stalled pending an inquiry. It later transpired that this meant that the cameras were not to be switched on. Ultimately, an agreement was reached for the cameras to be covered with bags. This gave an impetus to the campaigners to push for the complete removal of the cameras. On 4 July, a public meeting was held in the heart of the area where the cameras were located. Attended by more than several hundred members of the public, with speeches by leading civil rights campaigners, it brought a national dimension to this local issue. The West Midlands police were represented by Assistant Chief Constable Sharon Rowe, who made the following speech:

> I recognise, having reviewed Project Champion since Thursday, I recognise mistakes have been made. Mistakes have been made by West Midlands Police and I am sorry. I am truly sorry. My intention therefore is to make every effort to see how the scheme may properly proceed, how it can be used to combat crime in the area, which I believe we all have a common interest. So my update for you today on Project Champion is this: I will now take total responsibility for Project Champion within West Midlands Police. All elements of the

project will be past to me. There will be no longer any involvement from the Counter Terrorism Unit.

The opening line of the speech garnered a round of applause from the seated crowd, but clearly the intention was for the scheme to continue, but without the involvement of the CTU. What is clear here is that the soft arm of community policing (it is surely no accident that a woman was sent to engage with the audience) was being used as a way of diverting attention away from the campaign's basic demand for the cameras to be removed. As Naeem Malik, another campaigner, states:

> I mean, even at that. Although the 600 people decided at that meeting that the cameras must come down, before we'll consider anything else, the police authority from that meeting did not go away with the idea that they are going to bring the cameras down. We continued the pressure both on the Council, on the Police Authority, and on the government and on our local politicians that these cameras are just not acceptable in any form whatsoever.

But perhaps of more concern is not the fact that the public meeting was appeased in this way but the fact that what the Assistant Chief Constable was saying was not possible. The way in which the cameras were designed and installed meant that the feeds from many of them were going directly to the Central Terrorism Unit, with no involvement of the local West Midlands police force at all. Steve Jolly makes the point in a more pointed manner:

> It turned out that there was no facility for the local police to even view these cameras or even to access the information that they were gathering. It was whisked straight down to the Counter Terrorism Unit and was solely for their use. So any talk of local crime prevention or local policing, that these cameras might be a tool to help keep the local community safe, was a lie.

The increasing pressure on the police meant that in mid-July, a review of Project Champion was announced. It was to be carried out by the Chief constable of Thames Valley Police, Sarah Thornton, who was also the Vice Chair of the Association of Chief Police Officers Terrorism and Allied Matters Committee (ACPO-TAM), the body that gained the funding for Project Champion in the first place. This review clearly highlighted the contradiction for the police when they seek to carry out counter-terrorism operations, as Thornton (2010, p.49) states in the conclusion: 'There is no doubt that the security situation in 2007 was very grave, and the threat intense, however the response that was developed under Project Champion raised significant human rights concerns and has undoubtedly led to a loss of trust and confidence in the community.' In effect, police involvement in soft and hard counter-terror activities had the potential to lead to exposé and accusation. But this was not due to any internal contradictions within the police force but rather to the sustained pressure of the campaigning group. This is partially reflected in the tone of another inquiry, this time carried out by Birmingham City Council, which was released after the police review. In the local authority report the nature of the problem is expressed in a more forthright manner:

> There is a balance to be achieved between acceptable surveillance and excessive intrusion into personal freedom and privacy. We are clear that Project Champion overstepped this boundary and that the Project was unacceptable in the way it was constructed to target the Muslim community (Birmingham City Council 2010, p. 58).

Rather than any direct criticism of the police, the report concludes that it was the poor quality of the police communication that led to public disquiet. A more combative statement was made by Councillor Choudhry:

> What we still need is for somebody to be made accountable. Its easy enough saying, well I'm sorry I did it, won't happen again. But if this was in a private sector, somebody would be going to prison. Because you can't draw down 3 million pounds of funding and then invest it in the way they have, using the underhanded tactics that they did, they need to hold somebody to account. Whether somebody gets fired, whether somebody goes to prison. There needs to be that accountability, for the public, to officers to say, the police are just as accountable, if not more so than the local people.

It is of course the ultimate irony that an elected councillor, who was a part of the public processes of police accountability and communication, articulates a market model to ensure greater transparency. The mantra of the 'private sector' avoids the fact that it was the Association of Chief Police Officers, which is a private company with no democratic account-ability that applied for the money from the Home Office, and that it was private companies acting as consultants and implementing bodies that were involved each step of the way. Rather, the councillor should have been articulating a demand for greater democratic and public account-ability of police action. A further example of how neoliberal perspec-tives are unable to deliver on social justice can be seen in the way in which the police authority finally relented on the issue of the cameras. Subsequent to the releasing of the police and City Council inquiries, the Police Authority meeting of the 2 August 2010 resolved to remove the cameras and their poles as the best option.[16] However, the rhetoric of this report posits the Equalities and Community impact against the costs of removal. According to the logic of the report, if cost were taken into account, then the correct option would be to leave the poles and cameras in place (though not operational). But this option, though obviously preferred, is not possible because of the Equalities implica-tions. Indeed, four pages of the report go into the financial aspects of removal, building a case against taking the poles down. The concluding recommendation for taking the poles down begins by again articulating its cost as the second-best option in light of it being the best Equalities outcome. It is clear that the neoliberal imperative provides just as much potential for covering up social injustice as does the sham democracy of police consultation and council liaison.

Despite the decision to remove the cameras, it took a further six months before the cameras actually started being dismantled. In June 2011, the campaigners could claim a rare victory. As Naeem Malik put it:

> This is a victory for the people of Birmingham. This is a victory for the inner-city communities of Birmingham. This is also a victory for everybody whose actually fighting for human rights, civil liberties, both in Birmingham, in Britain and internationally.

Given the assault on civil liberties that is integral to the rhetoric of the War on Terror, this kind of campaigning is relatively rare. The push towards directly elected police commissioners in the UK may mean that in the future even the limited democratic accountability that enabled the exposure of the scandal may soon be narrowed.

Conclusion

Overt attempts by the state to survey and target a particular popula-tion could, arguably, be considered routine if the crude division between colonial and post-colonial spaces is collapsed. In terms of the management of unruly former colonial populations in Britain's urban centres, the role of the state was earlier conceptualised in terms of the hard arm, as in the police and the soft arm, as in social workers. In the new terrain of 'home grown' terror, the police are the soft arm, and MI5 and Counter terrorism Unit, the hard. This shift from soft and hard forms of securitisation in state action can be usefully viewed through the lens of racial neoliberalism, where the increasing withdrawal of the state from all activities other than security impacts overtly on racialised groups. Nonetheless, as in the earlier situation where coercive and hegemonic control were at play, spaces for resistance were always open. Even where the organisations and institutions that would lend support to black political mobilisations no longer exist, there remain moments of resistance and victory which should be highlighted. One such example is the case of the removal of CCTV cameras in Birmingham.

In an impassioned analysis of the corrosion of civil liberties since 9/11, Tariq Ali (2005, p. 73) despondently notes in the main body of his text: 'What can I do to stop this? With both major political parties pledged to the further destruction of civil liberties, Kennedy had no easy answer. Nor did I.' Perhaps, this pessimism arises from too many years of campaigning, but Ali's belief in activism only flounders for a page; in a footnote, he goes on: 'We need an organisation like the NCCL [National Council for Civil Liberties] again – an angry campaigning body, not a lobbyist' (Ali 2005, p. 74). The campaign to remove the cameras in Birmingham is of course a small dent in the overall repressive activities of the state. Yet it does provide a salutary reminder that it is only through organising and engaging that progressive change is possible. Even though analysis demonstrates the extent to which the state has become increasingly sophisticated in bypassing protections for citizen rights, this should not lead to paralysis. Indeed, one of the local campaigners in Birmingham expresses this point well:

> What we saw was a grass-roots campaign. I never thought the campaign would be as successful as it was. But we kept a consistent pressure on, to all the avenues possible, The Councillors put the pressure on, MPs put the pressure on and we used the media effectively to put the pressure on. And we constantly had the people, approaching the council, approaching the police. We did it. And I think if you do believe in something and keep on going, then sometimes you can win. (Jarrar Mughal)

Notes

1. www.levesoninquiry.org.uk
2. See Kapoor's chapter in this volume.
3. Such that any criminal activity involving Muslims contains as part of its rationale Muslimness itself. The grooming case (see Introduction) is a case in point, but this also operates at more subtle levels when it comes to financial misconduct or even petty crime. Much in the same way Caribbean and African communities were criminalised in the 1980s.
4. Though Kapoor's chapter in this book clearly shows the limits of the court when it comes to facing national pressure.
5. See http://www.guardian.co.uk/politics/2005/aug/06/terrorism.july7
6. http://www.parliament.thestationery-office.co.uk/pa/cm200910/cmselect/cmhaff/117/11707.htm
7. This is material gathered from personal interaction with members of the organisation involved. Names have been withheld for confidentiality issues.
8. Though of course the numbers of those actually arrested and charged with terrorist related activities is...
9. According to the 2001 Census of Birmingham, 49 per cent of Muslims in Birmingham live in the four wards of Sparkbrook, Springfield, Bordesley Green and Washwood Heath. Birmingham City Council. 2001 Population Census in Birmingham. Religious Groups Profile.
10. See Vron Ware's chapter in this volume for more details.
11. http://news.bbc.co.uk/1/hi/uk/6340935.stm
12. http://www.olivegroup.com/contents.php?contid=131
13. http://www.ohchr.org/EN/NewsEvents/Pages/Gunsforhire.aspx
14. All interviews that are quoted from were carried out by Tariq Mehmood and Ken Fero as part of the documentary, *Defeat of the Champion* (25 minutes/2011/UK/Dir: Ken Fero & Tariq Mehmood/Migrant Media), available at http://vimeo.com/35962437
15. http://www.no-cctv.org.uk/campaigns/moseley_antI_anpr.asp
16. http://www.west-midlands pa.gov.uk/documents/committees/public/2010/08c_PAuth_02Dec2010_Project_Champion_Scheme.pdf

References

Ali, T. (2005) *Rough Music* (London: Verso).
Awan, I. (2011) 'Terror in the Eye of the Beholder: The 'Spycam' Saga: Counter-Terrorism or Counter Productive?', *Howard Journal of Criminal Justice*, 50(2), 199–202.
Birmingham City Council (2010) *Scrutiny Review in to ANPR and CCTV Cameras* (Birmingham: Birmingham City Council).
Bowling, B. and Phillips, C. (2001) *Racism, Crime and Criminal Justice* (Essex: Longman).
Brown, K. (2010) 'Contesting the Securitization of British Muslims', *Interventions: International Journal of Postcolonial Studies*, 12(2), 171–82.
Fekete, Liz (2004) 'Anti-Muslim Racism and the European Security State', *Race and Class*, 46(1), 3–29.

Fiske, J. (1998) 'Surveilling the City: Whiteness, the Black Man and Democratic Totalitarianism', *Theory Culture Society*, 15(2), 67–88.

Gilroy, P. (1982)), 'Police and Thieves', in CCCS (ed.), *The Empire Strikes Back: Race and Racism in 70s Britain* (Birmingham: CCCS), pp. 141–81.

Hall, S., Critcher, C., Jefferson, T., Clarke, J. and Roberts, B. (1978) *Policing the Crisis: Mugging, the State, and Law and Order* (London: Macmillan).

Hillyard, P. (1993) *Suspect Community: People's Experiences of the Prevention of Terrorism Acts in Britain* (London: Pluto).

HM Government (2011) Prevent Strategy Presented to Parliament by the Prime Minister and the Secretary of State for the Home Department, by Command of Her Majesty, http://www.homeoffice.gov.uk/publications/counter-terrorism/prevent/prevent-strategy/prevent-strategy-review?view=Binary.

Norris, C. and Armstrong, G. (1999). *The Maximum Surveillance Society: The Rise of CCTV* (Oxford: Berg).

Pantazis, C. and Pemberton, S. (2009) 'From the "Old" to the "New" Suspect Community: Examining the Impacts of Recent UK Counter-Terrorist Legislation', *British Journal of Criminology*, 49(5), 646–66.

Patel, T. and Tyrer, D. (2011) *Race, Crime and Resistance* (London: Sage).

Peirce, G. (2010) *Dispatches from the Dark Side: On Torture and the Death of Innocence* (London: Verso).

Roth, O. (2010) 'A Fair Cop', New Local Government Network, www.nlgn.org.uk/public/wp-content/uploads/A-Fair-Cop.pdf.

Sivanandan, A. (1981) 'From Resistance to Rebellion', *Race and Class*, 23(2–3), 111–52.

Spalek, B. and Imtoual, A. (2007) 'Muslim Communities and Counter-Terror Responses: "Hard" Approaches to Community Engagement in the UK and Australia', *Journal of Muslim Minority Affairs*, 27(2), 185–202.

Spalek, B. (2009) 'Community Policing within a Counter-Terrorism Context: The Role of Trust When Working with Muslim Communities to Prevent Terror Crime', *Selected Works of Basia Spalek*, http://works.bepress.com/basia_spalek/1.

Stutzer, A. & Zehnder, M. (2012) 'Is Camera Surveillance an Effective Measure of Counterterrorism?' *Journal: Defence and Peace Economics*, iFirstarticle, pp. 1–14.

Thornton, S. (2010) *Project Champion Review: An Independent Review of the Commissioning, Direction, Control and Oversight of Project Champion* (Kidlington: Thames Valley Police).

Welsh, B. and Farrington, D. (2009) 'Public Area CCTV and Crime Prevention: An Update Systematic Review and Meta-Analysis', *Justice Quarterly*, 26(4), 716–45.

9
Extraordinary Extradition: Racial (In)justice in Britain

Nisha Kapoor

> There is a caged bird whose only wish is to be a bird again.
> There is a caged bird that yearns to fly free again
> And soar over the mountain tops and glide through the valleys.
> There is a caged bird that is no better than any other bird
> And no different to any other bird.
> There is a caged bird whose wings have been cut and voice has been muted
> Whose only desire is to be a bird again.
> That's why the caged bird sings.
>
> (Babar Ahmad, May 2007)

> The reigning doctrine is sometimes called 'American exceptionalism'. It is nothing of the sort. It is probably close to universal among imperial powers.
>
> (Noam Chomsky 2009)

In 2003 a new Extradition Act was fast-tracked into UK legislation without a formal consultative parliamentary process, scrutiny or debate. The Act made provisions for a unilateral agreement between the US and the UK whereby the UK would be expected to extradite any individual to the US on request, without the need for the US to provide prima facie evidence (only to invoke reasonable suspicion), and thus without allowing the individual called to challenge any evidence provided by the US in a British court of law. In contrast, in response to any requests made by the UK for extradition of subjects from the US, UK authorities are expected to provide enough evidence to demonstrate 'probable cause'. Accordingly, since its inception the Act has been at the centre of much controversy, most notably because it has made explicit the hegemonic position of the US in Anglo-American relations and brought to popular attention the limits of UK national sovereignty.

Specifically, it has been the unintended consequences of extradition which have laid focus on white British citizens that have dominated popular protest and parliamentary debate. The *Daily Mail*–backed campaign for Gary McKinnon received far more attention and notice than the campaign for justice for Babar Ahmad – Britain's longest-serving prisoner detained without charge or trial.[1] This dichotomy came to light in the response to the 149,000-strong petition to the Home Office against the extradition of Babar Ahmad, which secured, albeit reluctantly, a debate on the matter in the House of Commons. Despite the number of signatures totalling well over the 100,000-signature threshold required for a guaranteed debate on a particular issue in the House of Commons, the Government initially refused to allow such a debate to take place. Eventually they agreed to incorporate Ahmad's case into a wider debate on extradition arrangements, which took place in December 2011. Thus the state could appear to be staying true to its ostensible British democratic principles and processes – rights, supposedly, of all citizens – whilst the debate itself spoke to the rights of a particular faction of the population.

Within the back-bench debate, there was clear opposition against the Act from Members of Parliament (MPs) of all political persuasions, who argued that the legislation was completely at odds with the liberal principles of the British justice system and greatly eroded 'the liberty of our citizens'. In his introduction to the discussion, Dominic Raab, Conservative MP for Esher and Walton, argued that what was under threat was the 'cornerstone of British justice, innocent until proven guilty', asserting that 'in taking the fight to the terrorists and the serious criminals after 9/11, the pendulum [had] swung too far the other way' (House of Commons debate 2011, c82). Of ultimate concern was how a legal process stripped of all intent to due process, designed for targeting 'the terrorist', could also encompass the (white) British citizen. The consequence was to call for adjustment to legislation that was being delivered in a 'one size fits all' manner so that it could better distinguish between the two. The legitimacy of extradition was thus determined by its ability to racially distinguish, to invoke racism – racial division and stratification – to regulate the distribution of death (social and real), as has been historically normative. The House of Commons debate made clear that the extradition process was unfair because the distinction being made between those who must live and those who must die appeared racially incoherent.

The force of extradition as a governing device is of course informed by the escalation of militarisation and securitisation in the twenty-first century. The 9/11 attacks played a dual role in both acting as a signifying marker of threat to the US as global power and providing the justification for the US and its allies to heighten their use of aggressive militarised tactics in response to any perceived obstacle or threat within the nation and beyond. The attacks on 9/11, 7/7 and the numerous others against the West and its allies (Madrid, Bali, Mumbai) have been drawn upon by the US and the UK to gain popular consensus for their advancement of imperial aggression and their devaluation of human rights, and indeed, of human life. To follow Gramsci (1999), the discourse of the 'threat of terror' enabled a new mode of domination that was suitably universal and legitimate in its appeal while its basis in (racial) exploitation disappeared from view. The result was the preservation of US hegemony, with UK backing, and with consensus to more freely and openly employ its super-military powers in tandem with an increasing erosion of civil rights.

The legitimacy of the revival of extradition in recent times as a political and governing process was gained because of its stated purpose of assisting this fight against terror. Alongside a whole host of other measures passed in the name of the War on Terror which have drastically reduced rights and freedoms (Ali 2005; Kundnani 2007; Kapoor 2011), extradition to the US was agreed to be a suitable process for expelling the terrorist, for dispelling threat, and for enabling the sentencing and incarceration of those deemed the world's most dangerous men in the world's most sophisticated and secure prison systems. Extradition, in essence, formed part of a 'War on Terror complex', a system of militarised processes, procedures and operations instilled in the name of global security, designed to govern, control and discipline populations at the global level. This relies heavily on international co-operation between nation-states, with the US as commander in chief, as ultimate global sovereign. It is a system which oscillates between operating through the law (specifically through the creation of 'terror laws'), as Derek Gregory (2007) notes, and operating outside the law, bypassing international law completely (Prashad 2012) and asserting exemption by invoking the state of permanent war. By invoking present forms of Western imperial aggression as a defensive 'war' against the attack of *illegal* enemy combatants, the US and its Allies imply not just a parity between two sides, as has been typically the case, but claim their own victimisation from a threatening 'other'. Deflecting from what is in actuality a unilateral, continuous, colonial and imperial process, this approach consequently spares the Western allies from having to answer to ongoing acts of racial injustice. To speak of racism in the War on Terror thus becomes nonsensical, which in turn facilitates racism in the extreme. The War on Terror becomes the exception par excellence, and the War on Terror complex is the rountinised functioning of the state as the state of exception. It is the state of exception as the state of normalisation.

Britain's role in the War on Terror globally and its implications for Muslims living in the metropole can tell us a great deal about the state of race in Britain. While the legal framework which sanctions extradition exemplifies the perseverance of racial structuring just as legislative support for equality is weakened (Kapoor 2011) and how Britain, not unlike the US, begins to enforce the state of exception as the state of normalisation, the intricacies of the debate on extradition showcase the return to explicit and blatant racism, if racism not recognised as such. It is these two mechanisms that I present in this chapter highlighting, firstly, Britain's complicity and active role in the War on Terror, and secondly, through the exemplar of extradition, Britain's racial hypocrisy and continuing implementation of racial injustice.

The British State of Exception

During the parliamentary debate on extradition, the patriotic push made by a number of MPs, who argued that the ancient liberties of the British citizen enshrined in the Magna Carta and Habeas Corpus were being violated, and who contrasted the corruption of the US legal system to the fairness and equality of the British system was indeed curious (see House of Commons debate 2011). It had only been six months earlier that Barack Obama, in his first state visit to Britain as president of the United States, had been reverentially met with great applause when he emphasised the shared values of the two states.

> I have come here today to reaffirm one of the oldest, one of the strongest alliances the world has ever known. It has long been said that the United States and the United Kingdom share a special relationship ... The reason for this close friendship doesn't just have to do with our shared history, our shared heritage; our ties of language and culture; or even the strong partnership between our governments. Our relationship is special because of the values and beliefs that have united our people through the ages. (Obama 2011)

Rather astutely, Obama pointed out that the two nations had much in common. Hinting at the settler-colonial relationship, he paid homage to the Magna Carta, the English Bill of Rights, the Habeas Corpus, trial by jury and the English Common Law for providing the foundations of the American Declaration of Independence and the Constitution, making claims to the liberal foundations of both states. And in arguing the similarities, he did not fail to emphasise their joint imperial adventures, describing how as a unit it was they who had 'shaped a world in which new nations could emerge and individuals could thrive' and that there were few nations that 'stand firmer, speak louder and fight harder to defend democratic values around the world than the United States and the United Kingdom'. Massaging the egos of his hosts and paying homage to Empire, Obama whipped up Anglo-American nationalist fervour in a moment that conjured up the likeness of both. As Noam Chomsky remarks in the second epigraph to this chapter, Obama's narration of history, for all its distortions, drew attention to the fact that the reigning order was not simply a matter of 'American exceptionalism', but, in this case, 'Anglo-American exceptionalism', and in reality a doctrine taken on by all imperial powers. Though the US was hegemonic, it was certainly not exceptional.

In contrast, the suggestion by MPs that the British rule of law and approach was quite distinct from and separate to the US and other European countries was a gross oversight of the leading role that Britain has played in the Allies self-anointed War on Terror. It bypassed Britain's very active part in and support for the creation of an (il)legal global war strategy that, contra to UN human rights stipulations, has sanctioned rendition, illegal detention, torture, the increasing use of unmanned drones, and illegal occupation and war, in order to secure its own political and economic interests (Ali 2005; Peirce 2010). The claim in support of the preservation of liberal values said to be the foundations of the British state actually became a way of sidestepping, and presenting a suitable façade for, the array of punitive acts it was routinely conducting.

The War on Terror has reframed the boundaries of war, ultimately permitting the violation of human rights and the degradation of human life on global scales that had hitherto not been reached. By perpetuating and redefining the permanent state of war, the War on Terror is used to sanction an interminable state of exception, where the near-permanent militarisation of civilian life is justified as a necessary safeguard. In this regard, the legality of the War on Terror has drastically increased the power of the sovereign over its subjects, whilst simultaneously intensifying the vulnerability and precariousness of those under its control.

Within this paradigm shift, the figure of 'the (racially ambivalent) terrorist' is the most at risk of being treated with complete impunity and of being put to death.

If there had been uncertainty or ambivalence with regard to the normalcy of the state of exception in Britain, the British state's open response to 7/7 made explicit the permanency of the state of emergency through the number of draconian measures that were overtly put into operation to target the terrorist threat. In actuality, liberties that civil society has long taken for granted have been in the process of being whittled away for some time. The barrister Helena Kennedy QC (2004), for example, has pointed to New Labour's mass onslaught on civil liberties, well underway before 7/7. These measures included internment without trial for non-citizens suspected of terrorist links, repeated efforts to reduce trial by jury for all citizens, retrial of those who have been acquitted,[2] attacks on the independence of the judiciary, cuts to legal aid, severe limitations on the right to silence, and shifting the burden of proof on to the accused, to list but some. If many of these erosions had occurred to some extent under the radar to avoid protest or opposition from the population at large, post–7/7 Tony Blair could be more upfront about the state's increasing militarisation and securitisation. In support of his objectives, further terrorism legislation was quickly passed through Parliament in 2005, and Blair was nothing short of bold in declaring his commitment to use the law as a weapon with which to counter any right to 'human' that the terrorist might attempt to claim. Following the passing of the 2005 Prevention of Terrorism Act, he stated:

> Should legal obstacles arise, we will legislate further, including, if necessary, amending the Human Rights Act, in respect of the interpretation of the ECHR. In any event, we will consult on legislating specifically for a non-suspensive appeal process in respect of deportations. (Blair 2005)

Between 2000 and 2008 five pieces of terror legislation were passed, with one additional measure passed by the Conservative–Liberal Democrat Government in 2011. This legislation has worked to develop a legal frame which patches together a hotchpotch of measures (laws to counter laws), through which the sovereign conducts war. The War on Terror has relied on a glut of legislation, and the use of law to undo, redo, approve, remove, increase and reduce pre-existing legal measures such that the state of exception now operates, not always through a suspension of the law, but through the law

(Gregory 2007). As always, fundamental to war strategy is the de-humanisation of the enemy, the continuous reference and appeal to a 'fictionalised notion of the enemy' which the state then labours to produce (Mbembe 2003, p. 16). The imaginary of the terrorist as the inhuman death threat has longstanding appeal and thus legitimates the enactment of differential rights. Indeed, it permits the removal of rights altogether. The consequence is to re-institutionalise, and make more salient, racial categorisation (though with the denial of racial reference) as the determination of any possibility of equality before the law. The manipulation of the law to differentiate between the citizen and the other is of course nothing new. But of significance here is the vast amount of legislation passed to counter any access to legal rights and due process, even if it was only nominal to begin with. In essence, we have the institutionalisation of the state of exception. One of the key aims of the 2005 Prevention of Terrorism Act, for example, was to counter the decision by the Law Lords, who found the indefinite detention without trial of foreign nationals suspected of terrorism to be unlawful. The 2005 Act permitted the use of control orders, which essentially meant that suspects could be imprisoned at home, and went further by extending this to British nationals, too. The parliamentary Joint Committee on Human Rights expressed concerns about whether this was 'compatible with the rule of law and with the well-established principles concerning the separation of powers between the executive and the judiciary' (Kundnani 2007, p. 176). Their concerns, though, were disregarded and made irrelevant. Discussions pertaining to the human rights of a terrorist were a misnomer.

The consequence of this never-ending and geographically amorphous war is the sanctioning of an array of invasive and inhumane measures, including stop and search; the Prevent and Contest agenda (which incorporates numerous surveillance and pre-emptive interventions); detention without trial; the increasing use of the Special Immigration Appeals Court, which essentially conducts secret trials; and extradition. This is of course in addition to acts of illegal deportation, extraordinary rendition, torture and extrajudicial murder, where the law is more apparently suspended. These actions have a long history, embedded in colonial relations and governing techniques, so laws designed to permit acts such as preventative detention, used regularly to maintain imperial domination in the colonies, have now returned home (Ali 2005). Though links between the colony and the metropole have always been circular, since 2000 the growth of anti-terrorism legislation in Britain has institutionalised this imagining by in essence creating a secondary legal system for dealing with the terrorist. The consequence is the construction of a hyper-securitised state where everyday intrusions become the normalised experience of the terrorist figure just as such incursions are largely disregarded by the general population.

One of the key ways in which this tiered system is maintained is through the use of secrecy and coercion. The criminal actions of the state must be silenced and are done so in the name of national security. Of late there have been a number of cases attracting media attention which have brought Britain's complicity in torture and numerous other violent (and illegal) acts out of the shadows. In January 2010, the UN published a report on its investigation into torture and rendition across the globe in which it concluded that the British Government had been complicit in the mistreatment and possible torture of several of its own citizens during the War on Terror. Among the instances of a state being complicit in a secret detention, the report mentioned 'the United Kingdom in the cases of several individuals, including Binyam Mohamed, Salahuddin Amin, Zeeshan Siddiqui, Rangzieb Ahmed and Rashid Rauf' (Cobain 2010). One of those listed, Binyam Mohamed, is a British resident who was subjected to rendition by US authorities, incarcerated in prisons in Pakistan, Afghanistan and Morocco before being transferred to Guantanamo and tortured with the full knowledge of and direction from the British and US intelligence authorities (Peirce 2010). Following his release in February 2009 after almost seven years of imprisonment in the most inhumane of conditions, a legal battle against the then Foreign Secretary David Miliband evidenced how British intelligence (MI5 and MI6) had colluded with Mohamed's interrogators to the point of directing the questions he was asked. It transpired they were fully aware that he was being tortured and that they used the evidence obtained from him as a result of this.

Relatedly, on the illegal detention and torture of British citizens in Guantánamo Bay from the early days of 2002, the limited documentation that has been made public, which consists of a series of email exchanges, reveals ministers communicating that they did not want the men back in Britain under any circumstances and that the most satisfactory solution for the UK was for all to be transported (entirely unlawfully) to Guantánamo Bay. However, this was not to be until they had been held for a week (in unlawful conditions of extreme severity) so that they could be interrogated more conveniently by British intelligence agents. In the exchange it became clear that the orders were coming 'from No.10' (Peirce 2010, p. 100).

These cases and others concerning British citizens tortured by officials in Pakistan, who exchanged information with their British counterparts, placed the British Government in what Gareth Peirce (2010, p. 2) referred to as 'a moment of acute discomfort', not least because of the upset the public disclosure of CIA intelligence caused the US. Indeed, it was the potential harm that would be caused to the special intelligence relationship with the United States that was cited by David Miliband as reason enough not to disclose the notes which had been shared between the torture regimes, the CIA and MI5. And any attempt at a public inquiry or investigation into these injustices is limited in its terms from the start. As Gareth Peirce remarked on the Baha Mousa Inquiry, an investigation into the activities of the British military in Iraq, there was no intention of investigating 'the interaction of the British state with the US or the intelligence forces, or with any torturing foreign state. Instead the government will claim ... that any issue relating to the intelligence services, or the conduct of diplomatic relationships, should be confined entirely to special courts, or the evidence heard in large part in secret' (2010, p. 9). And this has been the response to evidence of complicity in torture. Resorting again to the law, this time for sovereign protection, to prevent further embarrassment and future costly compensation payouts by the state, the Secretary of State for Justice, Ken Clarke, has put forward a Justice and Security Green Paper which makes the case for secret court hearings in intelligence-related civil cases in order to prevent intelligence information from ever appearing in open court (HM Government 2011).

On Extradition

As one of the array of War on Terror weapons, the 2003 Extradition Act performed a specific and useful function. Aimed at targeting the terrorist, it acts in many ways as the legal equivalent of rendition, essentially making allowances for the terrorist ascertained under British control to be relocated under US jurisdiction – a legal system where 97 per cent of accused plead guilty due to the plea bargaining system in place (Home Affairs Select Committee 2012), thus making the legal distinction between suspect and guilty redundant. If one of the main aims of the War on Terror is to discipline and punish the terrorist, the US (and US jurisdiction, wherever that may be), as international court house, is the locale of choice for administering the punishment. It is thus not the result of short-sightedness that the US–UK extradition treaty appears unbalanced in its terms. It was never its intention to respect the sovereignty of each nation, but rather to ensure the terrorist could be treated with complete impunity.

However, of the numerous violations which the state carries out at its discretion, it is interesting that extradition is one of the few which has prompted upset and dissent. Between 2004 and July 2011, 73 UK nationals or dual nationals were surrendered from the UK to the US (Baker et al. 2011), not all on terror-related offences. In this process it has become apparent that the proliferating use of such practices means that there potential for them to impact segments of the population which they are not intended to target. It is the unintended consequences of extradition which have brought the issue so much attention, prompting national debate and calls for significant reform. As David Davis MP remarked:

> We should keep in mind that the rather draconian process that we have, which was put in place to defend us against terrorism, does not appear to have had much impact in that respect. In practice, the outcome is much more mundane. The truth of the matter is that we will have far more Gary McKinnons extradited than Osama bin Ladens. (House of Commons Debate 2011, c91)

In particular, it is the call for extradition of white British citizens such as Gary McKinnon, Christopher Tappin (who has been extradited) and Richard O'Dwyer which have raised the profile of the issue. Meanwhile the European Court's decision in April 2012, which ruled that five Muslim men accused of terrorism-related charges could be extradited to the US, received national public approval.[3]

Extraditing the Terrorist...

Babar Ahmad is the longest-serving prisoner in Britain detained without charge or trial. In December 2003, Ahmad, a British Muslim citizen and highly educated engineering graduate working in the IT Department at Imperial College London, was arrested at his London home under anti-terror legislation. By the time he reached the police station he had sustained at least 73 forensically recorded injuries, including bleeding in his ears and urine. Six days later he was released without charge.[4]

On 5 August 2004, Ahmad was re-arrested in London and taken to prison pursuant to an extradition request from the US in which they alleged that in the 1990s he had been a supporter of terrorism, committing terrorism offences in the USA from 1996 to 2003. The claim is that he had tried to solicit support for terrorism in Chechnya and Afghanistan using websites that supported Chechen and Taliban rebel fighters. The feeble link to the US is simply that one of the internet servers on which one of these websites was hosted was, for a short period, based in the US. During the entire period 'relevant to the indictment' Babar Ahmad was resident and in full-time employment in London. Despite the fact that the Crown Prosecution Service (CPS) repeatedly stated that the there was not enough evidence to prosecute him in the UK and, indeed, released him in 2003, the extradition request from the US has been deemed sufficient justification to detain him for eight years in high-security prisons in Britain. Between 2004 and 2007, he lost all his appeals against extradition in the UK domestic courts, and in April 2012, after waiting five years to hear the decision of his appeal to the European Court of Human Rights, Ahmad heard that together with four other terrorist suspects he could be extradited to the US. Following unsuccessful appeals, Ahmad and Talha Ahsan (along with three other Muslim men detained in Britain) were extradited to the US on 7 October 2012. They face spending the rest of their natural lives in prison in solitary confinement in US 'supermax', ADX Florence, Colorado, a maximum security prison which was described by a former warden as a 'clean version of hell' (CBS News 2009).

Ahmad's case has been riddled with controversy from the beginning. Following his horrific physical, sexual and religious abuse by the arresting police officers in 2003, in March 2009 the Metropolitan Police admitted their guilt, awarding him £60,000 compensation for damages. However, they offered no apology for the actions of their officers; and in a subsequent criminal trial in May/June 2011 where the police officers involved were charged with assault, all four were acquitted. The jury took only 45 minutes to reach their verdict, and it was reported that some of the jurors requested to meet the officers to shake their hands following the conclusion of the trial (BBC 2011). The stark contrast between the response of the Met Police to the officers' acquittal and their response to PC Simon Harwood's acquittal after he was accused of the manslaughter of Ian Tomlinson, who suffered a heart attack after being batoned by Harwood as he was walking away from the G20 protests in 2009, speaks to the entrenched racial hypocrisy within the criminal justice system. This hypocrisy is all too familiar to those who regularly experience its brunt. Despite the fact that PC Harwood was not charged, he was sacked for gross misconduct and his actions were described as 'discrediting the police service'. In Babar Ahmad's case, that the officers involved had a history of over 70 complaints of assault against them (predominantly on black and Asian men) was deemed inconsequential; none would face disciplinary hearings and all were returned to full duties.[5]

Racism within the police, upheld by society, was met with further controversy which come to the fore regarding the legality of the extradition process itself. In contra to the general assertion by the British authorities that there was not enough evidence to try Babar Ahmad in the UK, the European Court's interim decision in the case of Ahmad stated that it had an acknowledgement from the UK Government that he could be tried in Britain (House of Commons debate 2011, c101). Nevertheless, in July 2004, October 2006 and December 2006, the CPS and the Attorney-General declared that there was insufficient evidence to charge him with any criminal offence under UK law and that he should therefore be extradited. For Talha Ahsan, a second suspect associated with the same case also imprisoned awaiting extradition to the US, there has never been any domestic consideration of his case by the CPS, and he has never been questioned by British authorities. The determination of British authorities to discipline the terrorist within the US judicial system, if suspect before, was in no doubt when on 4 December 2011 Ahmad's lawyers received a letter from the CPS that admitted for the first time it was never given the evidence that was sent to the US, apart from a few documents. The bulk of the evidence was shipped straight to the US by the Met Police (House of Commons Debate 2011, c101). Secrecy uncovered, Britain's determination to extradite Babar Ahmad was not in doubt.

The revealing injustice of his case came to a head in April 2012 when the European Court of Human Rights finally came to a historic decision stating that the use of extreme isolation in US supermax prisons pre- and post-trial and the granting of lengthy sentences, such as life imprisonment without parole, or 80 to 100 years, prospects faced by Babar Ahmad and other terrorist suspects, did not violate Article 3 of the European Convention on Human Rights. This rather unusual decision from the European Court, which had previously spoken out against US human rights practices and suggested that such punishments might constitute what the law defines as torture (House of Commons Debate 2011, c101), came following David Cameron's aggressive lobbying to Strasbourg, as reported in the national press (Watt and Bowcott 2012). Here he argued that the European Court should be subsidiary to national authorities in guaranteeing human rights and that Britain need not be subject to the same stipulations as other 'less compliant' European countries which did not appropriately implement European human rights convention standards. It is not unlikely that behind the scenes discussions were very persuasive in influencing the court's final decision, such that when it was publicly announced Cameron could state he was 'very pleased with the news' (cited in Dodd 2012).

In spite of all this, and of the calls by the parliamentary Joint Committee on Human Rights that the Government change the law so that 'Babar Ahmad's perpetual threat of extradition is ended without further delay' (Hyde 2011), and even the call by Judge Geoffrey Rivlin QC at the conclusion of Babar's criminal trial against the Met Police officers that his ordeal be 'brought to an end as soon as possible' (BBC 2011), the thrust of the policy debate on extradition has been in support of, to quote David Davis, the 'Gary McKinnons'.

And the Non-Terrorist...

Thirteen months prior to Ahmad's first arrest, Gary McKinnon, a Scottish systems-administrator diagnosed with Asperger's syndrome, was indicted by a federal grand jury in the US, accused of hacking into 97 US military and NASA computers over a 13-month period between February 2001 and March 2002, using the name 'Solo'. The US authorities claim that, after gaining remote access to US military computing networks from the UK, he deleted critical files from operating systems, which shut down a US Army network of 2000 computers for 24 hours, and deleted US Navy weapons logs, rendering a naval base's network of 300 computers inoperable after the September 11 terrorist attacks. In addition, McKinnon is accused of copying data, account files and passwords onto his own computer. US authorities claim the cost of tracking and correcting the damage he caused was over $700,000 (*McKinnon v. USA 2007*). McKinnon was never charged with any espionage or terrorism offences,[6] though he does admit to leaving the following message on one computer:

> US foreign policy is akin to Government-sponsored terrorism these days... It was not a mistake that there was a huge security stand down on September 11 last year... I am SOLO. I will continue to disrupt at the highest levels (*McKinnon v. USA 2007*).

Arguably a gesture of solidarity in support of the many other forms of protest that attempt to expose the reaches and depths of US imperialism, the hegemonic response to the McKinnon case, in contrast to what might be the expected reaction to such a statement, has been to rally support for his defence, quite distinct from that which has greeted Babar Ahmad and Talha Ahsan. And it is this disparity which unveils the mindset of the racial state. McKinnon's defence rests upon his Asperger's syndrome, a condition his lawyers have linked to his explanation that he was looking for evidence of UFOs. His case has gained far-reaching support including a campaign backed by the *Daily Mail* which ensured that in their national election campaigns both David Cameron and Nick Clegg lobbied against McKinnon's impending extradition to the US (Robertson 2010). Committed to pursuing his promise, Cameron went further, raising the issue with President Obama on a number of occasions, and reporting in a joint press conference in 2010 that he hoped 'a way through' could be found (see Free Gary campaign website 2010). In March 2012, when raising the issue again, it was the 'controversial' cases of Gary McKinnon and Christopher Tappin that were raised, where their status as 'British citizens' was forefronted just as the Britishness of Babar Ahmad, Talha Ahsan and the numerous other British Muslim terrorist suspects was denied.

In this comparison it is of note that while McKinnon's diagnosis with Asperger's syndrome has been used to front his case and defend his innocence, Talha Ahsan's Asperger's syndrome, and, indeed, his case, has received scant attention. The racial distinction between the two was stated clearly by Dominic Raab MP and others in the House of Commons debate:

> The Gary McKinnon case is the leading case attracting great controversy at present. At root it is about the injustice in dispatching someone with Asperger's syndrome hundreds of miles from home on allegations of computer hacking when he was apparently searching for unidentified flying objects. Gary McKinnon should not be treated like some gangland mobster or al-Qaeda mastermind. (House of Commons Debate 2011, c84)

Unlike McKinnon, Ahsan's mental health was not deemed to have any worthy significance that would merit its being taken into consideration in the European Court of Human Rights's decision on his extradition to the US. Exemplifying the real motivation behind the parliamentary debate, in response to this decision, the same Dominic Raab who had brought the discussion to the House of Commons in a plea to call for reform was quoted in *The Telegraph* as commenting, 'To say that we couldn't extradite serious terrorist players to the US because they may get a long sentence in difficult, tough prison conditions would be ludicrous' (Holehouse 2012). Raab emphasised the decision as a 'moral matter' and as one necessary to uphold the whole basis for counter-terrorism extradition to the US. And here the real barriers to extradition reform come to light. Gary McKinnon's appeal through the European Court of Human Rights ended in August 2008, yet he remained on bail in Britain awaiting extradition while his case continued to be adjourned to give the Home Secretary and judiciary time to further consider psychiatric reports.[7] Aptly planned, in October 2012, ten days following the extradition of the Muslim men, Home Office–appointed psychiatrists decided that McKinnon was 'very likely to commit suicide' if sent to the US for trial, an assessment altered from earlier observations where they had noted that the risk was 'moderate'. Consequently, the Home Secretary halted his extradition. A predicament for the state who feared extraditing him because of the political clout his case held, but who also feared ruling in his favour lest they set a precedent for Muslim suspects with arguably worse health conditions than McKinnon,[8] once the Muslim suspects were extradited to the US legal arrangements could be reformed to save those deemed worth saving.

Tied to this distinction was the resurrection of the notion of Britishness as a racial identity. British exceptionalism relied on, as David Davis put it, the 'presumption of innocence', calling people 'sir' and treating them with dignity (House of Commons Debate 2011, c90). These were reasons to try British people in Britain – 'British justice for British citizens'. But clearly, the British justice which did 'not imprison people who are awaiting trial' did not apply to all those British Muslims detained indefinitely without charge. This presumption of innocence did not speak to the experiences of blacks and Asians, who remain significantly more likely to be stopped, searched and to die in police custody compared with the white population (Delsol 2012). It did not speak to the experiences of Jean Charles de Menezes, Smiley Culture, Mark Duggan, Mozzam Begg, Talha Ahsan or Babar Ahmad, to name but a few. The exception to those deserving British justice were those deemed a 'threat', and that threat was racially marked.

This distinction between the British citizen and the terrorist has framed the entire debate around extradition such that the whole basis of the discussion of the injustice of extradition has centred on the importance of retaining white privilege, obscuring the real injustice of racism. The Liberal Democrat Peer, Lord Carlile QC, in response to the decision that Babar Ahmad and other Muslim terrorist suspects should be extradited, said he agreed with the decision, commenting that it was 'perfectly reasonable that they should be tried where the crime was aimed' (Holehouse 2012), making a rather bizarre and tenuous link given that Ahmad and Ahsan were being accused of operating websites to support fighters in Chechnya and Afghanistan primarily during the 1990s. His comment was in complete contrast to the statement he made in 2010 in relation to the Gary McKinnon case. On this, his view was that 'there is no doubt that Mr McKinnon could be prosecuted in this country, given that the acts of unlawful access occurred within our jurisdiction (i.e. from his computer in North London)' (Slack and Seamark 2010). Lest there was any uncertainty that such reasoning might be used by terrorist suspects, Carlile made clear that McKinnon's case was a 'one-off'.

But it soon became apparent that McKinnon's case was not a one-off when Lord Carlile also felt compelled to speak out against the extradition of Christopher Tappin, a retired businessman extradited to the US in February 2012 for allegedly selling batteries to Iran to be used for missiles. A case of 'matter out of place' (Douglas 1966), Carlile was appalled by the legal conditions confronting Tappin and openly called for a public inquiry to examine 'whether it is acceptable for people to be sent back to the US to face their intimidating plea bargaining system', a system he claimed would not be acceptable under English law. Drawing on this apparent inverted racial order, Christopher Tappin himself saw fit to articulate the lack of appropriate racial distinction when speaking out on his impending extradition, stating, 'I have no rights. Abu Qatada is walking the streets of London today and we cannot extradite him. He has more rights than I have...I think it's a shame, a disgrace' (Whitehead 2012). In the discourse of postracial times, it was the racially privileged white middle-class male who could claim (much to popular appeal) he was the victim of inequality and injustice, declaring the ostensible elevated rights of the racially degenerate terrorist figure who could appeal for human rights.

And the 'Non-British' Terrorist...

The rights of citizenship if blurred and in the process of gradual suspension for British Muslims, are all the more prohibited from postcolonial nationals residing in Britain. The claim made advocating 'British justice for British citizens', which quickly comes undone when the rights and treatment of racially othered British subjects are considered, is all the more explicit in its distinction between the entitlement of British citizens and non-British citizens. In this regard, the sentiment is not just one aimed at re-invoking racially-coded notions of British nationalism but also speaks to, as it silences, Britain's ongoing role as a colonising power with all the differentiation between national and colonial subjects that this entails. Alongside the British Muslim subjects indefinitely detained without trial or charge are numerous cases of foreign nationals detained, often in liaison with US officials, who are granted few rights and without recourse to a sovereign national government. The erosion of sovereignty of the (post)colonial countries invaded and occupied by the Allies' War on Terror, reminding us that the colony is the space where the law is suspended (Mbembe 2003), is echoed in the treatment of colonial subjects in the metropole. That is, the special privileges of legal rights and protection reserved for British citizens, even as they become ever more fragile, do not apply. The division made between citizen and immigrant of course has longstanding appeal, but in the War on Terror which plays out on both domestic and international fronts, the connections between strategies of governance and discipline in the colony and in the metropole are all the more intertwined.

One such example is Abid Naseer, a Pakistani national who had come to Britain as a student. Naseer was arrested on 8 April 2009, along with eleven other men, on suspicion of planning an attack in the North West of England. Despite the fact that charges were dropped within 13 days of his arrest, ten of the men, all Pakistani nationals, were transferred to immigration detention. Naseer remained branded as an 'Islamist extremist', 'despite the *complete absence of any evidence* of the handling or preparation of explosives by Naseer and his alleged associates' (Mitting 2010; emphasis added). Following numerous legal battles to defend his right to stay in the UK and continue his studies, finding himself in legal limbo,[9] on 7 July 2010 Abid was re-arrested based on a provisional warrant issued by the US and was requested for extradition by the US Government on 1 September 2010. His case was thrown out from appeal to the European Court in December 2012 and he was extradited on 3 January 2013. In contrast with the cases of British citizens', Naseer's case was excluded entirely from the parliamentary discussion concerning sovereignty (as were the cases of Adel Abdel Bary and Khalid Al-Fawwaz). His case received little mention by the media except to assume his guilt.

Conclusion

Britain's ambivalence about naming race and racism is longstanding practice. The violence of colonial governance carried out under rule Britannia has always been imaginatively distanced from the way in which these racial ideologies have underlined the social structure and formation of the metropole. Though there have been key epiphanic moments where racism has been named as something more than the outcome of individual prejudice, such as the Stephen Lawrence Inquiry, these nods to a racially informed and thus unequal society have been few and far between, and when they do occur are quickly relegated to insignificance. This usually then follows with a return to racial denial. In the present conjunture, the silencing of racism is not only a reflection of this refutation, as has been historically the norm, but also a consequence of the expression that it has been overcome. As it becomes less fashionable to talk of, and indeed study and write of, racism, we find ourselves in an awkward predicament where the rather overt and heightened nature of racial injustice that occupies the current moment is muted by lack of social willingness to recognise it as such, in turn making it much more difficult to redress (Goldberg 2009).[10]

This sentiment is compounded by a situation of heightened racist violence carried out, and legitimated, under the banner of the War on Terror, through which the state achieves consensus for its criminal acts. The consequence of racism in the extreme which results from this has become as much a feature of the contemporary state of race in Britain as it has worldwide, different formulations and articulations notwithstanding. One of the useful functions of the War on Terror agenda in Britain has been to provide a novel way in which racial threat abroad can be linked to racial threat at home, where the nexus between imperialism and racism comes to light. The consequence of legislating for such purposes is the possibility that those not the target of intent may also fall victim to the law. In the case of extradition, this reality was acutely felt and articulated by Julia O'Dwyer, the mother of student Richard O'Dwyer, called to the US on charges of copyright infringement, who explained, 'if they can come for Richard, they can come for anyone' (Walker 2012). But in these times, the reality remains that a racial differentiation is made between those who deserve 'justice' and those who are just 'undeserved', those who are made 'human' and those who are 'inhuman', those who will be spoken out for and those who are silenced.

In the extradition debate in the House of Commons, Caroline Lucas MP of the Green Party made the point that 'one of the most fearful things about Guantanamo Bay – people being held without charge or trial – is happening on UK soil' adding 'at the behest of the US' (House of Commons Debate 2011, c100). When one considers this practice of indefinite detention alongside the array of other acts Britain has been complicit in, including the torture of British citizens and others, the racist foundations of the liberal democracy (Goldberg 2001) are (re)unveiled. But this deflection onto the US is surely a disservice to (perhaps even an injustice against) the iron will of Britain.

Acknowledgements

I would like to thank Babar Ahmad, Talha Ahsan, Hamja Ahsan and Virinder Kalra for their comments on earlier drafts of this chapter. To

Babar Ahmad, in particular, who offered detailed insight and spoke out for justice even as his liberty and right to a British trial were taken away. I dedicate this chapter to all those who battled extradition as I wrote.

Notes

1. That said, it should be made clear that the different lobbies against extradition, namely those leading the campaign against extradition for Babar Ahmad, Talha Ahsan, Gary McKinnon and Richard O'Dwyer, have made concerted attempts to show solidarity and campaign together. See http://wearebabarahmad.org/
2. It is interesting that it was this erosion of the double-jeopardy rule that was used to re-try Stephen Lawrence's murderers in 2012, when they were found guilty. This worked to gain mass popular support for an otherwise quite regressive legal tool.
3. Even *The Guardian,* which has been held as the more 'progressive' voice in the national media on these matters, came down in support of the ECHR's decision, declaring it 'was a powerful practical corrective to the shameless assumption that judges, and the European court judges in particular, do not inhabit the real world' (*The Guardian* 2012).
4. See Free Babar Ahmad campaign, http://www.freebabarahmad.com/
5. Fiona Murphy, Babar Ahmad's lawyer, commented on this hypocrisy and racial injustice in detail in *The Guardian* following the acquittal of the officers. See http://www.guardian.co.uk/commentisfree/2011/jun/05/babar-ahmad-metropolitan-police-ipcc
6. See Free Gary McKinnon campaign, http://freegary.org.uk/
7. In July 2012 they had been considering the reports for four years.
8. For example, consider Haroon Aswat in prison without trial since 2005, sectioned in Broadmoor Prison Hospital since 2008; Talha Ahsan, also suffering from Asperger's syndrome; Adel Bary, suffering from severe clinical depression; and Abu Hamza, who is a double amputee and diabetic.
9. Naseer and a second student, Faraz Khan, won their appeal against deportation on 18 May 2010 on the grounds that if they returned to Pakistan, their safety could not be guaranteed. Thus they were granted leave to remain on this second appeal, but the decision was a technical victory. Whilst officially they won the appeal and were able to remain in Britain, this was because it was agreed Naseer would be at risk of torture if he returned to Pakistan. At the same time, the court ruled that they were guilty of being Al-Qaida operatives, despite the absence of any evidence. They could not appeal against this declaration since they had 'won' their appeal.
10. The *Daily Mail* (2012) reported that a Labour councillor, Aaron Kiely, who, following the extradition of the Muslim men, tweeted 'British government deporting British citizens to the bastion of human rights that is the USA #shame' is under investigation, partly because of 'the views he has chosen to put in the public domain'. He had earlier also made 'controversial' remarks following the August 2011 riots, calling the Met Police 'institutionally racist'.

References

Ahmad, B. (2007) 'Cry of the Caged Bird', 25 May 2007, http://www.freebaba-rahmad.com/the-story/in-his-own-words/item/101-cry-of-the-caged-bird

Ali, T. (2005) *Rough Music: Blair/Bombs/Baghdad/London/Terror* (London: Verso).

Baker, Sir S., Perry, D. and Doobay, A. (2011) *A Review of the United Kingdom's Extradition Arrangements* (London: Home Office). http://www.homeoffice.gov.uk/publications/police/operational-policing/extradition-review?view=Binary

BBC News (2011) 'Babar Ahmad Police Officers Not Guilty of Assault', 3 June 2011, http://www.bbc.co.uk/news/uk-13638164

Blair, T. (2005) 'The Prime Minister's Statement on Anti-Terror Measures', *The Guardian*, 5 August 2005, http://www.guardian.co.uk/politics/2005/aug/05/uksecurity.terrorism1>

CBS News (2009), 'Supermax: A Clean Version of Hell' *CBS*, 21 June 2009, http://www.cbsnews.com/2100–18560_162–3357727.html

Chomsky, N. (2009) 'The Torture Memos', 24 May 2009, http://www.chomsky.info/articles/20090521.htm

Cobain, I. (2010) 'Britain "Complicit in Mistreatment and Possible Torture" Says UN', *The Guardian*, 27 January 2010, http://www.guardian.co.uk/world/2010/jan/27/britain-complicit-possible-torture-un

Daily Mail, The (2012) 'Fury as Labour Councillor Who Opposed Abu Hamza Extradition Claims £7,000 from Taxpayer Despite Attending Just One Half Hour Meeting', *Mail Online*, 10 October 2012, http://www.dailymail.co.uk/news/article-2215549/Labour-Councillor-Aaron-Kiely-opposed-Abu-Hamza-extradition-claims-7–000-taxpayer-despite-attending-just-ONE-half-hour-meeting.html

Delsol, R. (2012) 'London' Police Rethinks Stop and Search Tactics', Open Society Voices, 24 January 2012, http://www.soros.org/voices/london-s-police-rethinks-stop-and-search-tactics

Dodd, V. (2012) 'Abu Hamza Can Be Extradited to US, Human Rights Court Rules', *The Guardian*, 10 April 2012, http://www.guardian.co.uk/uk/2012/apr/10/abu-hamza-extradited-us-court

Douglas, M. (1966) *Purity and Danger: An Analysis of the Concepts of Pollution and Taboo* (London: Routledge and Kegan Paul).

Free Gary McKinnon (2010) 'PM David Cameron Raises the Gary McKinnon Extradition Case with President Barack Obama', blog entry, 21 July 2010, http://spyblog.org.uk.p10.hostingprod.com/freegary/2010/07/pm-david-cameron-raises-gary-mckinnon-extradition-case-with-president-barack-obama.html

Free Gary McKinnon (2012) 'Déjà vu after 20 months: PM David Cameron Raises the Gary McKinnon Extradition Case with President Barack Obama', blog entry, 14 March 2012, http://freegary.org.uk/

Goldberg, D. T. (2001) *The Racial State* (Malden, MA: Blackwell).

Goldberg D. T. (2009) *The Threat of Race* (Malden, MA: Blackwell).

Gramsci, A. (1999) *Selections from the Prison Notebooks* (London: ElecBook).

Gregory, D. (2007) 'Vanishing Points: Law Violence, Exception in the Global War Prison', in D. Gregory, and A. Pred. (eds), *Violent Geographies: Fear, Terror and Political Violence* (New York: Routledge), pp. 205–36.

The Guardian (2012) 'Abu Hamza: Europe's Judgement Call', *The Guardian*, 10 April 2012, http://www.guardian.co.uk/commentisfree/2012/apr/10/abu-hamza-europe-judgment-call-editorial

HM Government (2011) *Justice and Security Green Paper*, October 2011, http://www.official-documents.gov.uk/document/cm81/8194/8194.pdf

Home Affairs Select Committee (2012) 'The US-UK Extradition Treaty' 30 March 2012, http://www.publications.parliament.uk/pa/cm201012/cmselect/cmhaff/644/64403.htm#n29

Holehouse, M. (2012), 'David Cameron Frustrated at Wait to Send Abu Hamza to US', *Daily Telegraph*, 10 April 2012, http://www.telegraph.co.uk/news/uknews/terrorism-in-the-uk/9195292/David-Cameron-frustrated-at-wait-to-send-Abu-Hamza-to-US.html

House of Commons Debate (2011) 'Extradition Arrangements. Backbench Business' 5 December 2011, http://goo.gl/6Uk9v

Hyde, I. (2011) 'Stop the extradition of UK citizen Babar Ahmad: One Week Left on E-Petition' *Open Democracy*, 2 November 2011, http://www.opendemocracy.net/ourkingdom/i-hyde/stop-extradition-of-uk-citizen-babar-ahmad-one-week-left-on-e-petition

Kapoor, N. (2011) 'The Advancement of Racial Neoliberalism in Britain', *Ethnic and Racial Studies*, DOI: 10.1080/01419870.2011.629002

Kennedy, H. (2004) *Just Law: The Changing Face of Justice – and why it matters to us all*, (London: Vintage).

Kundnani, A. (2007) *The End of Tolerance* (London: Pluto Press).

Mbembe, A. (2003) 'Necropolitics', *Public Culture* 15(1), 11–40.

McKinnon *v.* USA & Anor (2007) EWHC 762 (Admin), 3 April 2007, http://www.bailii.org/ew/cases/EWHC/Admin/2007/762.html

Mitting, J. (2010) Special Immigration Appeals Commission Open Judgment. Abid Naseer, Ahmad Faraz Khan, Shoaib Khan, Abdul Wahab Khan and Tariq Ur Rehman *v.* Secretary of State for the Home Department, Appeal no: SC/77/80/81/82/83/09. 18 May 2010.

Obama, B. (2011), 'Obama's Speech to UK Parliament', 25 May 2011, http://www.bbc.co.uk/news/uk-politics-13549927

Peirce, G. (2010), *Dispatches from the Dark Side: On Torture and the Death of Justice* (London: Verso).

Prashad, V. (2012), 'Just Press the Button. The Drone Boom', *CounterPunch*, 2 April 2012, http://www.counterpunch.org/2012/04/02/the-drone-boom/

Robertson. G. (2010), 'Cameron and Clegg Must Now Do Their Moral Duty, and Save Gary McKinnon', *Mail Online*, 27 May 2010, http://www.dailymail.co.uk/debate/article-1281208/Cameron-Clegg-moral-duty – save-Gary-McKinnon.html

Slack, J. and Seamark, M. (2010) 'An Affront to British Justice: Gary McKinnon Extradition CAN Be Stopped, Says Lib Dem QC', *Mail Online*, 31 May 2010, http://goo.gl/iXifE

Walker, P. (2012) '"Piracy" Student Loses US Extradition Battle over Copyright Infringement', *The Guardian*, 13 January 2012, http://www.guardian.co.uk/law/2012/jan/13/piracy-student-loses-us-extradition?INTCMP=ILCNETTXT3487

Watt, N. and Bowcott, O. (2012) 'David Cameron Calls for Reform of European Court of Human Rights', *The Guardian*, 25 January 2012, http://www.guardian.co.uk/law/2012/jan/25/david-cameron-reform-human-rights?intcmp=239

Whitehead, T. (2012) 'Christopher Tappin to Be Held in Prison for a Week after Extradition to US', *Daily Telegraph*, 24 February 2012, http://goo.gl/SgDSp

10
Burying Asylum under the Foundations of Home

Ala Sirriyeh

In 2010, the former New Labour immigration minister Phil Woolas (in a rather dubious distillation of British identity) suggested that 'The simple act of taking one's turn is one of the things that holds our country together. It is very important that newcomers take their place in queues whether it is for a bus or a cup of tea' (*Daily Telegraph* 2010). He claimed that tensions emerge when some immigrants are not familiar with British cultural practices, such as queuing and 'playing fair'. The implication was that this disrupts the familiar rhythms and practices of home which 'hold our country together' and risks unmaking the host's home. Successful 'integration', therefore, depends upon well-behaved guests, leaving any complicating 'cultural practices' by the door as they cross the nation's threshold and adhere to a set of reasonable house rules laid down by the host.

Recent decades have seen the sustainment of immigration as a key policy issue taking a centre-stage position in many political and social debates within the UK and other European 'host' societies. Policies on immigration have attended to two key issues: first, the levels and forms of border controls and, second, the models for 'integrating' new migrants once they cross the threshold. The latter has been linked to debates about the nature of nation-states' cultures, identities, values and 'house rules'. UK Home Office statements on immigration and asylum routinely reiterate a recognition and celebration of 'diversity' and the UK's 'proud tradition of welcoming those fleeing persecution' (Home Office 2005; Darling 2009). Meanwhile, in the same breath they articulate the need for the exclusion and expulsion of the wrong type of migrant and the promotion of neo-assimilationist policies (Waite 2011) to guide the 'integration' of those migrants deemed good enough for the nation to be allowed to remain in the UK. The UK is, therefore, a place 'where diversity is publicly and officially celebrated, yet where not everybody qualifies to be recognised as the right kind of diverse subject' (Lentin and Titley 2011, p.176).

Despite the decline in numbers of people seeking asylum in the UK since the peak in 2002, and growing attention directed to Eastern European migrants, a recent study found that 'asylum-seekers remain one of the least popular groups of migrants, with a majority [of those polled] (56%) favouring reductions', reflecting a sense that the country is overburdened (The Migration Observatory 2011, p.13). This chapter draws on the example of UK asylum policy to outline how the restrictive policy and practice of the UK government in these arenas can be viewed as a reflection of a 'domopolitcs' agenda (Walters 2004), whereby, in response to perceptions that Britain had become 'addicted to immigration' (Damian Green, quoted in the *Daily Telegraph* 2011), feelings of increased economic and societal insecurity and a perceived 'crisis' in multiculturalism, governments have sought to reassure citizens through governing the state like a home. In some senses this may be a response to finding some meaning for the role of the nation-state in the context of globalisation. By presenting the nation-state as a domestic space, the thorny political problems that are often outside state sovereignty can be presented as manageable and localised. Indeed, the presence of asylum-seekers in the UK is due to commitment to international agreements rather than any response to a national demand. A domopolitics agenda enables UK governments to develop and implement policies that define the boundaries between those who pose a threat to this home and those who are guests (tolerated under our care and control) or potential household members; those who are 'at home' and those who are cast outside the threshold. In these approaches there is a suspicion of, and a need to control and integrate or exclude, particular types of mobile and liminal people who both threaten and cement particular national boundaries of home. In doing so, these policies have a negative impact on the ability of those people seeking asylum to (re)construct a sense of home (although as suggested later on, there are also opportunities for alternative frameworks of home that may be mobilised in this context). While it is not within the scope of this chapter to explore in detail the nature and direction of causality in relations between government policy and public attitudes, it includes some examples of how such ideas of 'home' and threats to home have also been visible among parts of established 'host' populations in the UK in their reception of refugees. Although the focus in this chapter is on the politics of home and asylum more broadly, these ideas developed as I conducted two studies with refugee and asylum-seeking young people in the UK. The discussion is, therefore, in parts, also attuned to ways in which immigration status and 'race' intersect with age and gender to affect people's positioning as inside or a risk to the nation-state home.

The first part of the chapter examines why migration, and in particular forced migration, has been linked to the destabilisation of home. It also explores immigration debates in the context of the 'postracial' discourse to examine who is placed outside the threshold and the denial of the role of race and racism in this process. Part two explores the concept of 'domopolitics' and how asylum has been articulated as a threat to home security, control of the house and 'home economics'. It examines restrictions and mechanisms that have been used to reinforce the walls of the house to control and exclude those who are cast outside. Finally, part three briefly outlines agendas for a situated politics of home and belonging that recognises mobility and potentially offers a more optimistic and inclusionary framework for home-making.

Migration and the threat to home

Migration has been associated with the destabilisation of home for those undertaking migration journeys, those in the 'host' countries, and those left behind in countries of origin. This is especially the case in the context of forced migration where movement is compelled and choices are restricted. In this approach migration is viewed as leading to the dismantling of the centre of people's worlds, particularly in conceptions of home which conceive home as fixed and bounded. In these ideas of home there is a notion of 'sedentarism' which 'locates bounded and authentic places or regions or nations as the fundamental basis of human experience' (Urry 2007, p.31). Therefore, forced migration with its association with uprooting, uncertainty and movement is positioned as a threat to the realisation of the home enclosure both for migrants and established host populations. However, as will be discussed later on in the chapter, such approaches have been critiqued by those who have recognised and highlighted the role of movement in home *making* (Sirriyeh 2010b; Ahmed et al. 2003).

The concept of 'home' combines spatial, social, psychological and temporal elements and is intimately connected with understandings of 'identity', 'place', and the relationship between the two (Sirriyeh 2010b). Home has been described as being formed at an intersection of identity and place, located in places where people feel it is most possible to ground their identities (Rapport and Dawson 1998), but also, crucially, where such ties are recognised by others who also see people as in place or 'at home' (Yuval-Davis, et al. 2006). In exploring the ties between people and place, Tuan (1980) recognised the emotional bonds and attachments to place that may be formed or challenged when he distinguished between an unselfconscious 'rootedness' to a place and a 'sense of place' based on a more reflexive identification. Casey (2001) links this 'sense of place' with Heidegger's notion of a 'dwelling', a 'thick space' where a dense network of embedded relations is established. A 'dwelling' is contrasted to 'thin places' where this network is looser and where, it is argued, there is greater exposure to difference and a potential weakening of bonds. It has been suggested that it is in thin spaces that some people seek to develop a 'sense of place', looking to re-create (the perhaps impossible) 'thick spaces' where they might attain greater security and stability (Easthope 2004).

The political significance attached to the emotional bonds to place and 'a sense of place' in the context of exposure to difference is reflected in Fortier's (2008, p. 98) discussion of multicultural politics, which, she suggests, increasingly addresses the internal state of citizens, how they 'feel at heart' about the nation and the cultivation of these feelings. Debates on immigration have been appended to wider debates concerned with the 'crisis' of multiculturalism and associated questions of home, belonging and citizenship as the existence of feelings for the nation among some racialised groups has been questioned and challenged. In the recent UK Government's emphasis on the need for meta-allegiance to 'shared values' and a rethinking of processes for acquiring and performing citizenship, some immigrants and other minority ethnic populations' feelings for the national home are seen as suspect and in need of interrogation and public performance and display. Balibar contends that such 'new' or 'cultural' racism has been developed within a process of European 'apartheid' protecting the interests of the 'European people' and operating through a program of exclusion in which 'cultural difference' becomes a basis for 'racial stigmatisation' (Balibar 2003, p. 122, quoted in Law 2010, p. 220). Law (2010, p. 219) points to a 'resurgence of coded, non-hierarchical racist discourse', of which a key feature is a strategy of denial. Within this vein Schuster (2003) has outlined how the xenophobic practices of European states targeting people seeking asylum have been disguised as a 'need for control'. Here, intersections of 'race', class and gender linked to global economic hierarchies have led to a 'hierarchy of the excluded'.

'It's not about race. It's not about culture. It's about numbers' declared a panellist on BBC's 'Sunday Morning Live' show in 2011, in a program which focused on immigration. The 'need for control' (Schuster 2003) to balance the books and manage numbers is often asserted in denials of accusations of racism or xenophobia by those in favour of increased immigration control. Race becomes buried under the weight of numbers. Immigration control becomes a matter of rational order, efficiency and good management, uncomplicated by the emotions of 'race' and culture. In efforts to discredit arguments highlighting a relationship between immigration policy and a 'new racism', the Conservative Party launched an election poster in the 2005 election campaign that claimed 'it's not racist to impose limits on immigration' (*The Independent* 2005). Those arguing for further restrictions on immigration often suggest that censorship has been applied to the topics of migration and asylum in policy debates because of a mistaken association between migration and race that implies that the impact of stratification, controls and exclusions on the basis of immigration status amounts to racism. Instead, those arguing for greater restrictions on immigration and asylum have sought to separate issues of immigration restriction from those of racial discrimination. By presenting immigration control as a rational and common-sense approach that seeks to match numbers to resources and the needs of the nation-state, proponents carefully distance themselves from the taboo of racism, which is constructed as an irrational sentiment exhibited by extremist individuals on the margins of public debates (Lentin and Titley 2011). However, as Capdevila and Callaghan (2008, p. 4) have cautioned, separating issues of migration from those of race 'enables the introduction of migration policy that certainly has both a racialised basis and racialised effects, while allowing challenges to the racialised nature of these policies to be dismissed as "playing the race card"'. With the assertion that racism is the irrational action of extremist individuals and a focus on the balancing of numbers and 'management' of migration under 'racial neo-liberalisation', 'race' and racism in these debates have been privatised and 'buried' (Goldberg 2009).

Underlying justifications for restriction is the view that certain forms of immigration are a threat to the nation's economic and societal security. Within a focus on practical and economic justifications for immigration restriction, asylum has often been conflated with other forms of immigration as a source of threat to security. In order to continue to assert that the UK has a proud history of providing hospitality and welcome to those fleeing persecution, while attending to concerns over security and the management of numbers, the original category of 'refugee' has been subdivided into 'good genuine refugee' and 'bad bogus asylum-seeker'. These contradictions are evident in the tensions between the discourses of security and ethics of care, both of which play an important role in a politics of home. The following section explores these issues further and outlines how asylum has been become subject to a domopoltics agenda.

Raising the drawbridge

The UK has a proud tradition of providing a place of safety for genuine refugees. However, we are determined to refuse protection to those who do not need it, and will take steps to remove those who are found to have made false claims. (UK Border Agency website, accessed 27/01/12)

In analysis of the reception and settlement of refugees, reference is often made to the analogy of the nation as a house or home, where hospitality is given by the 'host' and received by the 'guest'. The term 'host society' is used to refer to established populations already residing in the countries, towns and neighbourhoods into which refugees are received. The notion of hosting implies an offer of hospitality from those who hold ownership or control over the territory that is to be entered – the home owners host the strangers who cross the threshold. As the foregoing quote illustrates, the Home Office routinely uses asylum to allude to Britain's good-host status for having provided a welcome to 'genuine' refugees for generations (Home Office 2005). Yet as Derrida (2000a) illustrated, the concept of hospitality is imbued with an inherent tension, for in offering hospitality, the host claims ownership and control of the household in order to have the power and legitimacy to make this offer of hospitality. The word 'hospitality' is derived from the Latin *hostis* (stranger) and *potis* (power, control) (Gibson 2003). To offer hospitality there must be something to be hospitable with and to offer the guest. This hierarchical positioning of host and guest makes it difficult, if not impossible, to extend 'absolute' (i.e. unconditional) hospitality to the person entering. The guests cannot in practice make themselves at home under these terms because the agency required to do so also has the potential to violate and disrupt the host's order and control of the household (Derrida 2000a; Derrida 2000b). Derrida drew attention to the shared etymological route of the words 'hospitality' and 'hostility' in his neologism term 'hostipitalite' (Derrida 2000a). The stranger may be a unknown but welcome guest or, potentially, an alien invader (Kearney 1999). Increasing asylum control has been linked to fear of such stranger invasion and the need for power and mastery to be asserted in the defence of the nation-state home. The politics of home has the potential to exclude, while also maintaining narrow and conditional grounds for inclusion where some people are unable to escape the status of guest or even unwelcome and alien intruder.

In a 'domopolitics' agenda, the issue of home security is paramount, and, as a result of a process of securitsation, a discourse of security is applied to a range of policy areas. The securitisation of immigration and asylum policy has taken place so that 'the figure of the refugee and the asylum-seeker has been transformed from a political émigré to de facto criminal' (Back et al. 2002). The securitisation discourse on immigration has been partly explained as a tool in the promotion of the legitimacy of the nation-state in the context of globalisation. As Bauman (2004, p. 66) writes:

> State powers can do next to nothing to placate, let alone quash uncertainty. The most they can do is to refocus on objects within reach...those they can at least make a show of being able to handle and control. Refugees, asylum-seekers, immigrants – the waste products of globalisation.

Boundaries of exclusion and inclusion are applied through the increasing number of legal categories used to identify people seeking asylum and other migrants and the narrowly defined residence, economic and welfare rights that are tied to these. Research has recognised the complex and interrelated motivations for migration (Van Hear 1998). This has occurred as states increasingly choose to do the opposite by creating legal boundaries that distinguish amongst different categories of migrants on the basis of their motivations for migration and, in particular, making distinctions between political and economic motivations. Thick stories must be transformed into thin ones in order to fit through the narrow doors that offer possibility for residence. The processes of inclusion and exclusion resulting from immigration policies are an articulation of a particular politics of home in which notions of 'good' and 'bad' diversity play important roles (Lentin and Titley 2011).

Policies on asylum originated in the rights-based approach enshrined in the 1951 United Nations Convention and Protocol Relating to the Status of Refugees. However, although asylum was specifically marked as a humanitarian category in its inception, it has since been redefined in UK asylum policy, which since the 1990s has seen a move towards a narrowing and qualifying of the original humanitarian discourse and a raising of the drawbridge against those deemed 'bogus' and undeserving of hospitality. Contradictions between security concerns and ethical motivations are attended to by dividing asylum-seekers from 'genuine' refugees (Zetter 2007) and recasting these people primarily as objects of potential risk to security rather than as human subjects towards whom there is ethical responsibility and moral obligation. Meanwhile, the state's commitment to a duty of care towards the 'genuine' refugee is reiterated in statements otherwise outlining further immigration control as evidence of the tolerant hospitable and ethical home that the state seeks to maintain.

The following sections outline how asylum-seekers are recast as a risk to the nation-state home through their perceived threat to (a) home security, the nation's values and house rules, and (b) the nation's economic resources. Processes of surveillance, conditionality and sanctions are used to identify those considered 'genuine' refugees and to filter out and remove asylum applicants who are considered 'undeserving' and to attempt to constrain their ability to construct feelings of home and belonging.

The arguments are explored through findings from two studies. The first study (hereafter Study A) explored young refugee women's narratives of home in the context of migration to the UK and transitions to adulthood (Sirriyeh 2010a) and was based on 23 interviews and a Photovoice activity with young people, and 15 interviews with staff at services working with refugees and young people. The second study (hereafter Study B) explored the experiences of unaccompanied refugee and asylum-seeking young people in foster care (Wade et al., forthcoming). Fieldwork for Study B took place in four local authorities in England and consisted of analysis of local authority administrative data, a survey with 133 foster carers, 3 focus groups with young people and 4 with social workers and interviews with 23 foster carers, 21 young people and 4 team managers from the Children's Services' asylum teams. Eighty-eight per cent of looked-after, unaccompanied young people in these local authorities at that time were male, reflecting national proportions of males and females in this population at that time. Reflecting the time at which the research took place, approximately half of the sample in this study was young males from Afghanistan. Young people are referred to by pseudonyms (some chosen by the young people themselves). Those from countries with small populations in their UK locality are referred to by broader geographical regions.

Fortress Britain: threats to home security and house rules

In Fortress Britain, the home has been ruled to be a castle where the windows have been shut, the doors have been bolted, and the drawbridge has been raised against intrusion and the uninvited entry of those seeking asylum, leading, paradoxically, to a further obsession as its walls prove to be leaky and people continue to arrive, albeit in much smaller numbers than before. Asylum has become associated with criminality, and a stream of new immigration and asylum legislation over the past two decades since the first asylum legislation was passed in 1993 has introduced penalties for deception and the increased use of detention, criminalising refugees for seeking asylum (Zetter 2007). Following 9/11, the asylum system was also seen as a possible means of entry for potential terrorists into the UK (Huysmans and Buonfino 2008). In addition to a focus on terrorism, the UNHCR has also critiqued the UK Government's focus on questions of 'everyday' criminality (Seidman-Zager 2010), while the active citizenship agenda focuses on values and conduct.

Such discourses were evident in young refugees' accounts of settlement and interactions in UK communities. In Study A, Charmaine (Kurdish, aged 16) described her experiences of racism when she began school in the UK and linked them to perceptions other young people held about Iraq and violence. She said, 'They were generally racist to Asians, but more [to] us...they were like, these are Iraqis and they are like this and that. And [they made] stupid remarks like, "Have you got a knife in your bag?"' In research on racist attitudes and behaviour among young people, Lemos (2005) found that security fears and terrorism together were one of three key themes linked to feelings of hostility among young people towards refugees.

Meanwhile, in Study B with refugee young people in foster care, there was also evidence of an awareness of the focus on 'everyday criminality' and the citizenship agenda. Aspirations for young people to do well centred on a desire that they make the most of their time in education and achieve their potential. However, interest in educational progress was also tied into the recurring theme of future immigration pathways. Some young people and foster carers held hopes that educational progress might help young people with their asylum claims by demonstrating to immigration courts that they were building successful lives in the UK and becoming good prospective citizens. Young people and their foster carers worried about progress in education, exam results and social conduct at school for fear that slip-ups could portray young people as lacking good citizenship qualities and could jeopardise their chances of remaining in the UK. One foster carer concerned for her foster child had warned him, 'If you carry on like this, it's not going to be good when you go in front of the immigration judge.' Foster carers often advised young people to stay out of trouble, to walk away from situations and not to retaliate because 'It's too dangerous for you to get mixed up in that with your asylum process going [on]' (Leena, foster carer).

At the time Study B took place, Afghan males represented a large percentage of unaccompanied minors in the UK. In the context of the presence of British troops in Afghanistan, this nationality occupied a particular position in articulations of risk and security concerns. One social workers' focus group commented on the difficulties they had in locating foster placements for Afghan boys. A social worker said, 'Under the current climate of Afghanistan and people's views of Afghanistan, a lot of foster carers we've spoken to didn't want to take children.' It was thought that this was not always because foster carers did not want to foster these young people, but rather that they were concerned that their families, friends or neighbours might object, particularly in communities where a number of neighbours had relatives or friends in the army. Rashid (aged 18) had been anxious about telling people he was Afghan because he was concerned that there might be hostility directed towards him because of the war. Aarif's foster carer spoke of the bullying at school directed towards Aarif (aged 17) and other Afghan boys:

This is bullying in a big way, whether it's to do with him being a Muslim, or the Afghanistan War, soldiers dying. And both my boys they've only got to see it on television. If any soldiers die, they really get upset.

Meanwhile, the discourse of asylum-seekers as threatening 'Others' and a danger to the safety of the nation has often been embedded in the image of the racialised and sexualised young male body (Judge 2010). Perceptions of intersecting risky identities were evident in the reception of some young people into foster care. In one placement a foster carer who had fostered Afghan boys fitted alarms on the doors of her teenage daughters' bedrooms and spoke of her sense of discomfort. In another case the foster carer's daughters and Afghan foster children eventually developed close and happy relationships, but the daughters had initially been anxious and expressed doubts.

Both my daughters were a little bit concerned, which I suppose is understandable when, you know, the situation, like, in Afghanistan. My daughter, my oldest one, was like, 'Oh my God, what if they try and bomb the house, or they do this or they do that? I want a lock on my door,' and stuff like that. But once they came and we got to know them, you know, everyone was fine. (Stephanie, foster carer)

In a few cases racialised stereotyping and perceptions of sexuality and masculinities had also been a source of tension in interactions with other young people in school and in the wider community. In one case the racist bullying and victimisation of an Afghan young person had incorporated accusations of sexual advances and inappropriate behaviour towards a female peer, and a set-up in which the boy was led to a location by a girl to be physically attacked by a group of boys and men who were there waiting for him.

There were a number of reports of racism encountered by young people, particularly those living among predominantly white populations where there was little history of immigration or ethnic diversity. Young people are often on the 'front line' both as targets and perpetrators of racist violence and hostility (Hemmerman et al. 2007). Two months into his foster care placement, Abbas (aged 16) began attending a local youth club and was involved in fights with white boys at the club. Abbas' explanation touched on the risks in hospitality and indicated that initial hostilities expressed towards him were based on entwined motivations centring on his status at that point as an unknown stranger in the area, the stranger enemy (Kearney 1999), in addition to more particular racialised perceptions relating to his nationality and ethnicity.

Now, it's – They know me, who I am ... what I'm not ... the first thing is, because when you not speak English, how can you even know someone, like, "Who is him? Where he stay?" ... "Why are you staring?" And you can't speak English, and so he think ... he want the trouble, but you really don't want the trouble ... And now it's everything is fine for me 'cause everything's – the boys know me, everyone know me, so I have peace, you know? (Abbas)

Abbas' story indicates the unease that surrounds the stranger whose intentions and feelings remain unknown. Since 2001 a new integration discourse has emerged in the UK in response to the perceived crisis in multiculturalism and such forms of unease (McGhee 2008). The new discourse still voices a respect for diversity, but with what McGhee

(2008, p. 83) describes as 'a new level of meta-allegiance through establishing shared values'. This is reflected in policies concerned with the integration of refugees. Despite suggestions that integration starts from day one of arrival (Castles et al. 2002), the UK's integration strategy is only directed towards those with refugee status who have proved that they are 'genuine' refugees. In the national integration strategy, *Moving on Together* (Home Office 2009), there was an emphasis on refugees' duty to integrate by abiding by existing 'British' values.

> We are seeking to ensure that migrants, including refugees, completing the journey to citizenship understand and abide by our shared values...We also believe that refugees should play an active part in the community, as many currently do, to attain the quickest path to citizenship. (Home Office 2009, p. 8)

Having become named and known, refugees, alongside other migrants, are required to demonstrate and express how they 'feel at heart' for the nation (Fortier 2008) to finally quash their status as potential risks to home. While termed 'integration', such a process is more along the lines of neo-assimilation (Back et al. 2002; Waite 2011). As Woolas' statement on queuing indicated, refugees and other migrants are perceived to need induction and schooling in the nation's house rules. In addition to immigration, the citizenship agenda has also been directed at young people who are positioned as unsettled and in a state of transition, and who, therefore, occupy a risk status and need an education in citizenship (Sirriyeh 2010b). As well as their status as immigrants in need of integration, young refugees, like other young people, are also positioned as 'becomings' and adults in the making (Sirriyeh 2010b). In Study B social workers, foster carers and young people discussed the intersection of age and immigration status in the processes of instituting or negotiating house rules in foster care.

Home economics

The criminalisation of people seeking asylum and their high-risk status extends beyond threats to safety and security to also include concerns over the protection of the nation's economic resources. In 2003, *The Sun* newspaper ran (what was shown to be an unfounded) story under the headline 'Swan Bake: asylum-seekers steal the Queen's birds for barbeque.'. That same year the *Daily Star* produced the headline, 'Asylum-seekers ate our donkeys', alleging that nine donkeys had been stolen from the Greenwich royal park by asylum-seekers (Greenslade

2005). Asylum-seekers were accused of stealing the nation's resources while also apparently showing marked disrespect to British institutions and traditions – 'our' royal family and famed love of animals. They were portrayed as eating the nation out of house and home.

A major argument evoked in calls for imposing limitations on migration and asylum has been based on concerns over the allocation of public resources (Bloch and Schuster 2002). Policy debates about immigration, the economy and the welfare state have become increasingly entangled as they all undergo significant changes in the current era (Schierup et al. 2006). As Waite (2011, p. 2) states:

> Migration trends pose a challenge to traditional Westphalian notions of national citizenship that were traditionally envisaged as a set of exclusionary rights that established claims to collective resources in territorially-bound nation-states.

Since its emergence during the twentieth century the welfare state has played a significant role in ideas of citizenship (Schierup et al. 2006) and concern over 'free riders' has been a defining factor in influencing how 'host' populations from the early twentieth century onwards have viewed immigrants (Lucassen 2005, p.15). The development of an idea of citizenship that included economic and social welfare entitlements (and responsibilities), and the relationship between citizenship and the nation created new dimensions of belonging. It transformed economic resentment and suspicion of immigrants from concerns over economic competition to also incorporating concerns over the protection of national belonging and citizenship.

There is a continuation of the notion of 'deserving' and 'undeserving' members of society as immigration status has become a marker of rights (Sales 2002). This is reflected in the increasing distinctions between the legal definitions given to different types of immigrants and the entitlements that are attached to these categories. The welfare system has become appended to this immigration system. Through a 'tiering of entitlement' (Dwyer and Brown 2005) conditionality is applied to distinguish and order deserving potential members of the household from those who are cast outside. The distinction between the immigration status of 'refugee' and 'asylum-seeker' has become increasingly important in this process and in an entitlement led debate people must prove they are 'real' refugees to obtain support.

The propagation of myths about asylum-seekers' access to excessive material goods and financial support, and the concerns discussed above are compelled by a fear of loss of mastery and control over the national home. It is such fears and hostility that constrain the possibility of hospitality and 'compels the conditional' and the creation of 'bare life' (Darling 2009; Agamben 1998). Darling (2009, p.656) asserts that 'For bare life the predominant relation is one either of the *in*hospitable, of confinement, refusal, and rejection, or of a conditioned temporary refuge centred almost exclusively around the need to not be "too welcoming."' Under such conditions basic essentials are provided as a service rather than through an offer of hospitality.

Many of the young women in Study A took photographs of poor housing conditions. Esther (West Africa, aged 19) was housed in a block of flats that were being emptied of 'citizen' tenants in preparation for its demolition. She took photographs of a broken window, leaking drains outside the entrance, broken appliances, and a flooded bathroom. Describing poor security and open post-boxes in her building, Oceane (Congolese, aged, 18) said, 'Because we are asylum-seeker or refugee we don't have rights or confidentiality'. Her status was that of someone who lacked the 'right to rights' (Arendt 1951) who was subject to the power of the sovereign without recourse to political rights or law that a citizen has (Agamben 1998). The framework of asylum has been hollowed out from its earlier conception to become defined by provision of duty, rather than care and humanitarian response.

Living with this containment and curtailment of rights makes 'you feel like you in prison' said Ella (Kurdish, aged 18) who was waiting for the outcome of her family's asylum claim after living in the UK for four years. Young people, like asylum seekers of all ages, faced foreshortened horizons. However, this was particularly pertinent for many who had arrived as teenagers because 'Youth is conventionally understood as 'a time of change(s); a moment of acceleration past life-course landmarks' (Hall et al. 2009, p.555); and they were in contexts where their peers were considering and planning for future education pathways and careers. Without access to refugee status, young people faced overseas student fee rates and no right to seek employment in the UK. Their ability to access higher education and employment became limited and their planning for the future was often suspended or ambiguous. At the age of 17.5 Harroon, (Afghan, aged 18) (Study B) had applied to extend his leave to remain in the UK and was waiting to hear the outcome. (He was refused shortly after). Describing his social worker's attempts to get him to consider his plans for the future he said, 'She said, "What is Plan B and C?" and I was like, "No, Plan B and C", so I want to stick to this one, so, and if this get ruined and everything is ruined'. Faced with the impossibility of contemplating his future outside of the UK and uncertain prospects within the UK, home-making and planning for the future was a challenge.

The application of such processes of conditionality and sanctions affects people's ability to assert choice and control. In Study A, alongside priorities of safety and family young women spoke of the importance of having choice and control over their lives in order to feel at home (Dupuis and Thorns 1996). This was often limited by the asylum system. For example, young women described how they were allocated accommodation through the dispersal system, in which asylum-seekers are sent to live on a no choice basis in accommodation outside of London and the South East of England (Robinson et al. 2003).

> We just had a letter saying go to this hotel and then this person came and took us and said 'after a few days you will have to go to this area of London and there are lots of people and you will go on a coach to this place' and we didn't know where this place was and it was Huddersfield...and then after that we were taken to a hostel in Huddersfield. (Esrin, Kurdish, aged 18)

Accompanying the application of conditionality and sanctions are the acts of surveillance that are embedded within the asylum system. As asylum-seekers enter and live in the UK alongside citizens, borders between householders and guests are potentially weakened and leakages may occur. Internal borders are reasserted to avoid this through conditionality and the regulation of entitlements. Surveillance is undertaken to ensure that the solidity of these borders is maintained. This occurs before people even arrive in the UK (through extra-territorial border controls) and at the UK border, but is also built into the asylum support system through the dispersal process to allocated housing, financial support through vouchers for some, reporting requirements and immigration detention. In Study A, young refugee women's feelings of being at home, or not at home, were often expressed through notions of comfort and discomfort. Ahmed (2006, p. 134) describes feelings of comfort as being achieved when an individual is so at ease in their environment that they 'sink' in. To fit so comfortably and to sink into one's environment suggests a feeling of freedom and of no need to explain or justify oneself. The 'surfaces of bodies' (ibid) disappear and one is not visible as a body out of place. Postcolonial racism has been described as a 'racism of surveillance' (Law 2010, p. 220), and surveillance has been utilised within the asylum system as a means of making sure some bodies are marked as bodies out of place and outside the borders of home.

Sites of sanctuary in a politics of home

In Study A, the attainment of refugee status was seen by young women as a catalyst for establishing future feelings of home, but being given refugee status was also seen as recognition and confirmation of existing feelings of home and belonging in the UK that were sometimes already being practiced and felt. While the UK government's domopolitics approach can be exclusionary, an alternative politics of home potentially offers opportunities for recognising a more inclusionary and flexible approach to understanding people's sense of belonging and attachments and incorporates mobility. Through drawing on the development of anti-essentialist 'routes' approaches to theorising 'home', which 'destabilize a sense of home as a stable origin and unsettle the fixity and singularity of a place called home' (Blunt and Dowling 2006, p. 198), claims to and practices of 'home' simultaneously offer points of resistance and opportunities for counter-narratives to such exclusionary approaches. People's lived experiences are informed, but not completely bound by, legal and policy categories and discourses. Constructions of home can be a complex and ongoing negotiation. What may be positioned as transitional zones or 'temporary shelters' in official discourses can also be made habitable by people as they seek to negotiate 'homely' spaces within a wider 'unhomely' environment (Sirriyeh 2010b).

Essential humanity

While the suggestion that there are racialised effects of asylum policy has been dismissed by some, this is not necessarily a perspective shared by many of those who have been subjects of these policies. Oceane, (Congolose, aged 18) (Study A) who was seeking asylum, took a photograph while attending a 'Diversity Week' event with a friend which highlighted for her the prominence of the diversity discourse. During her three years in the UK she had noticed the attention give to the language of 'diversity' and anti-discrimination in the UK. Yet this had made her acutely aware of the distance between such statements and her experiences here. In her discussion of this photograph, she said:

> They talk about discrimination and when they are talking I just think why do they teach people about discrimination and they still have it! ... We are all the same. Refugee, asylum seeker, white. If God creates

everyone the same he couldn't make it possible that black people stay in this country or white people go this country. He knows we are the same and we might need help from each other.

In her critique of racialised immigration policies, Oceane used a language of essential humanity and equality to assert her rights. In an earlier study I conducted with asylum-seeking young people, a young person had also declared along similar lines, 'I am from Africa ... so that's why you say me I am not supposed to be here ... but me I am free. I am a citizen of the world' (Sirriyeh 2008). Commenting on the universal principle of human rights discourse Yuval-Davis (2011, p.172) writes that, 'human rights have been ... a rallying cry for recognition and the entitlements of people all over the world, not as citizens of specific states or as members of specific cultural or religious community, but as part of the human race'. Marginalised groups, such as asylum-seekers, who have been excluded from 'the human' (and their supporters) often use these human rights principles as tools for resistance and struggle for inclusion and equality. However, as Hoffman (1997, p.131) wrote in 'Lost in Translation', 'essential humanity is all very well but we need the colors of our time and the shelter of a specific place ... we exist in actual homes'. While recognising the role of movement in home-making, it is important to note that people also live in situated places and home is a 'situated event' (Fortier 2001, p.420).

Situating sanctuary

In Study A and Study B young people described how they worked to construct homely places and enclaves within a wider unhomely environment (Sirriyeh 2010b). Sometimes these were particular spatial locations. For example, in Study A some young women described the safety and comfort they felt within their bedrooms where in the context of asylum, but also some experiences of sexual and physical violence, intergenerational family relations and other forms of household relations, it was a space where these young women could exert control over space and apply their sense of order within a wider household space where this was not always possible. In addition to being particular spatial locations, some were also sites of social relations. For example, young women in Study A spoke about public places such as parks, bus stations and shopping centres where they spent time with friendship groups. In Study B some young people in foster care felt a sense of belonging within their foster families where they had developed 'like-family' relationships (Mason and Tipper 2008), despite their temporary immigration status and uncertain future where they were positioned outside the national home of UK citizens (Wade et al. 2012).

Reviewing the recent emergence of the UK based movement 'City of Sanctuary' in the Northern, former Steel town of Sheffield, Darling (2010) and Squire (2009) have described how this campaign and action has recognised the situated process of home-making. 'City of sanctuary' is advertised as 'a movement to build a culture of hospitality for people seeking sanctuary in the UK'. A City of Sanctuary is a place where 'the skills and cultures of people seeking sanctuary are valued, where they are included in local communities and able to contribute to the life of the city' (City of Sanctuary website, accessed 29/08/2011). The emergence of the campaign in localised city spaces recognises existing practices of belonging and home-making that refugees undertake in part through their engagements with more established local residents. It also seeks to develop this further through supporting more of these kinds of relationships, and influencing policy makers and public attitudes to asylum-seekers and refugees. Squire (2009) argues that it disrupts the dichotomy between citizens and non-citizens, asylum-seekers and 'host' community because it is organised around groups and institutions such as schools, religious congregations, community groups and trade unions. Refugees and asylum-seekers are members because of membership of these groups, not on the basis of their refugee, asylum-seeker or 'citizen' status. Meanwhile, Darling (2010, p.127) describes how the City of Sanctuary movement in Sheffield has attempted to recognise the situated nature of hospitality and home-making, while also linking to wider humanitarian responsibility and human relations. He writes that, 'The political challenge of relational thinking might be captured in accommodating the negotiations of *both* proximate diversity and distant connectivity'. The movement has focussed not only on the role refugees and migration have played in making and contributing to the identity of the city of Sheffield, but also how Sheffield as a place formed through flows of people and ideas is tied into wider networks and relational ties and can look outward to these. While not without challenges, this politics of home seeks to embrace mobility and flows within its foundations and gains strength and support from facing outwards rather than retreating behind rising fortress walls.

Despite a considerable decline in the numbers of people seeking asylum in the UK since the peak in 2002, the weight of numbers continues to leave an imprint in the minds of those who seek to enforce greater levels of immigration control. Through the application of increasingly exclusionary immigration controls, governments have attempted to hollow out the notion of asylum in approaches that feature some key elements of postcolonial racism including denial, (false) respect, a reactive racism and a racism of surveillance (Law 2010). In efforts to dispel accusations of racism and a hierarchy of exclusion UK governments have utilised the language of rational 'migration management', balancing the books and matching numbers to resources and supply to demand. The tensions inherent in the notion of hospitality are evident as governments routinely reiterate their recognition and celebration of 'diversity' and the UK's proud tradition of welcoming and hosting refugees, while in their application of border controls and integration strategies they subdivide diversity into good diversity or risks to the nation. On this basis a domoplitics agenda is pursued in which a preoccupation with numbers and legal status is ordered around the exclusion of those who are deemed to threaten a destabilisation of home.

Bibliography

Agamben, G. (1998) *Homo Sacer: Sovereign Power and Bare Life* (Palo Alto, CA: Stanford University Press).

Ahmed, S. (2006) *Queer Phenomenology: Orientations, Objects, Others* (Durham, NC, and London: Duke University Press).

Ahmed, S., Castaneda, C., Fortier, A. M., and Sheller, M. (eds) (2003) *Uprootings/ Regroundings: Questions of Home and Migration* (Oxford: Berg).

Arendt, H. (1951) *The Burden of Our Time* (London: Secker and Warburg).

Back, L. et al. (2002) 'The Return of Assimilation: Race, Multiculturalism and New Labour', *Social Research Online*, 7(2), http://www.socresonline.org.uk

Balibar, E. (2003) *We, the People of Europe? Reflections on Transnational Citizenship*, trans. J. Swenson (Princeton, NJ: Princeton University Press).

Bauman, Z. (2004) *Wasted Lives: Modernity and Its Outcasts* (Oxford: Polity Press).

Bloch, A. and Schuster, L. (2002) 'Asylum and Welfare: Contemporary debates', *Critical Social Policy*, 23(3) 393–414.

Blunt, A. and Dowling, R. (2006) *Home* (London: Routledge).

British Broadcasting Corporation (BBC) (2011) 'Sunday Morning Live', 28th August 2011.

Capdevila, R. and Callaghan, J. (2008) 'It's Not Racist. It's Common Sense'. A Critical Analysis of Political Discourse around Asylum and Immigration in the UK', *Journal of Community and Applied Social Psychology*, 18(1), 1–16.

Casey, E. S. (2001) 'Body, Self and Landscape: A Geophilosophical Inquiry into a Place-World', in P. Adams, S. Hoelscher, and K. E. Till, *Textures of Place: Exploring Humanist Geographies* (Minnesota: University of Minnesota Press), pp. 403–25.

Castles, S. et al. (2002) *Integration: Mapping the Field* (London: Home Office Immigration Research and Statistics Service).

Daily Telegraph, The (2010) 'Immigrants to Be Taught How to Queue', 13 February 2010, http://www.telegraph.co.uk/news/uknews/immigration/7230274/Immigrants-to-be-taught-how-to-queue.html

Daily Telegraph, The (2011) 'Britain Is "Addicted to Immigration" Warns Minister', 6 April 2011, http://www.telegraph.co.uk/news/uknews/immigration/8430001/Britain-is-addicted-to-immigration-warns-minister.html

Darling, J. (2010) 'A City of Sanctuary: The Relational Re-Imagining of Sheffield's Asylum Politics', *Transactions of the Institute of British Geographers*, 35(1), 125–40.

Darling, J. (2009) 'Becoming bare life: Asylum, Hospitality and the Politics of Encampment', *Environment and Planning D: Society and Space*, 27(4), 649–65.

Derrida, J. (2000a) 'Hospitality', *Angelaki*, 5(3), 3–18.

Derrida, J. (2000b) *Of Hospitality, Anne Dufourmantelle Invites Jacques Derrida to Respond*, trans. Rachel Bowlby (Palo Alto, CA: Stanford University Press).

Dupuis, A. and Thorns, D. (1996) 'Meanings of Home for Older Home Owners', *Housing Studies* 11(4), 485–501.

Dwyer, P. and Brown, D. (2005) 'Meeting Basic Needs? Forced Migrants and Welfare', *Social Policy and Society*, 4(4), 269–380.

Easthope, H. (2004) 'A Place Called Home', *Housing, Theory and Society*, 21(3), 128–38.

Fortier, A. (2001) 'Coming Home: Queer Migrations and Multiple Evocations of Home', *European Journal of Cultural Studies*, 4(4), 405–24.

Fortier, A. (2008) *Multicultural Horizons: Diversity and the Limits of the Civil Nation* (London: Routledge).

Gibson, S. (2003) 'Accommodating Strangers: British Hospitality and the Asylum Hotel Debate', *Journal for Cultural Research*, 7(4), 367–86.

Goldberg, D. T. (2009) *The Threat of Race: Reflections on Racial Neoliberalism* (Malden, MA: Blackwell).

Greenslade, R. (2005) *Seeking Scapegoats: The Coverage of Asylum in the UK Press*, Asylum and Migration Working Paper 5 (London: IPPR).

Hall, T., Coffey, A. and Lashua, B. (2009) 'Steps and Changes: Rethinking Transitions in Youth and Place', *Journal of Youth Studies*, 12(5), 547–61.

Hemmerman, L. et al. (2007) *Situating Racist Hostility and Understanding the Impact of Racist Victimisation in Leeds* (Leeds: Centre for Ethnicity and Racism, University of Leeds).

Hoffman, E. (1997) *Lost in Translation: A Life in a New Language* (London: Minerva).

Home Office (2005) *Integration Matters: A National Strategy for Refugee Integration.* (London: The Stationary Office).

Home Office (2009) *Integration Matters: A National Strategy for Refugee Integration* (London: The Stationary Office).

Huysmans, J. and Buonfino, A. (2008) 'Politics of Exception and Unease: Immigration, Asylum and Terrorism in Parliamentary Debates in the UK', *Political Studies* 56(4), 766–88.

Independent, The (2005) 'Tory Election Poster Sparks Complaints of Racism from Students and Teachers', 7 February 2005, p. 6.

Judge, R. (2010) *Refugee Advocacy and the Biopolitics of Asylum in Britain: The Precarious Position of Young Male Asylum Seekers and Refugees*, Refugee Studies Centre Working Paper No. 60 (Oxford: University of Oxford).

Kearney, R (1999) 'Aliens and Others: Between Girard and Derrida', *Cultural Values*, 3(3), 251–62.

Law, I. (2010) *Racism and Ethnicity: Global Debates, Dilemmas and Directions* (London: Pearson).

Lemos, G. (2005) *Challenging and Changing Racist Attitudes and Behaviour in Young People* (York: Joseph Rowntree Foundation).

Lentin, A. and Titley, G. (2011) *The Crisis of Multiculturalism: Racism in a Neoliberal Age* (London and New York: Zed Books).

Lucassen, L. (2005) *The Immigrant Threat: The Integration of Old and New Migrants in Western Europe since 1850* (Chicago: University of Illinois Press).

Mason, J. and Tipper, B. (2008) 'Being Related: How Children Define and Create Kinship', *Childhood*, 15(4), 441–60.

McGhee, D. (2008) *The End of Multiculturalism? Terrorism, Integration and Human Rights* (Buckingham: Open University Press).

Rapport, N. and Dawson, A. (1998) 'Home and Movement: A Polemic', in N. Rapport and A. Dawson, *Migrants of Identity: Perceptions of Home in a World of Movement* (Oxford: Berg), pp. 39–60.

Robinson, V., Andersson, R. and Musterd, S. (2003) *Spreading the Burden: A Review of Policies to Disperse Asylum Seekers and Refugees* (Bristol: The Policy Press).

Sales, R. (2002) 'The Deserving and the Undeserving? Refugees, Asylum Seekers and Welfare in Britain', *Critical Social Policy*, 22(3), 456–78.

Schierup, C. U., Hansen, P. and Castles, S. (2006) *Migration, Citizenship and the European Welfare State* (Oxford: Oxford University Press).

Schuster, L. (2003) 'Common Sense or Racism? The Treatment of Asylum Seekers in Europe', *Patterns of Prejudice*, 37(3), 233–55.

Seidman-Zagar, J. (2010) *The Securitization of Asylum: Protecting UK Residents*, Refugee Studies Working Paper No. 57 (Oxford: University of Oxford).

Sirriyeh, A. (2010a) *Inhabiting the Borders: A Study of 16–25-Year-Old Refugee Women's Narratives of Home*, unpublished PhD thesis (Leeds: University of Leeds).

Sirriyeh, A. (2010b) 'Home Journeys: Im/mobilities in Young Refugee and Asylum-Seeking Women's Negotiations of Home', *Childhood*, 17(2), 213–27.

Squire, V. (2009). *Mobile Solidarities: The City of Sanctuary Movement and the Strangers into Citizens Campaign* (Milton Keynes: Open University Press).

The Migration Observatory (2011) *Thinking behind the Numbers: Understanding Public Opinion on Immigration in Britain* (Oxford: University of Oxford).

Yuan, Y. F. (1980) 'Routedness versus Sense of Place', *Landscapes*, 24, 3–8.

Urry, J. (2007) *Mobilities* (Cambridge: Polity).

Van Hear, N. (1998) *New Diasporas: The Mass Exodus, Dispersal and Regrouping of Migrant Communities* (London: UCL Press).

Wade, J., Sirriyeh, A., Kohli, R. and Simmonds, J. (2012) *Fostering Unaccompanied Refugee and Asylum Seeking Young People in the UK* (London: BAAF).

Waite, L. (2011) 'Neo-assimilationist Citizenship and Belonging Policies in Britain: Meanings for Transnational Migrants in Northern England', *Geoforum*, doi.10.1016/j.geoforum.2011.08.009

Walters, W. (2004) 'Secure Borders, Safe Haven, Domopolitics', *Citizenship Studies*, 8(3), 237–60.

Yuval-Davies, N. (2011) *The Politics of Belonging: Intersectional Contestations* (London: Sage).

Yuval-Davies, N., Kannabiran, K. and Vieten, U. (2006) 'Introduction', in N. Yuval-Davies, K. Kannabiran and U. Vieten, *The Politics of Belonging* (London: Sage), pp.1–14.

Zetter, R. (2007) 'More Labels, Fewer Refugees: Making and Remaking the Refugee Label in an Era of Globalisation', *Journal of Refugee Studies*, 20(2), 172–92.

11
Afterword: Racial Futures

Nisha Kapoor

During the course of putting this collection together, five Muslim men, three of whom were British citizens, were extradited to the US on terrorism-related charges. Despite the fact that the charges against them were for quite distinct and unrelated events, they were collectively grouped behind one of those indicted, and referred to as 'Abu Hamza and others'. Abu Hamza, depicted as a pantomime villain, became a convenient trope for characterising the terrorist threat, behind which the remaining men could be grouped, pathologised and disposed of, othered as the ultimate enemy within. Brought to the fore was the problematic Muslim male, useful and used for retaining/sustaining embedded racial hierarchies, essentially enabling a biopolitics which in turn could be remobilised for the state's own ends. In an act revealing the continuation of explicit racial distinction, ten days after their extradition, the Home Secretary, Theresa May, finally ruled against the extradition of Gary McKinnon, finding that his Asperger's syndrome put him at high risk of committing suicide were he to be incarcerated within the US prison system. Stressing that this was an 'exceptional case', perhaps not least so because it was a decision postponed until after the Muslim men – who between them also suffered from Asperger's, severe clinical depression and physical disabilities – had been extradited, it was clear that the real exception was the state's suspension and re-articulation of the law for its own protection. Having made the distinction between the citizen and the terrorist, the spectacle of threat, which the public act of extradition came to represent, has in turn facilitated the push for a greater repeal of rights, liberties and freedoms. Perturbed by the length of time it took to banish the Muslim men from British shores, Home Secretary May vowed to ensure that the extradition process was further reviewed so that in future it might be possible to 'shorten the process' by curtailing entitlements to appeal in the juridical process. This position fed into the ongoing lobbying of the Conservative–Liberal Democrat Government to replace the Human Rights Act with a UK Bill of Rights because 'of problems we have in being unable to deport people who *perhaps* are terrorist suspects' (BBC 2011, emphasis added). Speaking to the Parliamentary Assembly of the Council of Europe in January 2012, in a fight to ensure that British prisoners were not granted voting rights and to halt the interference of European courts in the British state's 'democratic' decisions to deport and extradite (racially defined) terrorist suspects, David Cameron pushed for immediate reform of the European Court of Human Rights. Part of a wider agenda that aims to re-articulate the dialectic between justice and security, between citizenship, national security and human rights, this push for legal reforms, as it further empowers the executive and delimits the notion of an 'independent' judiciary, comes to reflect the shifting cartographies of the British racial state. This determined pursuit to repeal any sense of entitlement – to rights, to law, to life – is a moment where even the premise of formal equality before the law is revealed as tentative, dependent on ascriptions of subjecthood and belonging. It is a moment where the formalism of law can be undone in the postracial, and where the claim to 'equal opportunities' is lost in the postracial. Those who are racially excluded are done so explicitly, blatantly, with the retort of racism deemed absurd.

From a number of different perspectives the chapters in this collection have sought to highlight, problematise and critique the operations of the state. The extradition case explicitly highlights the racial state at its most blatant and belligerent. It also highlights the transnational stage upon which these supposedly local issues are played out, from the European courts to the US penitentiary system. David Cameron's statement on Abu Hamza that 'I'm delighted on this occasion we've managed to send this person off to a country where he will face justice' (Jones and Bowcott 2012) spoke volumes, and echoed Theresa May's statement that 'It is right that these men, who are all accused of very serious offences, will finally face justice.' For what reasons could Abu Hamza not face justice in Britain? What was it about the British judicial/ prison system that was not equipped to deal with the terrorist in the way the US could? Was it that Britain was ill equipped to deal with a subject-turned-object in full spectacle of a liberal society that prides itself on tolerance, or was it something more sinister? Perhaps the security agencies had gained all the intelligence they could from Abu Hamza, and now he needed to be disposed of in a way that would not come back to haunt British state authorities. Perhaps it was a combination of both.

Nevertheless, his extradition into the US prison system means his case is now a US issue. But likewise, the European Court of Human Right's ruling that a sentence of 80 to 100 years in a US supermax prison in solitary confinement is not tantamount to torture pushes the declining powers and 'protection' of Europe, and makes this case, and issue, as European as it is US American.

In speaking to the state of race – the condition of the racial state – in Britain, the issues raised in this collection concerning immigration, asylum, the asserted failure of multiculturalism, and the associated threats to national security which front the motivations to curtail even arbitrary notions of human rights, and are used to justify deportation and extradition, necessarily require us to consider the global formations of racism. Shifting modes of global capitalism and the advancement of the neoliberal security state transgress not only the borders and boundaries of the nation state, but the very idea of the nation state as well. The shifting cartographies of labour and capital, as well as of geopolitical formations, have gone hand in hand with re-articulations of sovereignty and the law. The state of race is, by implication, global. Still, the specificities of the local need to be located within these wider trends, and thus our specific examples demonstrate a tenuous positioning between Europe and the USA. As Britain moves away from European ideals of equality and universalism and towards a system of outsourcing its justice system to the US, what comes to the fore is a position of oscillation between US-style imperial racism and European fascism. On the one hand the US protects its 'own' by restricting extradition back to the UK. On the other hand, Europe purports to defend its own: British citizens Babar Ahmed and Talha Ahsans' protracted cases were due to the European Human Rights Court's intervention rather than any legal protection offered in British law. A progressive Europe versus an imperial USA with the UK negotiating in between is an analytic that is often proffered, but this is not the usual contour for understanding global state practices. Rather affirmative action, the embedding of civil rights into various institutions, and the election of Obama, all point to impossible futures for (mainland) Europe. Britain in this context is seen as a beacon of tolerance when compared with *Hijab*-banning France (a policy spreading virus-like across Northern Europe) and neo-facist Austria. The extradition case draws our attention to the Muslim subject as the object of the harshest operations of the racial state. Racisms as they operate across Britain clearly impact on a range of subjects, but the issues covered in this book aim to highlight those moments which transcend the tensions of a 'tolerant' Britain, revealing the structures of state power. It is this ambivalent, but also centring, position that Britain holds, which draws wider connections to the state of racism in mainland Europe and to the US, that provides an international thematic for the specific cases covered in this volume.

The connections and interactions amongst Britain, mainland Europe and the US function on a routine, regular, almost banal basis. The transatlantic trafficking of ideas, strategies and resources to manage the racial threat has a longstanding history and continues to traverse both formally and informally. This has been articulated in terms of whiteness and the white working class, as well as through the management of ethnic minorities. The tactics of 'hard' policing which make use of surveillance, stop and search, and indefinite detention to target suspect immigrant communities frequent daily life in the Pakistani and Arab neighbourhoods of New York as much as they do in the black and Asian communities of Birmingham. Taking its cue from the British Preventing Violent Extremism strategy, launched in 2007 and based on a longer-term philosophy of policing terrorism 'at home' in Britain, in August 2011 the White House released its own 'Empowering Local Partners to Prevent Violent Extremism in the United States' document, outlining a broad, outreach-based strategy for reducing the threat of 'violent extremism', mimicking the British approach. At the same time, these connections have not escaped those on the far right campaigning against the 'Islamization of the West'. Pamela Geller, who heads the inflammatory organisation 'Stop Islamization of America' joined forces with Dutch anti-Muslim extremist Geerst Wilders, who was charged with hate incitement in the Netherlands in 2009, inviting him to speak at the Ground Zero Mosque rally in May 2010. Likewise, she invited the English Defence League (EDL) to speak at a second rally in September 2010, describing them as 'courageous English patriots'. A report in *The Observer* revealed that Geller had been instrumental in aligning the EDL with the American Tea Party movement, providing the former with access to significant financial resources (Townsend 2010).

And the transatlantic borrowing and interaction extends to the 'softer' liberal ideologies concerning approaches to integration of these otherwise 'ungovernable' communities. Such exchanges are backed by state financial support through programmes such as Our Shared Future. Funded by the British Council, 'Our Shared Future aims to improve the public conversation about Muslims in the US, Europe and beyond by providing access to the evidence-based arguments and research findings of reputable academics and experts' (British Council 2012). Promoting a flurry of academic work and dialogue, this program has prompted prolific discussion and knowledge transfer across the Atlantic focusing explicitly on the 'problematic' Muslim community, forefronting liberal ideals of tolerance as it silences (il)liberal acts of state terror. In many ways this conflation is epitomised through the Prevent programme's 'education arm', where liberal notions of tolerance are used to discipline and coerce Muslim youth. The similarities, though, are not limited to approaches of state governmentality but extend to responses from Muslim communities themselves. Across the Atlantic we witness intense declarations of patriotism from those otherwise racially excluded, just as we witness their increasing alienation and marginalisation.

The focus in this collection on Muslims is to indicate the operations of state racism at their sharpest and keenest. These techniques and strategies also apply to other racialised groups in the British (and European) polity. A necessary distinction between our use of Muslim as a political identity which can impact (and of course has done) on the rights and lived realities of all of those who are open to be mistaken (the names Balbir Singh and Jean Charles de Menezes roll off the tongue) with a group of people who might identify themselves as Muslim is critical to our approach. Policing in the UK still disproportionately impacts young African/ African-Caribbean males (some of whom may also identify as Muslim), but our issue is not with the catalogue or litany of oppressed groups. In the Euro-American context the list is long, and empirical work on particular groups is, as we argued in the introduction, perhaps the dominant form of academic study, reflecting a politics of representation as well as a certain kind of neoliberal neglect of the role of the state. We are conscious of the policy domain in which community cohesion, interfaith dialogue and tolerance have become the focus, to replace equality, anti-racism and oppression. It is for this reason that the main thrust of this book has been to explore the way in which *Mussalman* has come out of the camp into the mainstream. Rendered now as the figure upon which the state can practice new techniques of repression and control, it is this that is critical about the various arenas in which we have examined state racism.

Our theoretical intervention is aimed at evoking the consequences and strategies that are enabled by thinking through the British state as racial and neoliberal. A recognition of the global reach of racial neoliberalism does not mean that it settles in the same way in the particularities of a nation state, or even the different urban spaces within it. Rather, we have shown the ways in which the local contours of racial neoliberalism are played out in specific contexts, with outcomes that are almost always demeaning and dehumanising. These demand in themselves an urgent response for which our academic writing is often not sufficient. If this book is a relentless account of the destructive and disruptive operations of state power, this is not something about which we are apologetic. Rather, this is a necessary counter to the descriptive and celebratory literature which, though at some level humanising, also provides (in) adequate excuses for the state to marginalise those upon whom the greatest violence is wrought. It is at the limits of tolerance that racial neoliberalism is most usefully exposed, and the mundane examples of schooling and security cameras indicate that there is no arena in which racial hierarchies are not created and maintained. A critique of this position might demand a more subtle reading of the state in that the forces of neoliberalism have equally hollowed out its base, such that without considering the role of private corporations, our analysis is limited. In response, we hope we have indicated that despite and to some extent through these changes, such as enhancement of securitisation and the withdrawal of social welfare, that racial hierarchies are strengthened and material inequalities entrenched. We also recognise that it is not sufficient just to state or analyse these processes. A response is urgent and necessary and one that links across local struggles, be they deaths in police custody, racist attacks or extradition. Part of the work of thinking with racial neoliberalism is that it potentially provides a binding mechanism to a range of particular cases and offers a space to campaign on a broader platform.

References

BBC (2011) 'Home Secretary Theresa May Wants Human Rights Act Axed', *BBC News*, 2 October 2011, http://www.bbc.co.uk/news/uk-politics-15140742.

British Council, 'Our Shared Future', *British Council* website, http://usa.british-council.org/our-shared-future

Jones, C. and Bowcott, O. (2012) 'Abu Hamza Arrives in US after Extradition', *The Guardian*, 6 October 2012, http://www.guardian.co.uk/world/2012/oct/06/abu-hamza-us-court-extradition

Townsend, M. (2010) 'English Defence League Forges Links with America's Tea Party', *The Observer*, 9 October 2010, http://www.guardian.co.uk/uk/2010/oct/10/english-defence-league-tea-party

Index

CPI Antony Rowe
Eastbourne, UK
September 11, 2019